THE Ultimate Personal Recording Studio

Gino Robair

THOMSON
COURSE TECHNOLOGY
Professional ■ Technical ■ Reference

Publisher and General Manager, Thomson Course Technology PTR: Stacy L. Hiquet
Associate Director of Marketing: Sarah O'Donnell
Manager of Editorial Services: Heather Talbot
Marketing Manager: Mark Hughes
Executive Editor: Mike Lawson
Marketing Coordinator: Meg Dunkerly
Project Editor and Copy Editor: Marta Justak
PTR Editorial Services Coordinator: Elizabeth Furbish
Interior Layout Tech: Stephen Ramirez
Cover Designer: Stephen Ramirez
Indexer: Kevin Broccoli
Proofreader: Karen Gill

ISBN-10: 1-59863-210-8
ISBN-13: 978-1-59863-210-1

Library of Congress Catalog Card Number: 2006923272
Printed in the United States of America

07 08 09 10 11 TW 10 9 8 7 6 5 4 3 2 1

Thomson Course Technology PTR, a division of Thomson Learning Inc.
25 Thomson Place
Boston, MA 02210

THOMSON
COURSE TECHNOLOGY
Professional ■ Technical ■ Reference

Acknowledgments

Writing a book about music technology is a difficult task. Not only are music-production tools continually changing or becoming obsolete, but the ways people think about and create music are constantly evolving as well. Consequently, it takes the eyes and ears of many people to keep up with the developments.

The Ultimate Personal Recording Studio borrows heavily from articles that originally appeared in *Electronic Musician* magazine and were later assembled for the book, *Making the Ultimate Demo.* As writer, editor, and curator of *The Ultimate Personal Recording Studio*, I have updated and refined the text and added new information where needed. My goal was to seamlessly integrate various sources into a step-by-step guide for building and using a personal studio.

The writers who have contributed valuable source material to this book are Neil Brighton (Chapters 6, 8, 12, 19, and 23), Jeff Casey (Chapters 20 and 25), Geoffrey Goacher (Chapter 3), Gary Hall (Chapter 24), Brent Hurtig (Chapter 21), Brian Knave (Chapters 5, 10, 13, 14, 16, 17, 20), Scott Mathews (Chapter 25), Michael Molenda (Chapters 15, 16, 17, 25, and 26), Larry the O (Chapters 7 and 12), Steve Oppenheimer (Chapter 1), Chris Pelonis (Chapter 3), George Petersen (Chapter 9), and Scott Wilkinson (Chapter 22). I would like to thank Marta Justak for her patient editorial assistance;

Stacy Hiquet for getting the ball rolling; Chuck Dahmer for his excellent technical drawings; Mike Lawson for his encouragement; Steve Oppenheimer, editor in chief of *Electronic Musician*, as well as the rest of the magazine's staff, for making "work" fun; and my family for their love and support.

About the Author

Gino Robair is a senior editor at *Electronic Musician* magazine and has composed for Shakespearean theater, Indonesian gamelan, and modern dance. His commercial credits include themes for Starbucks, Comedy Central, and MTV, and he served as music director for the CBS Saturday morning cartoon *The Twisted Tales of Felix the Cat*. As a drummer, Robair has recorded with Tom Waits, Anthony Braxton, Lou Harrison, Peter James, and Pink Mountain, among others. He is one of the "25 innovative percussionists" included in the book *Percussion Profiles* (SoundWorld, 2001).

Contents

Introduction

Don't fall prey to the myth that all you need is a roomful of expensive gear to make good music. Professional-sounding recordings can be made anywhere, and on almost any budget. Talent, knowledge, inspiration, and—above all—hard work are the key ingredients to recording memorable tracks.

The Ultimate Personal Recording Studio is designed to help you acquire the basic recording skills needed to get maximum results from a minimum amount of equipment. Everything you need to know—from picking the right recording equipment and setting up your studio space to recording and mixing your songs—is covered in these pages.

The Ultimate Personal Recording Studio is designed to be a reference tool; it's not meant to be read once from cover to cover and shelved. Keep it handy, make notes in the margins, underline important items, and mark the sections that you find useful so that you can easily relocate them. Using the book in this way will help you raise the quality of your recordings and perhaps suggest new avenues of exploration.

No matter what your proficiency is as a home recordist, or your intention for the finished product, *The Ultimate Personal Recording Studio* will help you take your sound to the next level.

Who This Book Is For

The Ultimate Personal Recording Studio will give you the tools you need to get professional results from your own recordings, whether you have any previous engineering experience or not. The book was designed for musicians—professional and amateur—of any level, as well as beginning to intermediate-level recording hobbyists. This book will also be useful for seasoned musicians who may never have set foot into a control room or fully learned how the various parts of a studio work together.

How This Book Is Organized

The first section, "Getting Your Studio Together," provides an easy-to-follow overview of the components that make up a modern recording studio, including microphones, mixers, monitors, and multitrack recorders. This section will also help you determine which room to use for your studio and how to get the most out of it acoustically and ergonomically.

The nine chapters of "Recording Techniques" will show you how to use your studio gear to record a variety of instruments. These instruments include drum, acoustic and electric guitars, electric bass, synthesizers, piano, and—of course—vocals. The last chapter in this section, "The House Is Rockin'," will show you how to take full advantage of the unique acoustics in the various rooms of your home when recording.

The third section, "Effects Basics," shows you how each of the common studio effects operate, and how they are used by the pros. This includes dynamics processors (compression, limiting, expansion, and gating), EQ (graphic and parametric), reverb, and delay.

By the time you reach the section on "Mixing and Mastering Your Demo," you will be ready to take your project through its final stages and prepare it for release. In "Creating the Ultimate Mix," you will learn how to make each instrument sound its best when combined with other instruments. The chapter will also give you insights into how professional engineers create an enhanced stereo spread and add depth to their recordings. The final chapter, "Mastering Your Mix for Reproduction," tells you what you can expect when you take your finished mixes to a mastering facility as it is prepared for release on compact disc.

Together, the chapters in *The Ultimate Personal Recording Studio* show you how to make CD-quality recordings, from the conceptual stages of building a studio and shopping for gear to adding the final touches to your songs.

Part I

Getting Your Studio Together

CHAPTER 1

Holistic Studio Design

Many musicians assemble or expand their personal studios by simply buying gear that catches their fancy. But if you're trying to build a workable recording studio, it's not enough to check out pieces of gear and buy what excites you (assuming you can afford it).

Even when you buy quality equipment and use it in accordance with the manufacturer's instructions, the results can sometimes be disappointing. Some equipment doesn't play well with others, causing interfacing problems, degraded audio quality, software conflicts, and so forth. Features are wastefully duplicated, and money flows to buy more gear to make the gear you bought do what you thought it would do to begin with. Poor ergonomics can make working in the studio unproductive or even unpleasant. Eventually, this gets frustrating, which dulls the enjoyment of producing music. What's a personal studio owner to do?

The Holistic Model

Admittedly, we all get surprised sometimes by "gotchas" that couldn't have been anticipated. But in many cases, you can avoid these problems with advanced, systematic planning. You must carefully analyze your studio needs and plan how the elements will integrate into a functional whole. In short, a well-integrated studio can be thought of as one complex machine.

How does one go about analyzing a studio in this way? I suggest you apply a structural-functional model in which you conceive of your studio as a holistic system that has a structure—that is, an organized arrangement of parts. Each part of the system—each piece of gear—has a function, which is the contribution that part makes to the whole system. The parts occupy "statuses"—sound source, controller, effects processor, acoustic conditioner, cable, etc.—in a network made up of the relationships between individual pieces of equipment.

The studio exists in a physical environment, which is a room of a certain size, with structurally determined acoustics and considerations, such as outside noise, ventilation, temperature, humidity, and so on. The studio's growth depends on available resources: your time, space, and money. By considering all of these aspects, you can plan a total studio system with functional unity.

Define Your Objectives

Of course, a recording studio serves a definable purpose, so let's start there. Consider what you plan to do with the studio now, tomorrow, and a few years down the line. Are you doing preproduction, with the intent of mixing the final product in a commercial studio? Are you producing music CDs, audio for picture, live recordings, or something else? What styles of music do you want to produce? Will you have outside clients, or will you record only your own music? Will some of the gear be used on stage or hauled to other studios in addition to serving in your studio?

Next, thoroughly analyze all aspects of your production methods until you clearly understand how you like to work. Do you feel comfortable recording with a computer? If not, perhaps a hardware multitrack recorder is right for you. How important is MIDI sequencing? Maybe a keyboard workstation that includes a built-in sequencer and sound library will fit the bill.

Do you need complex audio editing features? If so, you will want to investigate computer-based systems.

Based on your objectives and preferred working style, consider which functions are necessary to achieve your goals. Will you use only electronic sound sources, or will you record acoustic instruments and vocals? If the latter, for example, you probably need to take a look at mics, preamps, and dynamics processors. Or perhaps you will work completely "in the box," so you will need a fast computer, lots of RAM, and a USB or FireWire keyboard controller/interface with plenty of knobs, sliders, and pads for working with soft synths and effects.

Static Versus Dynamic Systems

Of major importance is whether your studio will be a static system or a dynamic system that will undergo change in the foreseeable future. Small, tightly integrated studio-in-a-box systems (such as MIDI keyboard workstations and various types of integrated audio mixer/recorders) are generally easy to use and require minimal maintenance, troubleshooting, and expense. If you are likely to keep doing the same thing in essentially the same way, this type of system might be an excellent choice. On the other hand, an all-in-one system is relatively inflexible by definition.

As noted earlier, a well-integrated studio is, for practical purposes, one machine. As with many machines, depending on how you design it, you might be able to reshuffle its components, changing its structural type. In many cases, you can even absorb it, as an integral part, into a larger studio. Following that line of thought, if you expect your needs to change any time soon, your studio should have the ability to admit new links with gear you don't even have yet. The continuity of the studio's structure should not be destroyed when you change parts, forcing you to dump central pieces. Component systems are generally much more flexible than all-in-one systems in this scenario.

Remember that no change occurs in isolation; each part in a system is linked to other parts. If you expect that your studio will change, you need to design a system of components that ideally have multiple uses, are expandable, and have an assortment of connections.

Rapid change promotes problems, though, so make changes in increments. In addition, you will save money, frustration, and time if you can build onto what already exists. If old, familiar gear is still in good shape, why not keep it in service, perhaps in a different role? In addition, it's easier to remain productive if you don't try to completely reinvent your work habits overnight.

Compatibility and Connectivity

As you consider various components, analyze the relationships you will set up among them. Before buying a new mic or mic preamp, test the interaction between the mics and mic preamps you're considering. Think about which synths complement each other sonically for your purposes. Determine whether the software and audio interface you want to use are compatible.

Beware of mixing gear that operates at different audio levels (i.e., +4 dBu and –10 dBV) or that uses incompatible types of I/O. Make sure your cables and connectors are of high quality and are appropriate for their intended uses. (Good cables make more of a difference than you might imagine.) Where you must mix and match, be sure to use the proper adapters and format converters. Sometimes, you may be forced to improvise here, but then you risk degrading the audio quality. Keep your cable runs short wherever possible, especially with audio cables. And make sure you have separate physical paths for audio and power cables, so that your audio cables don't pick up unwanted noise.

Ergonomics

An important and often overlooked issue is where you will locate everything to achieve optimal ergonomic and sonic results. It's crucial to design a comfortable working environment, or you won't want to work there.

The gear should be strategically placed so that the things you use most, such as keyboards and controllers, are within easy reach. The ultimate setup allows you to sit in your monitor's sweet spot and have full control of everything in your studio without having to leave your chair.

Noisy gear—anything with a loud fan, such as a hard drive or computer—should be moved into an equipment closet and accessed remotely. If your personal studio has more than one room, the Frontier Design Groups TrazPort lets you control your digital audio workstation (DAW) wirelessly. It can be mounted on a stand in the tracking room, or placed next to you in the control room (see **Fig. 1.1**).

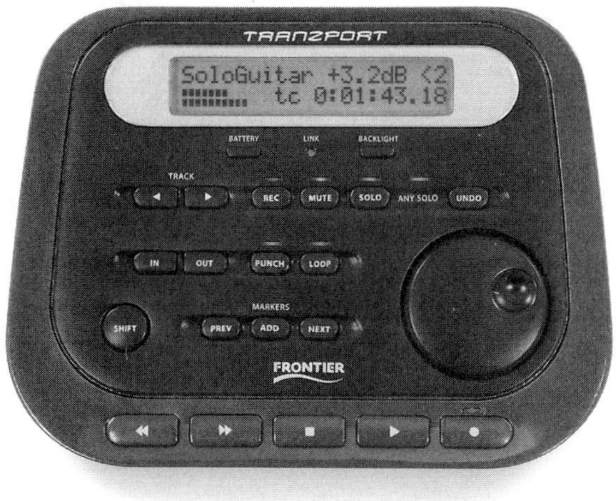

FIG. 1.1:
The TranzPort, by Frontier Design Group, is a compact wireless unit that lets you control recording devices remotely. It works with all the major digital audio sequencers, and it can even be used to control Apple iTunes.

What's the Plan, Man?

By now, hopefully, you get the point: To design a studio that you can use productively and want to use, you should look at the bigger picture and plan ahead on many levels. The structural-functional method I've presented isn't a magic solution, but it can provide a useful framework for designing a studio or live-performance system. (For that matter, the same principles apply to planning an album or a mix.) Just keep in mind that, as important as it is to choose the right tools for the job, success is far more likely when you configure and use them properly.

Well-designed studio furniture, such as this Pro Station by Omnirax, can help you work within your monitoring sweet spot, minimize system clutter, and prevent problematic tonal reflections and resonances.

CHAPTER 2

Gear Checklist for the Ultimate Personal Studio

In terms of setup and purpose, there's a big difference between the professional recording facility and the typical personal studio. The pro studio contains enough equipment to handle any project that may come up. Whether in Los Angeles, New York, or a midwestern suburb, studios have to fight for business in a highly competitive marketplace. With the rise in quality and drop in price of home recording gear, pro facilities have to work harder than ever to get clients in the door. Some of the ways studios do this are with great-sounding rooms, top-notch engineers, and state-of-the-art gear. All of these things come with a hefty price tag, which ultimately gets passed along to the customer.

At the other extreme is the highly personalized home studio. Everything in it is ideally suited to the needs of the person using it. The personal studio can be as simple as a cassette recorder with a built-in microphone, or as complex as, well, a multimillion-dollar pro recording facility. And there are infinite possibilities in between. Where does your studio fit in this continuum, and how will you know when you have everything you need?

For starters, the kind of gear you need for a personal studio depends on your goals, talents, and budget. Remember that many classic recordings have been made on equipment that seems modest, even primitive, by our present standards. For example, in the earliest days of recording, the musicians crowded around a single microphone, with the "mix" created in part by the physical arrangement of the musicians in the room. When it was done right, the results were incredible, and producers today sometimes strive for a similarly natural sound.

Personalized Setup

The most common scenario for beginning recordists is to assemble every piece of sound equipment they own into one room and work from there. If this describes your situation, start by taking an inventory of everything you have, so that you can see the holes or weak links in your system. When you're done, make a wish list based on what you think you will need to record the kind of music you work with.

Next, divide the list into two categories: essentials and non-essentials. That way, you can avoid making impulse purchases when the salesperson puts the pressure on. If this is your first time building a studio or your first time upgrading to higher quality gear, you may be wondering how to determine what the essentials are. Essentials include both new gear and equipment upgrades. For example, if the recorder you have doesn't have the features you need or the sound quality you want, it's essential that you get a new one. Spend some time clarifying your artistic and business goals, and you will begin to see which items your studio truly needs to facilitate your artistic pursuits.

As you assemble your gear list, keep in mind that a studio is something that is never complete—it's always in a state of flux or transition. That's not to say that you shouldn't have everything set up for your particular needs. It's just that there is always room for improvement. For instance, as you hone your studio chops, you will begin to feel that some of your gear needs upgrading. Remember that being a musical artist is as much about process as it is about product, and home recording is no different.

Anatomy of a Studio

On the most basic level, a recording studio contains four distinct elements:

- Sound producer
- Transducer (for recording)
- Storage device
- Transducer (for playback)

The sound producer is whatever the artist makes music with: voice, guitar, turntable, synthesizer, drums, etc.

A transducer is something that converts one kind of energy into another. In the recording studio, the two main transducers are the microphone and the loud speaker. The mic converts sound waves into electrical energy that can be stored in a recording device. To hear this stored information, we use another transducer—the speaker. Electrical energy causes the speaker cone to move, which in turn creates sound waves that we can hear.

The storage device is what you'll use for recording and playback. This serves as both a notebook and the final canvas on which you'll create your masterpieces.

If you have gear that fits into each of these categories, you already have the makings of a personal studio. However, there are a few other things you will need to make the basic elements work properly, such as microphone preamps and a power amp for the monitors. And to add greater flexibility when working, there are a few other things a personal studio might include, such as a mixer, digital converters, and effects processors. Often, a single device will incorporate a number of these items. Digital mixers, for example, include microphone preamps, effects, and digital converters, among other things.

Typical Studio Components

Anyone who plays music can recognize a microphone, mixer, and monitor. However, there are subtle factors that determine the quality of each of these items. Without getting too technical right away, let's look at the most common studio items one at a time. Each of these will be explored in greater detail in subsequent chapters.

Microphones. The microphone is one of the most important (yet often undervalued) pieces of gear in the studio. The first microphone most of us own is usually an inexpensive dynamic mic that we use on stage. It's probably the first mic we recorded with as well. However, once you've decided to build the ultimate personal studio, you will need to be more selective about mics, and you may want to find mics that are suitable for specific studio situations. For example, if you are a singer, the first thing you will want to do is find a microphone that makes your voice sound its best on recordings. Remember, as transducers, microphones are the "ears" your recording device uses to "hear" your music. Therefore, it's important to make sure you have the right mic for the job.

Mics made for the stage are built to handle loud volume levels for long periods of time and are made to withstand years of abuse. As ears, stage mics are not necessarily the most sensitive transducers. Consequently, they might sound good on some instruments (such as electric guitars or snare drums), but lousy on others (for example, piano, violin, or bass clarinet). These kinds of mics also tend to be the least expensive, so many beginning recordists start with one or two of these to get the ball rolling.

Microphones made specifically for studio recording, on the other hand, often have a greater sensitivity (that is, they are more accurate and have a wider dynamic range and frequency response) than stage mics. They tend to be more delicate and require a little more care and knowledge on the user's part than a stage mic. Studio mics are usually more expensive, although their price tag doesn't guarantee that they will sound good on everything. A well-rounded microphone closet will have a mix of different kinds of mics, including cheap and expensive mics, because, like people, each microphone has its own personality.

How many mics does a personal studio need? That depends on your budget as well as how you plan to record. A talented engineer can produce great recordings with only two mics—for example, a multipurpose condenser and a quality dynamic mic. (For more on the different microphone types, see Chapter 6, "Microphones Made Easy.")

The Red Microphones Type B combines a transformerless, Class A, solid-state preamp body with a removable large-diaphragm cardioid capsule. Other modular capsules, with different polar patterns, are available.

If you are a singer/acoustic guitarist, you can get the job done with one, two, or three mics. If you want to record acoustic music—played by a jazz group, string quartet, or solo harpsichordist—direct to a stereo recorder, a matched pair of high-quality condenser mics may be sufficient. If you plan to do multitrack recordings of your band, and you want to be able to record several instruments simultaneously, four or five mics should do the trick.

To Tube or Not to Tube

With the help of the digital recording revolution, vacuum-tube technology has made a comeback. Many engineers have recognized that a well-designed tube device can help a signal sound better when going to tape or disc. This has caused a sensation in the audio industry, with manufacturers scrambling to include tubes in many of their products to cash in on the craze.

A tube is used to change the gain of a signal in a circuit. As the level of the signal going through the tube is increased beyond its design tolerances, you get a kind of distortion that many people find more pleasing than distortion from solid-state devices. Tubes (known as *valves* in the UK), therefore, are found not only in microphones and mic preamps, but also in signal processors, such as compressors, equalizers, and even direct boxes.

The recent hype about vacuum tubes has led many consumers to believe that having a tube in the circuit is automatically going to give the right kind of "warmth" and "color" to the "cold" sound of a digital recording; this is simply not the case. While it is true that tube gear can provide coloration to the signal, tubes can also be used in such a way that they are transparent in the signal path, just as they were used back when today's vintage gear was contemporary.

Tube devices priced within the budgets of the personal studio often do not have this transparency. The design and engineering of the circuitry make the greatest difference in the sound quality of a tube product; a badly designed circuit cannot be saved by the presence of a tube. Do some research before you buy, including a comparison of features and specifications, as well as listening tests whenever possible.

Many engineers who strive for high-quality recordings won't use more than one tube device in a signal path (i.e., a tube mic preamp with a tube microphone). However, more than one tube stage in the signal path may create exactly the sound you need for a given application.

If you do purchase a device that contains tubes, remember to do the following: warm the tubes up, handle the glass with care, follow manufacturer's recommendations when replacing tubes, and use a dedicated power supply.

Choosing the right mics for your studio is a matter of personal taste and usually requires a combination of research and trial and error. Begin your research by asking other musicians about their mic preferences. Perhaps this will lead to a chance to try their favorite mic, either in their studio or your own. If you're not in a hurry—and you shouldn't be, because this is a lifelong process—begin reading microphone-related articles and reviews in magazines such as *Mix*, *Remix*, and *Electronic Musician*. This will not only give you an idea of specific products, but it will also give you insights into recording technique and theory.

When you finally do go shopping, don't rely solely on the word of the salesperson (unless you already have a working relationship with him and trust his judgment). Manufacturers often give salespeople incentives to sell their products, especially new releases. Before you buy, find out what the store's return policy is for microphones. The mic you choose may be the darling of the press, but if you get it home and it's not right for you, take it back for a full refund. Above all, trust your ears. You will know when you have found the right mic.

One more word of advice: Don't be surprised to find that, after a period of time, your taste in microphones has changed. This is just an indication that your ears are maturing, and you are beginning to hear the strengths and weaknesses in each microphone. Take that as a positive sign, and understand that you may still want that old mic for a project down the road.

Recorder. A few years ago, choosing a recorder was a relatively easy task: You simply had to decide on the number of tracks you wanted to record and determine your budget, and the choice was just about made for you. For a 4-track recorder, you had your choice between reel-to-reel and cassette tape decks. For another thousand dollars, you could move up to eight tracks. Today, however, there are different choices when it comes to recording formats, with budget being only one of the determining factors.

In the desktop studio, all of your recording and playback is done using a personal computer. Many programs allow you to do multitrack recording, MIDI sequencing, and conventional music notation within one application. Software packages range in price from around $1,000 for a full-featured program to well under $100 (and in some cases, free) for basic recording, editing, and sequencing features.

The Digidesign Digi002 is the centerpiece of a Pro Tools LE digital audio workstation. It combines a mixer with mic inputs, a control surface, and a multichannel digital interface in one device. It can also be used as a stand-alone mixer in a concert setting.

Programs that can record audio and sequence MIDI are referred to as *digital audio sequencers*. The digital audio workstation, or DAW, is a sequencing and recording program that includes a hardware interface with digital inputs and outputs (I/O). Many digital audio sequencers and DAWs are bundled with other software, such as effects processors or synthesizers, or programs for burning CD-Rs and creating MP3 files.

The M-Audio Ozonic is a 37-note keyboard MIDI controller and 24-bit, 96 kHz FireWire audio interface. The sliders and knobs can be assigned to control virtually any parameter in a digital audio sequencer.

A number of manufacturers realized early on that some musicians want an inexpensive, easy-to-use, all-in-one multitrack recorder that is also portable and rugged enough to take on the road. Companies such as Roland, Boss, Yamaha, and Korg offer personal digital studios that include the features you need to record, mix, and master a recording project, such as a mixer, mic preamps, a CD-R burner, and effects. Personal digital studios are available in a wide range of configurations and prices. It's important to note that these recorders offer a fixed number of tracks that can be played back at one time, as well as a fixed number of tracks that can be recorded simultaneously, so make sure that whichever recorder you choose matches the kind of recording you plan to do. For example, if you want to track a full drum set using five mics, plus bass, guitar, and vocals, you will need a recorder that can record at least eight tracks simultaneously.

The Roland VS-2480 is a digital multitrack hard disk recorder that gives you 24 tracks (with 16 virtual tracks each), two stereo effects processors, 17 motorized faders, and support for 24-bit, 96 kHz recording.

Another type of hardware multitrack recorder and sequencer is the keyboard workstation, which combines a hardware keyboard instrument with a multitrack sequencer and recorder. These enhanced instruments are often more intuitive for songwriters to use, because the keyboard, sequencer, sounds, and effects are tightly integrated. The more expensive models include multiple inputs and outputs, high-quality sound libraries, a CD-R burner, and digital ports to connect the keyboard workstation to your computer for backing up files or loading new sounds.

The Korg OASYS is a top-of-the-line synthesizer keyboard workstation that offers multitrack audio recording, MIDI sequencing, sample playback, physical modeling, digital signal processing, a color touch-screen LCD, and a 40 GB hard disk.

All the multitrack recorders mentioned previously are based on tapeless, disk-based, nonlinear recording and editing formats. Some of the benefits of a nonlinear digital format include nondestructive editing, multitrack flexibility (e.g., the ability to add numerous "virtual" tracks), and the amount of time you can record. The downside is that you can lose an entire recording project if you have disk failure, and you can't do any further recordings until your disk is up and running again.

Tape-based digital and analog multitrack formats are also available. Although fewer and fewer manufacturers are supporting them each year, there are reasons why engineers gravitate toward tape-based recorders. Overall, tape is a robust medium that can be stored for long periods of time, and these formats have a proven track record of stability under the stress of the studio.

Using a linear tape format means you will spend time rewinding or fast-forwarding to hear different songs. Although this seems trivial on paper, you will eat up plenty of studio time moving from one section of the tape to another. In addition, any editing you do will be destructive, because although you can edit open-reel analog tapes with a razor blade, you can't do so with digital tape (at least not in the common semi-professional formats).

Multitrack recording to analog tape, in particular, remains popular, because of the excellent sound quality the format provides. However, analog tape machines require regular maintenance and calibration if you want to get the most out of the format. In addition, analog tape isn't cheap, and the resources for new tape stock are dwindling. But if you are looking for vintage vibe and beefy drum sounds, tape is where it's at.

Mixer. As the name suggests, a mixer allows you to combine, or mix, multiple signals at one time. Typically, a mixer includes other items the recordist will find useful, such as mic preamps, EQ, digital converters, and signal processing. Mixers come in many shapes and sizes, including virtual ones within computer programs.

The Mackie Onyx 1620 is an analog mixer with eight phantom-powered mic preamps. An optional FireWire card is available so you can use the mixer as a digital interface.

In a basic multitrack studio, where several instruments are recorded at a time, a small mixer with a couple of microphone and line-level inputs could serve an artist well. For a studio that needs a little more flexibility, a mixer with a greater number of inputs and outputs, as well as mix buses, multiband parametric EQ, digital effects, and fader automation may be a better choice. Generally, the larger and more complex the mixer is, the more expensive it will be.

As mentioned earlier, portable multitrack digital recorders often have built-in mixers with EQ, effects sends, and mic preamps. Again, depending on the size of your budget and the kind of projects you will be doing, one of these all-in-one devices could be perfect for your studio.

If you plan to do your work on your computer using a digital audio sequencer, a virtual mixer is an integral part of the program. Software mixers offer features that would be difficult to achieve with a hardware mixer, such as unusual automation possibilities and track expandability through software.

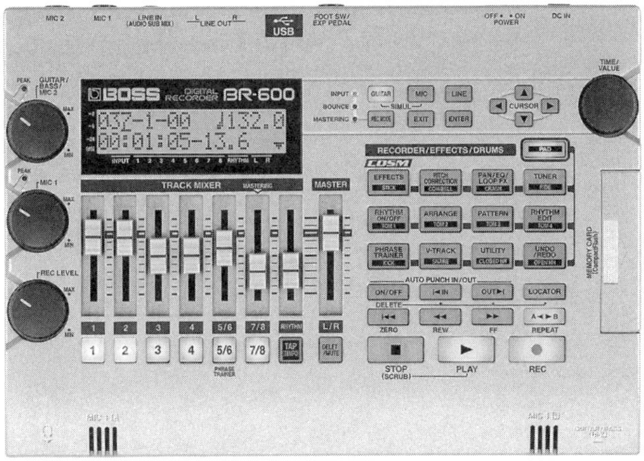

The Boss BR-600 is a lightweight 8-track digital recorder that supports 64 virtual tracks and uses CompactFlash memory cards. The BR-600 also includes an effects processor, a built-in stereo mic, and an onboard drum machine with Velocity-sensitive pads.

Signal Processors. This broad category includes any hardware device or software plug-in used to modify your music, either during the recording stage or while mixing. Processors are typically divided into several categories: spatial effects (reverb, echo), dynamics processors (compression, limiting, gating), equalizers (parametric and graphic), and saturation-type effects (distortion).

One of the most useful effects for recording is the compressor. A compressor allows the recording engineer to get the hottest possible signal to tape while keeping the dynamics consistent. This helps avoid peaks that would overload the recorder while also making the quieter sounds more audible. Compressors are often used when tracking or mixing electric bass, vocals, and drums, but they can be used on any instrument if needed.

A reverb unit is a useful effect to have when it comes time to mix. It allows you to put a "room" around the instruments and can make a good track sound great.

Monitor Speakers. Like the microphone, the playback system is typically one of the last things the recordist thinks about. Since you probably already have a home stereo, you may be tempted to incorporate it into your recording setup. Unfortunately, home stereos are not designed to give the listener an accurate representation of a recording.

The KRK's V8 is an example of a powered, 2-way close-field studio monitor, with an 8-inch woofer and a 1-inch tweeter.

Monitor speakers designed for use in a studio environment have a flat frequency response, meaning that they reproduce every frequency, from the highest to the lowest, at the same intensity. Home stereo speakers, on the other hand, often have bumps in the frequency response, to exaggerate different areas of the frequency spectrum (such as the low and high ends). If you record and mix using a pair of speakers with exaggerated characteristics, the results you get may not translate well onto other playback systems. By working with accurate studio monitors, you can be sure of what you're hearing as you mix.

Just like in a home stereo system, your studio speakers are driven by a power amp. However, the power amp in your stereo receiver may not match the level of your recording gear. By getting a dedicated studio power amp, you further guarantee the accuracy of your playback system.

A recent development on the home-studio scene is the low-cost, powered close-field monitor. Powered monitor speakers can be plugged directly into the main outputs of your mixer and have the advantage of factory-matched components for optimized accuracy and performance. Powered monitors cost more than unpowered, passive monitors, but they may be the perfect solution if you're going for a high-quality, yet simplified, studio setup.

Accessories. Beyond choosing a recording format and assembling the major studio components into a system, you should budget for several smaller items that are no less important. Typically, these items will include various kinds of cables and removable media for your recorder, headphones, mic stands, and keyboard stands, as well as racks and studio furniture.

Don't skimp on studio cables. Look for high-quality products such as low-capacitance shielded cables. These have a low-resistance shield and a braided (rather than solid) internal conductor. Never twist, bend, or knot your cords after winding them up, as this will eventually damage them. Problematic cables with intermittent shorts should be replaced so that you don't accidentally use them. A cable tester can be used to identify bad cables.

Points of Purchase

There are a number of ways to purchase pro audio gear. Most metropolitan areas have at least one store that sells equipment suitable for the personal studio. You can also shop by mail or online.

There are also online auctions specializing in used pro-audio gear. Some of these auctions are run by pro-audio dealers that guarantee everything they sell, so they're worth investigating if you know what you want to buy.

However, be careful when buying equipment sight unseen. Make sure you're dealing with a reputable dealer and that you fully understand the warranties and return policy.

Checkout

Personal studios are a hot topic these days, and there are many ways to learn about new gear and how to use it. One way is via the Internet, where you can find online discussion groups devoted to every aspect of recording, and at almost any level. Talking to other recordists can be very helpful when it comes to questions about gear—you're likely to learn more about a particular piece of equipment than you wish to know!

Ultimately, having the finest gear in the world doesn't ensure creative success. However, owning and knowing how to use quality equipment will give you the tools you need to make your recording stand out among the rest. By building your studio slowly over time and making informed purchases, you can bet that the gear you get today will serve your needs well into your creative future.

Powerful Protection

Most professional and semipro gear can tolerate moderate variations in voltage. However, constant fluctuations in level cause stress to your gear over the long term. At the worst, sudden power surges and spikes can cause immediate harm to sensitive equipment such as computers and hard drives.

Luckily, there are quite a few devices that can help prevent sudden disaster and prolong the life of your studio equipment. These devices have multiple power outlets that you plug your audio equipment directly into. The most common are the surge protector, power conditioner, voltage regulator, and uninterruptible power supply.

Surge protectors are inexpensive devices that resemble a multi-outlet power strip and act like fuses to protect your equipment against strong surges and spikes. They are generally inexpensive and can be found in any electronics or computer store.

Power conditioners are used to suppress high-voltage surges and transients as well as filter out radio-frequency interference (RFI) and electromagnetic interference (EMI) from incoming power.

Voltage regulators are used to deliver a stable AC current to sensitive electrical equipment. They work by continuously monitoring the incoming power level and modifying it when voltage irregularities (such as brownouts, overvoltages, or sags) occur in the AC line. Voltage regulators can also perform the job of a power conditioner, removing RFI and EMI, as well as large power spikes.

An uninterruptible power supply (UPS) is a larger, more expensive device that runs on rechargeable batteries. In the event of a power failure or brownout, the UPS will immediately switch over to battery power and continue to provide current long enough for you to save your work and shut off your equipment. Some UPSs also condition the power to minimize line noise, spikes, and surges.

CHAPTER 3

The Personal Studio Makeover

Most personal studio builders have neither the budget nor the room to transform their studios into professional-caliber facilities. You can't expect to get million-dollar sound for a few hundred bucks—or even a few thousand. But there are techniques you can use to greatly improve the acoustics of your studio space, even if it's a rectangular room with parallel walls. These tips will help you get optimal performance from your personal studio, no matter how modest it is.

Basic Considerations

Before we get into acoustics, though, you'll need to make sure you don't have any weak links in your monitoring system. First, monitoring systems for critical listening must have a fairly flat frequency response, ranging from 60 Hz or lower to at least 16 kHz, and the lowest distortion spec possible. Fortunately, most studio-grade, powered close-field monitors on the market do a fine job of meeting these specifications. Therefore, selecting the "right" system is often just a matter of personal taste. (See Chapter 9, "The Monitoring Milieu," for more detailed information about monitors.)

It is also important to set up the monitoring system symmetrically within the room. The distance between speakers should be the same as the distance from each speaker to your ears, forming an equilateral triangle (see **Fig. 3.1**). For close-field monitoring, the distance between speakers should be two to four feet, depending on their size and dispersion and what is ergonomically most feasible. Also, the center of this equilateral triangle should be equidistant from each of the room's walls.

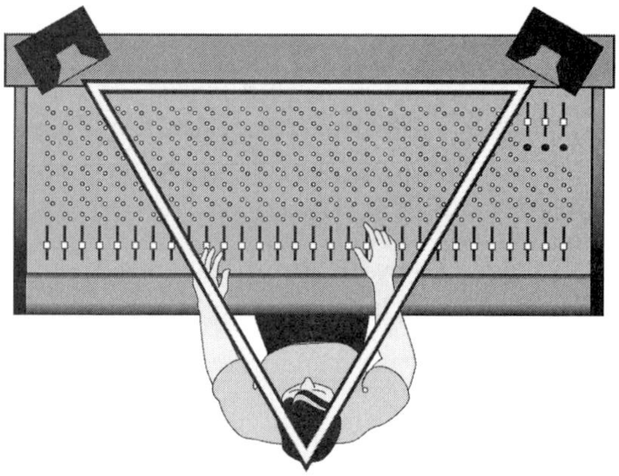

FIG. 3.1:
The distance between speakers should be the same as the distance from each speaker to your ears, forming an equilateral triangle. The center of this triangle should be equidistant from each of the room's walls.

However, even when you've placed high-quality gear symmetrically in the room, your setup may still fall short of sonic accuracy. The overall sound might be boomy and muddy, the bass too loud or too soft, the high-end dull or harsh-sounding, and the imaging blurry and undefined. Room acoustics can play a significant role in both creating and reducing these problems.

In professional studios, room acoustics are a top priority. Typically, the owners spend a good deal of money on professional consultation, premium construction, and first-rate sonic treatments, sparing no expense to achieve a trouble-free, acoustically "neutral" monitoring environment. Luckily, acoustic problem solving is not outside the financial realm of the personal studio owner. Expect to spend at least the same sum of money for acoustical treatment as you did for your monitors.

Finding the Right Room

A comfortable and spacious studio is something to be thankful for. Knowing where everything is and that it is all going to work each time is quite liberating, especially if you're planning to spend serious time at your craft.

Which room you use for your studio probably depends on considerations other than artistic, acoustic, or ergonomic ones. In a perfect world, you not only would be able to choose the best-sounding and most inspiring space to make your musical home, but you could also determine the exact placement of each piece of gear in the room (perhaps by using Feng Shui) and then have the money to acoustically treat the room to make the mixing position sound the sweetest.

In the real world, most personal studios are assembled in any room the recordist can usurp from the rest of the household, regardless of the potential problems that isolation from the outside world and interior sonic dilemmas present in the basements, attics, walk-in closets, and garages we are often forced to inhabit.

If you're one of those lucky people who has a choice of rooms, how do you decide which will be right for your studio? Let's look at some particulars that can make the difference between a troublesome and a trouble-free studio.

Isolation. In addition to preventing the outside world from hearing your band rehearsing and recording, it is important to keep as much external sound out of your studio as possible. Unless you own your home, have lots of money to spend on renovating its structure, or have a landlord willing to let you do major modifications, you're going to have to accept marginal isolation. Therefore, you will need to think about how much sonic disturbance you're willing to tolerate.

Begin your quest for the perfect studio by sitting quietly in each room you have available. Is the room on the noisy side of the house? For example, can you hear traffic outside the window? Chances are your microphones will hear it as well. On the other hand, it may be the better of two rooms if your only other option is an unused bedroom that shares a wall with an easily annoyed neighbor.

Weather conditions. If you are thinking of using an attic or basement, imagine the worst-case scenario for any weather conditions you may encounter in your area. Does your basement have a problem with moisture when it rains? Does it flood?

Water damage can also be a concern in the attic. If you have an old roof, it may take only one severe storm to cause a leak to develop.

If you're still considering the attic, remember that heat rises. Is there adequate ventilation in the attic during the hot summer months, or during the winter when the heat is on downstairs? In either situation, it could be too hot to work upstairs with the heat from your recording gear, combined with the sweat from your performances, while every window and door is shut for isolation purposes.

Wiring. If you have a separate circuit for the room you choose, consider yourself lucky. When your audio equipment shares a household circuit with the refrigerator or air conditioner, you hear annoying audible artifacts each time the appliances switch on or off. In addition, sharing circuits with the rest of the house increases the possibility of a circuit overload, which could abruptly power down your system and unexpectedly ruin a session. If the circuit is shared by major appliances somewhere else in the building, consider hiring an electrician to help you find a solution.

Before you move your gear into the room, determine the number of circuits you would like in your studio. The best situation is to have your computer, audio gear, and lighting all on separate circuits. It may require a bit of planning to make this work, but you will be happy with the results.

Speaker Placement

Your first consideration should be the orientation of the speakers in the room. Assuming that your space is rectangular, it is best to point the speakers down the longest dimension so that low frequencies have a chance to develop before hitting the back wall. Next, consider the position of your speakers in relation to the listener, adjusting them until you get the most accurate bass response. This is critical for every studio.

The way that low frequencies behave in a room is dictated largely by the room's dimensions. Certain frequencies, due to the lengths of their respective sound waves, will be reinforced as they move along the room's boundaries—the walls, floor, and ceiling—creating resonant boosts in volume at those frequencies (see **Fig. 3.2**). These resonances are commonly referred to as *standing waves*. You can estimate the most prominent resonant frequencies of a room by using the formula:

$$f_1 = 1{,}130/2L = 565/L$$

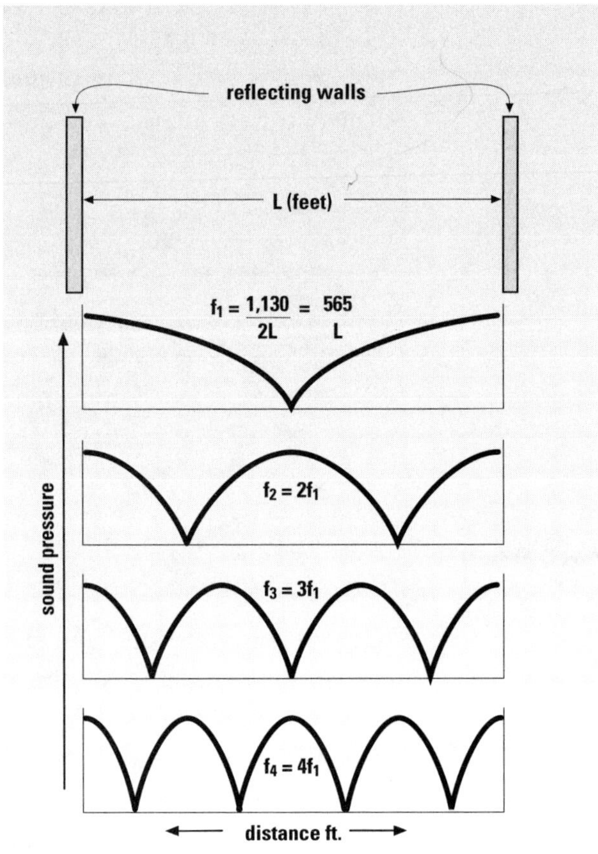

FIG. 3.2: When a wavelength is twice as long as the distance between room boundaries, "standing waves" reinforce that frequency and its harmonics, which boosts their volume.

In this formula, f_1 represents the resonant frequency, and 1,130 is the speed of sound through air under normal conditions (defined as one atmosphere of pressure at sea level at 21 degrees Celsius). L represents the length of the room in feet. For example, if the room is 10 feet long, there will be a natural resonant volume boost in the room at 56.5 Hz. In addition, natural boosts in volume will occur at multiples of this frequency: f_2 = 113 Hz, f_3 = 169.5 Hz, f_4 = 226 Hz, and so on.

The resonances are closer together and their volumes are more diminished as you move up the frequency spectrum. In small rooms, therefore, resonances are typically not as problematic above 200 Hz.

By nature, low frequencies are omnidirectional. When you are using free-field rather than flush-mounted speakers, low frequencies reflect from all nearby room boundaries. The result is that the bass sounds as if it's coming from different directions (see **Fig. 3.3**). These slightly delayed reflections of the original signal cause comb-filtering peaks and dips within the range of frequencies above the modal resonance range (typically 200 Hz in a small room) to an upper limit of approximately 500 Hz. The increasingly directional nature of sound above 400 Hz makes speaker/boundary interference less of a problem for mid and high frequencies.

Standing waves and speaker/boundary interference can cause deviations in frequency response as high as 15 dB. This amount of variation could keep you guessing about proper levels for all the bass frequencies you mix. Your goal is to find a speaker position that minimizes these types of interference.

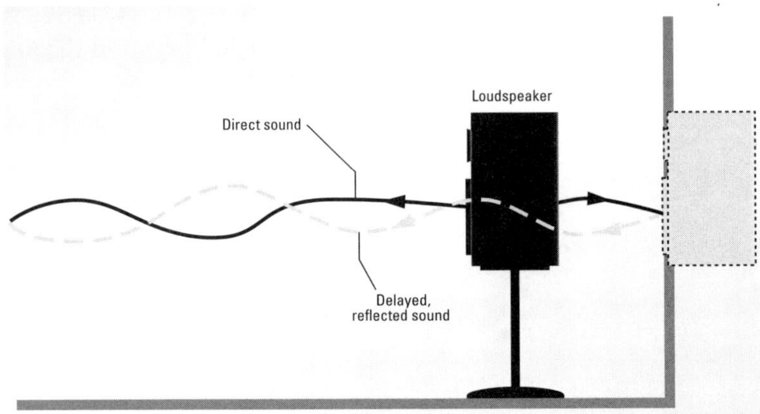

FIG. 3.3:
The omnidirectional nature of low frequencies causes them to reflect from all nearby room boundaries.

Software Route

First, locate the best listening position and then acoustically treat the walls and ceiling based on this position. You can locate the "sweet spot" using specialized studio-design software that does predictive analysis. These programs ask you for the dimensions and characteristics of the room so that the software can mathematically determine which position in the room is the most accurate for listening.

To find the sweet spot in real time, you will need a real-time analyzer (RTA), a calibrated measurement microphone, and a pink-noise generator. If you have furniture and equipment in the room already, using an RTA will give you greater accuracy in positioning your listening station. You can also use the real-time approach to verify the software analysis.

Set the microphone where you would prefer to sit. Then run pink noise through one speaker only and move that speaker in 4- to 6-inch increments in every direction until you find the position where the bass response is flattest. Once you have located the best spot for the first speaker, measure its distance from the microphone and mirror it with the other speaker to form an equilateral triangle.

JBL's affordable LSR4300-series monitoring system offers a convenient and easy-to-use Room Mode Correction feature. Each monitor in the system has a built-in analyzer to measure and compensate for problems created by standing waves and boundaries in a room. The system includes a calibration microphone, a wireless remote control, and Control Center software.

Another approach is to place one of the speakers where you want it and then search for the optimal seating position by moving the microphone. When you find the sweet spot, make your measurements and place the other speaker to form your equilateral triangle.

If you're using enclosed monitors with separate woofers and tweeters—known as *discrete*, rather than *coaxial* or *concentric*, monitors—position them so that the speakers are in a vertical line, one on top of the other. (Putting them on their sides, with the woofer and tweeter horizontal to each other, creates phase problems.) Be sure that the speakers are placed high enough to project over the console.

Rays Versus Waves

Once you've established the speaker and listening positions, the next step is to treat the room to reduce unwanted reflections. You'll need to address two areas of acoustics: ray acoustics and wave acoustics. Understanding how sound behaves in the rectangular confines of a personal studio, where dimensions are usually fixed and space is tight, is the key to the proper application of sonic treatment.

Ray acoustics apply to the mid and high frequencies. These frequencies have very short wavelengths that arrive at a boundary surface completely developed. These frequencies behave in much the same way as beams of light—for example, hard and irregular surfaces diffuse and scatter beams randomly, whereas more absorptive surfaces are less reflective (see **Fig. 3.4**).

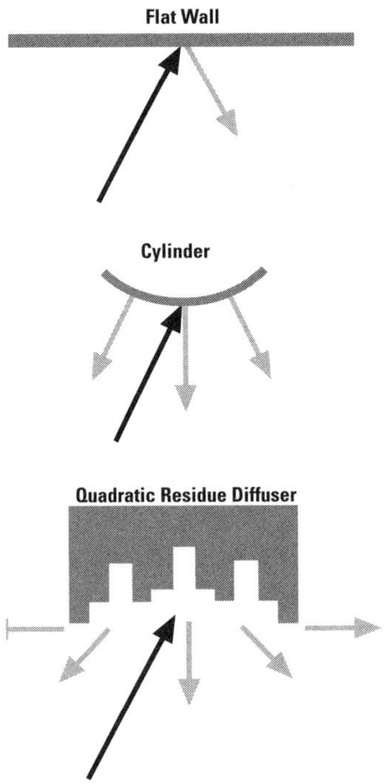

FIG. 3.4:
Diffusers and cylinders scatter reflections in many directions.

The biggest detriment to mid- and high-frequency accuracy is the presence of early reflections. When you listen to your monitors, you hear the direct sound from the speakers, followed by reflections of that sound from the walls, ceiling, and other hard surfaces in the room. When reflections arrive at our ears "early"—within 20 milliseconds of the direct sound—we hear them as part of the direct sound. Because sound waves travel about one foot per millisecond, most of the first reflections that make their way to the listening position in a small room qualify as early reflections.

Commonly, the frequency range of early reflections extends from 500 Hz on up. This range critically affects the accuracy of the monitoring system's imaging, as well as its mid- and high-frequency tonality. Early reflections often add audible comb-filter distortion to the direct signal, tainting the frequency response with a variety of boosts and dips. Early reflections also tend to blur the stereo imaging between the speakers, making it difficult to hear the exact position of sounds within the stereo field.

If you have the luxury of constructing a studio from the ground up, you can minimize early reflections by avoiding parallel surfaces. When modifying an existing room, though, it's necessary to apply acoustical treatment to the walls and ceiling. Additionally, you'll need to know the dispersion characteristics of your monitors when determining which areas to treat; fortunately, these specs are provided by most monitor manufacturers.

Wave acoustics deal with the behavior of low frequencies—from 20 Hz to 500 Hz. If the room's acoustics are balanced, the bass and low mids will be full and warm. If the room has significant frequency boosts in this range, the resulting sound will be boomy, muddy, or both. Dips in low frequencies will result in a thin and hollow sound. The goal is to flatten out the room's low-frequency response so that you don't erroneously mix your music to compensate for boosts or dips caused by the acoustic environment.

Atmosphere and Ambience

An important aspect of your studio is how it makes you feel when you're in it. Everything from the color of the walls to the lighting can make the difference between an invigorating space and an energy-sucking hole. Before you run out and buy a can of paint in your favorite color, take a moment and consider how color affects a room.

If you have a low ceiling with water pipes running along the length of it, consider painting everything a uniform and neutral color. To avoid a claustrophobic feel, refrain from painting the ceiling beams and pipes in contrasting colors.

Recording studios often have subdued lighting. Fluorescent lights are too harsh for daily use and produce a terrible sound, while discreetly positioned lamps can throw enough light for you to see your work without annoyance. However, you may want to have one strategically placed fluorescent fixture that you can use when you're cleaning or rearranging the studio. Even if you only use it once a year, this can be a real eye-saver.

Placing Absorption

For now, let's assume that your speakers have a 90-degree dispersion in the mid to high frequencies. From the front of the monitor, position a laser pointer or a small flashlight to point

45 degrees toward the right wall, then 45 degrees toward the left wall, and then 45 degrees toward the ceiling. These are prime areas where absorption will eliminate early reflections in the listening area.

In large commercial studios, if the first splay of the side-wall is 135 degrees from the face of a speaker, the dispersion of the mid and high frequencies will run parallel to that wall. When designing a room from the ground up, you would apply absorption to this area to clean up any mid- to high-frequency reflections that are more than 90 degrees from the speaker's face, as well as any reflections that may occur from other parts of the room. In a personal studio with parallel walls, this treatment is mandatory.

The most common way of dealing with these reflections is by covering 1- or 2-inch-thick pieces of fiberglass (typically with a density of three to six pounds per cubic foot) with panel fabric (a fire-rated material that is acoustically transparent). If you're on a tight budget, you can substitute duct liner or sound-deadening board. If you have the space to spare, you can create hinged panels that allow you to easily change the way you offset the parallel surfaces.

Lowdown

To absorb low frequencies in a commercial studio, the room's dimensions are designed to focus the frequencies into an area where a bass trap has been built. However, a bass trap takes up quite a bit of space, and therefore may not be practical in a personal studio. Instead, you can apply a combination of broadband bass absorption and full-band absorption/diffusion in the back of the room. But keep in mind that the modal response of a room can change as you bring in more equipment and people, thereby reducing the effectiveness of tuned absorbers.

One place that low frequencies accumulate is in the corners of the room. An affordable method of controlling the corners is to line them with loose insulation. Place a panel of 4-inch fiberglass (with a density of three pounds per cubic foot) covered in panel fabric across each corner. In the rear corners, behind the listener, the panels should have a pegboard surface between the fiberglass and the cloth (see **Fig. 3.5**). The effect will be less absorption in the mid and high frequencies and a bit more ambience in the rear of the room. The corner traps in the front of the room do not need the pegboard. Another option for the rear wall is to put a V-shaped panel across it built of pegboard or thin plywood lined with fiberglass (see **Fig. 3.6**). This offsets the parallel surfaces and increases bass absorption.

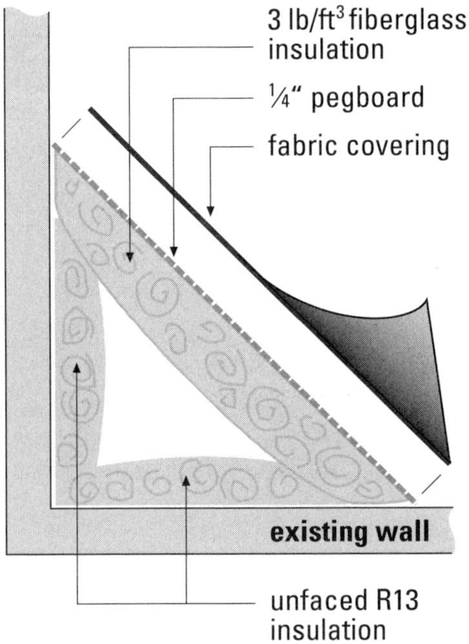

FIG. 3.5: Bass traps for the rear corners of the studio should include a layer of pegboard covered with panel fabric. Unfaced insulation lines the wall inside the trap.

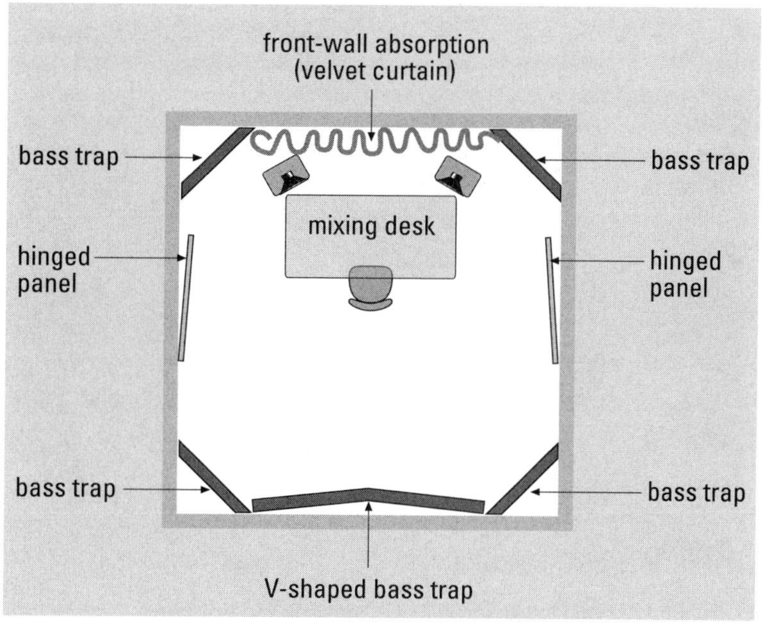

FIG. 3.6:
The use of corner bass traps, strategically placed absorbers, and back-wall diffusers can significantly improve room acoustics and monitoring accuracy. Notice how the hinged panels can handle sound emitted from speakers that have a 90-degree dispersion.

For an accurate listening environment, it's essential to eliminate the standing waves between the floor and ceiling, especially around the console and speaker areas. If you have a standard 8-foot ceiling, there are a few affordable options for treatment. The preferred method is to attach panels of cloth-covered 4-inch fiberglass (again, with a density of three pounds per cubic foot) on the ceiling (see **Fig. 3.7**).

In the rear 30 to 50 percent of the room, install RPG's Binary Amplitude Diffsorber (BAD) panels over the fiberglass ceiling treatment. (RPG calls the panels *diffsorbers* because they combine the characteristics of reflection, absorption, and diffusion into one product.) Keep the ceiling panels at least two feet away from the walls to avoid a dead room.

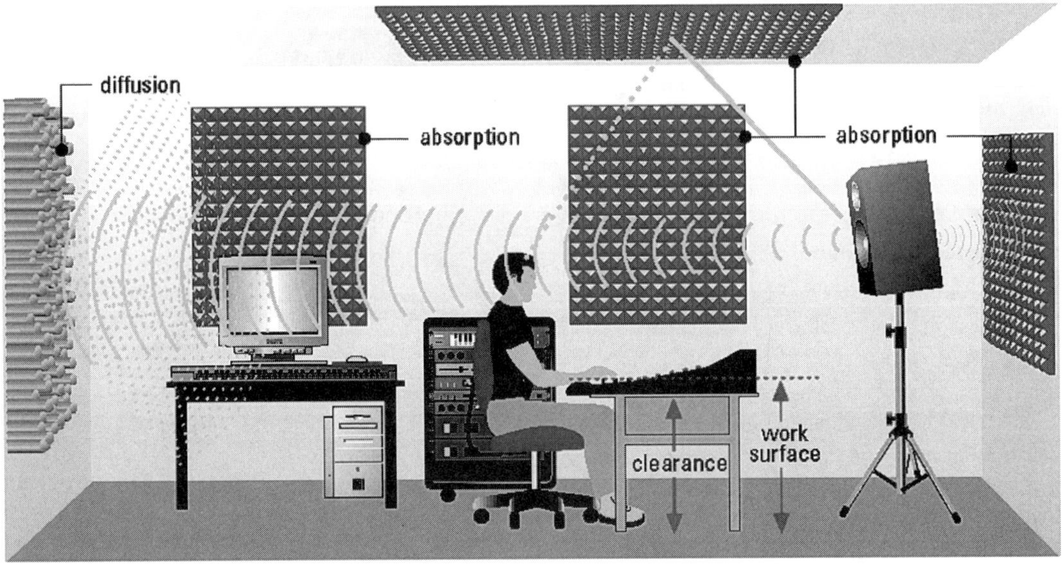

FIG. 3.7: For an accurate listening environment around the console area, standing waves between the floor and ceiling must be eliminated.

The final area requiring treatment is the front wall. Equipment racks and the back side of the console typically end up sending reflections toward the front wall. A panel similar to those used on the side walls will help. You can also use flannel-backed velvet curtains that weigh at least 14 ounces per square yard. By hanging the curtains over a couple of inches of fiber-glass treatment, you extend the low-frequency absorption and further eliminate front-to-back standing waves.

Moving In

Once you've positioned your speakers and acoustically treated the walls and ceiling, you're ready to install your equipment. Try to keep its layout as symmetrical as possible, and keep your racks and other furniture to a fairly low profile. A height of 30 inches is ideal; nothing should be taller than 36 inches. If possible, mount your monitors on stands behind the console, rather than placing them on the console by the meter bridge, to diminish the reflections from the console's surface. Avoid cavernous spaces entirely—any large, empty racks or similar items should be filled with something, even if it's only blank panels.

Arrange your equipment as ergonomically as possible. Position your gear so that it's within easy reach, but be careful not to close yourself in (see **Fig. 3.8**). Finally, to keep things tidy, you may want to run the wiring down one side of the room while keeping the other side clear for traffic.

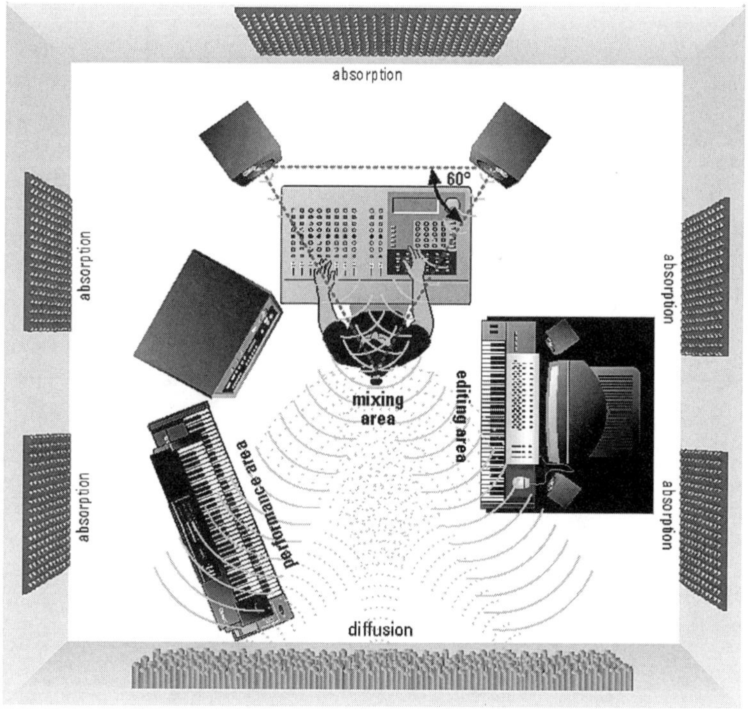

FIG. 3.8: Arrange your gear so that everything is within easy reach.

Mission Accomplished

If you're creating your studio on a limited budget, be realistic about what you can accomplish. With a little know-how and some creative exploration, you can turn any room into a reasonably accurate listening environment.

CHAPTER 4

Choosing a Multitrack Recording Format

With so many recording formats and so many ways to record, how do musicians choose the format that's right for them? Considering the large variety of recorders on the market, it's not as difficult as it may seem. Simply use your musical needs and goals, as well as your budget, to guide you.

The More, the Merrier

Two top-priority attributes of a piece of recording gear are its price and how easy it is to use. The success of analog cassette multitracks (also called *ministudios* because they include a mixer and other useful components) reflects an unmistakable demand by musicians to work quickly and simply, even if it means sacrificing audio fidelity. In this case, the basics—recording, overdubbing, and mixing—are usually enough. Many musicians prefer the straightforward approach of these devices because the technology doesn't get in the way of the creative flow, and the cost of the recorder and blank media is low.

However, if you want to create CD-quality work, the practical and creative priorities are different. Price and ease of use are no longer the only criteria to be met; audio quality and feature set become important, as well. The user interface must also be considered, because it will determine the ways in which you work.

Often, musicians will have more than one format at their disposal to cover a variety of situations. For example, a person might use a portable CompactFlash-based recorder for making informal stereo recordings of live performances. That same musician might bring an 8-track portable digital recorder on the road to use as a multitrack scratch pad. When it comes time to lay down the basics of a song destined for release, he may rely on the superior sound quality of a high-end digital audio workstation (DAW) or open-reel analog tape deck. Each of these formats has its own personality, and the trick is to find the one that best suits your circumstances and style of working.

I've divided the multitrack formats into two major categories: analog and digital. Many of the formats are no longer supported by manufacturers, but I have included them anyway because they are still widely used, and you are likely to run across them at some point in your career. In addition, many of these obsolete formats are an excellent choice if you're looking for an inexpensive, secondhand hardware recording system.

Analog Recording Considerations

The secret to getting excellent sound from analog tape is to use the widest tape at the fastest speed with the fewest tracks possible. The more physical space that each track has on the tape, the better the sound reproduction will be. The same goes for tape speed; the sound gets more space on the tape the faster the tape is moving. This is why a recording made on a 2-inch, 8-track machine at 30 inches per second (ips) sounds far superior to a cassette 4-track recording made at 3.75 ips. On the other hand, a cassette multitrack provides a recorder and mixer in a single unit, for a fraction of the cost of a high-quality open-reel recorder.

With all analog-tape formats, the audio quality degenerates slightly each time you play the tape. This is more noticeable on cheaper machines, with smaller tape formats, and at slower tape speeds. If you're the sort of person who will do 100 takes of a solo to get it right, remember that each time you rewind and play the tape, the other tracks suffer a slight signal loss. However, many musicians are willing to trade minor signal degradation for the sonic benefits of analog tape, such as the perceived "warmth" that tape gives to certain instruments.

With that in mind, here are the two analog multitrack formats you will encounter.

Analog cassette multitracks. The home-recording craze really began with the advent of the 4-track cassette recorder. The popularity of the Tascam Portastudio and the Fostex Multitracker was largely due to their low price and ease of use. For the first time, everything the musician needed to record a project (other than the microphones) was included in one unit—mixer, EQ, an effects send, etc.—and musicians began referring to them as *portable studios*. All of these features combine to make the portable cassette multitrack a great audio sketch pad for home or traveling. Some portable cassette recorders can even run on batteries.

Unfortunately, the sound and facility of the cassette recorder are not up to today's recording standards. Cassette recorders often have problems with wow and flutter, especially with longer cassette tapes, and rewind time is quite slow in comparison to other tape formats.

When it comes to editing, other formats, especially digital ones, outshine cassette recorders. Tape-splice editing is out of the question because of the cassette housing (except in the case of repairing a broken tape, when splicing is the way to go). Seamless punching in and out is difficult with cassette machines. And if you want to synchronize a sequencer with your audio, you have to dedicate a track to do it.

A 4- or 8-track cassette ministudio may be technically unable to clearly reproduce scores of stacked instrumental tracks (see **Fig. 4.1**). The width of the cassette tape, the number of tape tracks, a slow tape speed, and track crosstalk often work against large-scale orchestrations. To get the best sound from this format, you should record with a relatively sparse instrumentation to avoid overwhelming the recorder with more information than it can cleanly and accurately reproduce.

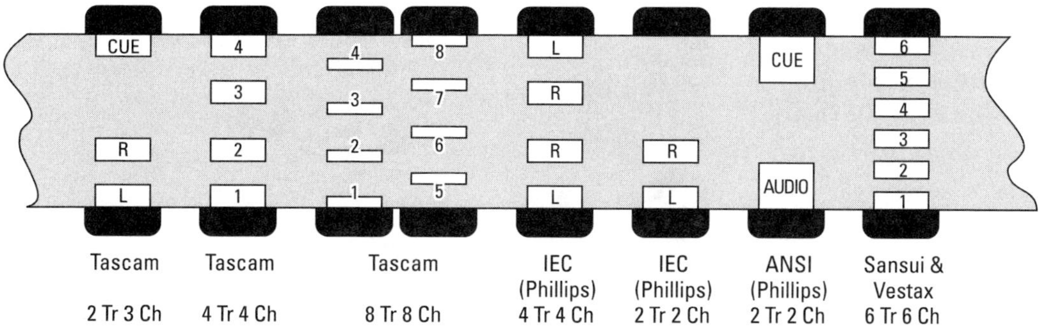

FIG. 4.1: Cassette tapes were divided into various track configurations. From left to right, the configurations depicted here are Tascam 2-track plus cue, Tascam 4-track, Tascam 8-track, quarter-track stereo, half-track stereo, ANSI/Philips mono plus cue, and Sansui/Vestax 6-track.

If you want to use a cassette multitrack recorder for more than just sketching ideas, consider spending a little extra and buying the best-sounding unit you can afford. Also, use the highest-quality blank cassettes you can find, as well as the fastest tape speed, if the unit gives you a choice.

Analog open-reel multitracks. The reel-to-reel format is where multitrack recording began, and most of the multitrack-recording techniques we use today (whether in the analog or digital domain) were developed on these machines. Overdubbing, track bouncing, punching in and out, and tape splicing are easily accomplished with open-reel recorders (see **Fig. 4.2**). Analog tape is a very robust and reliable format, with the potential for high-quality sound and very little risk of complete media failure. Unfortunately, consumer-priced reel-to-reel recorders are no longer commercially produced, so you will have to find one secondhand if you're interested in working in this format.

FIG. 4.2:
In a typical open-loop tape transport, the tape encounters the erase head first, then the record head, and finally the repro head.

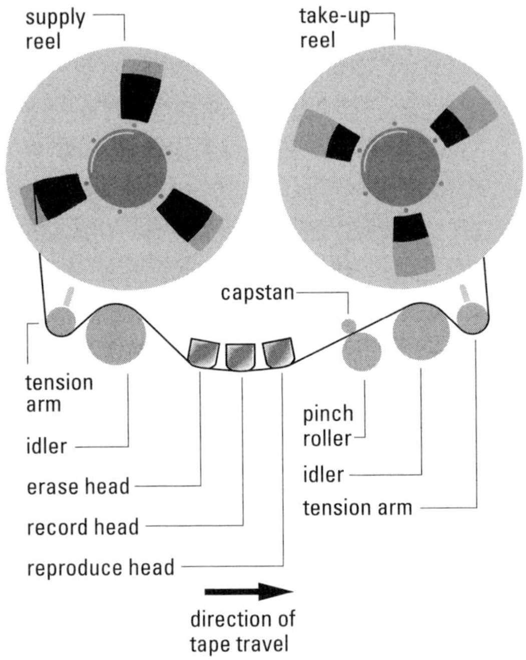

The number of tracks on open-reel decks ranges from 4 to 16 for consumer-priced machines; tape widths range from 1/4-inch to 2 inches; and tape speeds run from 7.5 to 30 ips. (Some recorders give you a choice of two speeds.) The wider the tape and the more tracks you have, the more expensive the recorder will be, and blank reels of wider tape are also more costly.

The most popular reel-to-reel formats include 1/4-inch 4-track and 8-track machines; 1/2-inch 8- and 16-track machines; and 1-inch 16-track machines. Tascam and Fostex even manufactured 1-inch 24-track recorders for a short period of time.

Remember that open-reel recorders do not include mixers, mic preamps, effects, or other useful features that the various portable studio formats (both analog and digital) provide, so further investment will be needed to get your studio up and running. In addition, compare the price of large-format tape reels ($200 and up for a 1-inch reel that yields about 15 minutes of recording time at high speed) to the price of an ADAT tape (less than $20 for 60 minutes of recording time on 8 tracks), and you will see why MDM recorders became popular.

One thing that you can't do with an ADAT or cassette is tape-splice editing. To splice a tape, you literally cut out a portion of the tape with a razor blade, and then attach it to another piece of recording tape using special adhesive splicing tape. For decades, editing with a razor blade was the easiest way to rearrange entire sections of a song. Because of this, knowing how to splice tape was an essential skill for anyone working with an analog multitrack.

Tape splicing is a physical (and very satisfying) way of moving data around, which today's generation of computer-savvy musicians may never experience. On the other hand, it's also dangerous compared to editing on a computer, because the potential of damaging your master is much greater. But in the hands of an experienced recording engineer, tape splicing can produce remarkable results.

Digital Recording Considerations

Digital recorders don't suffer from the same limitations that analog tape formats do. Nonetheless, each digital format has its own strengths and weaknesses that the recording artist must consider.

Two primary considerations are bit resolution and sample rate. Bit resolution, also referred to as *word length*, is the number of bits per sample that a digital device uses to convert or store data. The greater the number of bits in a digital sample, the more accurate the digitized description of the audio waveform will be. Compact discs use 16-bit resolution. However, it's now common to record 24-bit word lengths. One thing to remember is that the greater the word length, the more digital storage space you will need to hold it.

To get the most out of your digital recorder, you will want to record at the highest audio levels possible without getting distortion. This allows you to use the analog-to-digital (A/D) converter's full bit resolution, resulting in a better representation of the analog waveform in the digital domain.

Sample rate (or sampling frequency) refers to the number of samples taken per second. The most common rates are 44.1 and 48 kHz, as well as their multiples—88.2, 96, and 192 kHz. The higher the sampling frequency, the more accurate the recording will be.

The sample rate for compact discs is 44.1 kHz. If your music is destined for CD release, you should consider recording at that sample rate (or a multiple of it, such as 88.2 kHz) to avoid awkward sample-rate conversions. Although sample-rate conversion is a fairly common practice, converting in the digital domain (say, from 48 to 44.1 kHz) can sometimes yield less-than-satisfying results. If this happens, you're better off going back into the analog domain through a digital-to-analog (D/A) converter and resampling the music at 44.1 kHz.

Often, the quality of the built-in digital converters in a recorder can be improved with a dedicated outboard converter. This is particularly important with the A/D converter because it determines the accuracy of the bits going to tape or disk.

Although outboard converters are sometimes as expensive as the recorders themselves, the resulting sound quality is well worth the money. High-quality A/D converters give you a wider dynamic range, greater clarity, and improved frequency response.

Let's look at the most common digital multitrack formats.

Digital audio workstations. If you already have a computer, you can use it for recording, mixing, and MIDI sequencing by purchasing the specialized hardware and software needed for a DAW. Because DAWs are computer-based, they offer the greatest possibility for expansion. For example, recording time is limited only by the amount of disk space at your disposal, while the number of tracks you can run at one time is often software expandable (see **Fig. 4.3**). DAWs can be fortified with various third-party applications and plug-ins so that an entire virtual recording studio can reside in your computer.

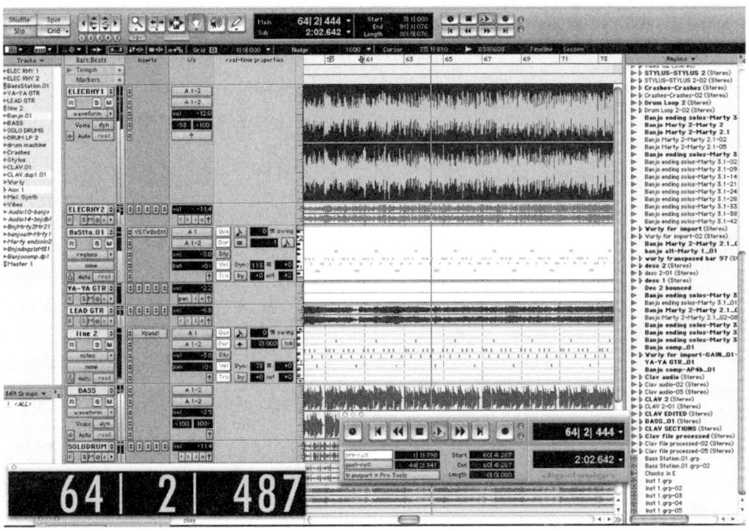

FIG. 4.3:
Digidesign Pro Tools is a DAW that is used in both professional and personal studios. The more affordable version, Pro Tools LE (shown here), is fully compatible with the more expensive TDM version.

A DAW can give you the greatest amount of flexibility of all the recording formats we've examined. Besides covering the basic functions of a multitrack recorder, you have the ability to nondestructively cut and paste portions of audio and MIDI files (together or individually), use effects in unusual ways, create virtual audio tracks, automate the mixing environment, and burn a CD-R of the final product.

Sample rate and bit resolution are determined by the software, digital converters, and amount of disk space you want to use. The higher the bit resolution, for example, the more disk space you will need for your sound files. If 16-bit CD-quality audio is fine for your needs, then every sequencer on the market will work for you.

The downside of using a DAW is the risk of total media failure. If your computer crashes during a session, you could lose everything you were working on, and you wouldn't be able to continue the session until you got it up and running again.

Personal Digital Studios. On the surface, these all-in-one recorders bear a slight resemblance to cassette-based multitrackers, but their feature set is far more advanced than their analog brethren. Portable digital studios are well-integrated hard-disk recorder/mixer combinations offering nonlinear, random-access cut-and-paste editing, digital mixing, manual and automated punch-in and -out capabilities, digital effects, and, in some cases, computer connectivity, and sequencers with dedicated rhythm tracks, percussion pads, and sample libraries. As the name suggests, a *keyboard workstation* marries a piano keyboard with the functionality of a digital multitracker. All of these devices are capable of CD-quality audio—16-bit, 44.1 kHz—but many of them offer much higher fidelity.

Another interesting feature of these kinds of recorders is the virtual track. Virtual tracks give you a number of tracks to record beyond the recorder's regular track count. The catch is that you can only play back a limited combination of these tracks simultaneously. For example, a 16-track unit might offer 96 virtual tracks, but you can play back only 16 of them simultaneously.

The number of tracks you can record simultaneously is also limited on personal digital studios (see **Fig. 4.4**). Obviously, the more expensive machines give you more tracks and more features, such as a greater number of auto-locate points and a CD burner.

FIG. 4.4:
At 24-bit resolution, the Korg D3200 lets you record 12 tracks and play back 16 tracks simultaneously. The number of tracks you can simultaneously record and play increases to 16 and 32, respectively, when you decrease the resolution to 16 bits. The D3200 also offers 272 virtual tracks, eight phantom-powered mic inputs, and 52 effects algorithms.

The interface of the portable digital studio resembles other types of portable studios, with basic transport controls and familiar mixer knobs and faders. These devices are simple to use in record and playback modes. Things can be a little trickier, however, when it comes time to edit or bounce tracks. Be sure to investigate the user interface when you're considering a specific recorder, because each company implements its features a little differently, and it is important that these features match the way you want to work.

Other Digital Formats

Modular digital multitracks (MDMs). The release of Alesis ADAT recorders in 1991 engendered such a strong resurgence of home recording that, for the first time, the livelihood of professional studio engineers was threatened. Suddenly, musicians could afford multitrack recorders that gave them sound quality rivaling that of many large-format multitrack recorders.

This 8-track digital-audio format boasted better-than-CD sound quality and used standard S-VHS tapes that were inexpensive and easy to find. The best part was that up to 16 ADATs could be combined for a maximum of 128 tracks. Other companies quickly got into the game, and the field of MDM was born.

There are currently three MDM formats to choose from. The original ADAT (now referred to as *Type I*) is a 16-bit format that uses S-VHS tape. Type I units have a maximum recording time of 67 minutes using a T-180 tape. Examples of Type I units include the Alesis (original) ADAT and XT, the Fostex RD-8 and CX-8, and the Panasonic MDA-1.

The ADAT Type II (sometimes called *PDAT*) is a 20-bit format that also uses S-VHS tape. The maximum record time is also 67 minutes when using a T-180 tape. Type II units include the Alesis LX20, XT20 (see **Fig. 4.5**), and M20, and the Studer V-Eight. Type II ADATs will record and play back both 16- and 20-bit tapes, so they can also read tapes made on Type I units.

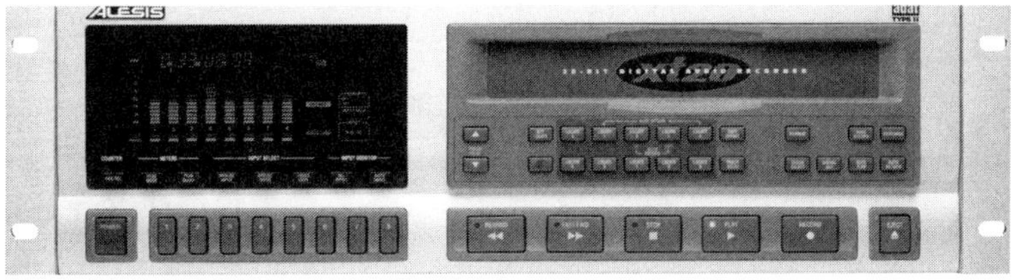

FIG. 4.5: The Alesis ADAT XT20 is a Type II ADAT recorder that offers 20-bit resolution.

DTRS (Digital Tape Recording System) is a 16-bit format that uses Hi-8 mm videocassette tape and gives you a maximum record time of 108 minutes. DTRS units include the Tascam DA-38, DA-88, DA-98, and the Sony PCM-800.

Unlike analog multitracks, MDMs can bounce tracks and make digital backups of your master tapes with no data loss or signal degradation. And because the recording media are cheap compared to open-reel tape, you don't have to worry about ruining your budget by doing another take of a song, which gives you more room to experiment with basic tracks and overdubs.

Multitrack MiniDisc. MiniDisc (also referred to as *MD*) was originally conceived as a consumer format to compete with cassettes. Instead, it became popular in the United States for radio broadcasting, as well as for fixed-installation sound exhibits, such as in amusement parks and museums.

The MiniDisc is a robust optical-storage format that is wear resistant, handling heat, dirt, and shocks relatively well. There are two types of MDs—audio and data. The audio MiniDiscs are 2-channel devices that consumers use like Walkman-style stereo cassette players. The data MiniDisc (MDD), which was originally designed to store computer data, is the format used in the 4-track ministudios manufactured by Sony, Yamaha, and Tascam.

Multitrack MiniDisc recorders are similar in design to cassette ministudios, incorporating a basic onboard mixer; simple routing options; XLR, 1/4-inch phone, and RCA connectors; and a small, tabletop footprint. But besides sharing the ability to bounce tracks, MiniDisc recorders, unlike cassette multitracks, allow you to perform simple edits using markers. This kind of editing is ideal for quickly rearranging parts of a song, copying and pasting rhythm or background parts, or cutting together ideas from several takes. Although crude in comparison to waveform editing on DAWs, digital splicing works fine for the songwriter who simply wants to manipulate the parts of a song arrangement.

Another feature of this format is that the discs can be played back on any MiniDisc machine, regardless of its manufacturer. However, your editing markers are only readable on machines from the same company. One more thing to be aware of is that many of the MD recorders lack a digital output or computer connection. Without this, there is no way to make backups or digital clones of your work, which you can do with other digital recorders.

The sound quality of the MiniDisc is superior to cassette ministudios but not as good as CDs. To record as much data as possible, MiniDiscs use a form of data compression developed by Sony called *Adaptive Transform Acoustic Decoding* (ATRAC), which reduces the amount of information that is stored on the disc by a nearly 5:1 ratio. ATRAC lets you record up to 650 MB of audio (which equals the amount of music on a CD) on a 140 MB MiniDisc.

Manufacturers use data compression when recording to a medium that has a limited storage capacity or data-transfer rate, and MiniDiscs are one such medium. Data compression is not the same as dynamics compression in the audio world. Rather, data compression uses complex algorithms to remove specific amounts of digital information that the human ear shouldn't notice is missing when the audio is played back. Most musicians, however, will notice a difference in sound quality between CDs and MiniDiscs.

Taking the Plunge

As you can see, each format has its positive and negative sides. Nonetheless, great music has been made in every one. But before you make your final decision, think about what you will be using the recorder for. If you simply need a place to record ideas quickly and easily, an inexpensive multitrack cassette recorder could be the answer. However, if you plan to make a professional-sounding release, and you want extensive editing and sequencing capabilities, you should consider setting up a DAW in your studio.

Once you have narrowed down your format preferences, spend some time investigating the different models available. The more time you spend, the more likely you will find the one that best fits your style and budget.

High-Bandwidth Cables

When making digital transfers using AES/EBU or S/PDIF coaxial connectors, use a cable that is specifically designed for this application (see Fig. 4.6). Although the connectors are the same, regular audio cables with XLR and RCA phono connectors cannot handle the high bandwidth that digital signals use. Common problems caused by improper cabling during digital transfers range from mysterious and intermittent tics and pops to garbled and distorted data. Several pro-audio companies make cables designed specifically for digital transfers. Always use the cable that's right for the job, and keep the cable runs as short as possible.

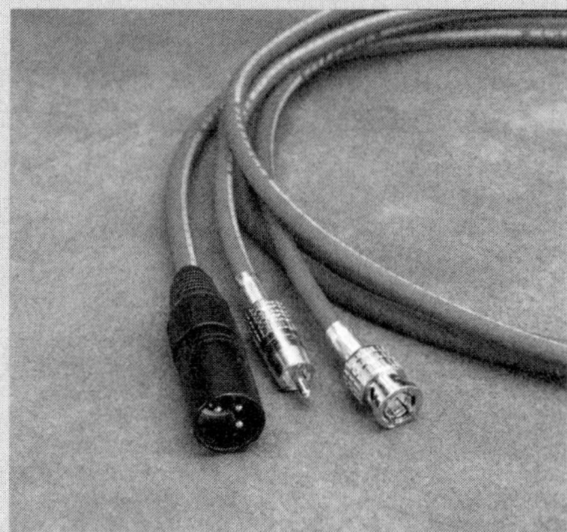

FIG. 4.6: Apogee Electronic's Wyde Eye cables are designed for use with digital-audio devices. The connectors shown here include XLR for AES/EBU signals, RCA/coaxial for S/PDIF signals, and BNC, which is typically used for word clock I/O.

CHAPTER 5

Making the Right Connections

There's nothing more maddening than getting underway with a recording session only to discover that you can't proceed because you're missing some particular cable, adapter, or other link required to complete the signal path. At best, you have to postpone the session for however long it takes to assemble the piece you need—assuming you have the parts on hand, as well as the tools and skills to assemble them. Then again, you might have to make a run to the closest pro audio or electronics shop, and if you're working nights or weekends (as musicians tend to do) you won't find the stores open when you need them. At that point, you have little choice but to abort the session—all because of a relatively inexpensive accessory that you didn't think to stock up on.

In this section, we'll get acquainted with various in-line adapters that can accommodate whatever connections you need to make. Most of these devices are available ready-made from cable manufacturers and distributors or can be ordered on a custom basis. We'll also go over the basics of signal levels, impedance matching, and polarity—issues that are critical to making proper connections.

After taking stock of the various connections in your studio, as well as the adapters you already own, you can peruse the adapter chart (see **Fig. 5.1**) to determine potential missing links in your selection. Or, if you typically solder your own cables and such, this article may inspire you to assemble your own adapters. The point is to be prepared. Then you're not only ready to handle the unexpected, but you have extra tools on hand for creative applications.

Basic Grab Bag

Some studios are static (the gear and connections don't change from one session to the next), while others get reconfigured regularly to accommodate outside artists and gear. This makes it difficult to suggest a batch of adapters that will prove sufficient for all studios. Just the same, here are some adapters that just about any studio will need at some point:

- 20 dB pad
- Ground lifter
- Phase reverser
- impedance transformer (low-Z to high-Z)
- ¼" M to RCA F (2 or more)
- ¼" F to RCA M (2 or more)
- ¼" M to minijack (both TS and TRS)
- ¼" F to miniplug (both TS and TRS)
- ¼" TRS F to ¼" TS M (stereo to mono)
- Gender benders: ¼-inch F (2), RCA F (2), XLR F & M
- Variety of Y-adapters

a. 3-cond. XLR F to 1/4" TRS M
b. 3-cond. XLR M to 1/4" TRS M
c. 3-cond. XLR F to 1/4" TRS F
d. 3-cond. XLR M to 1/4" TRS F
e. 3-cond. XLR F to RCA M
f. 3-cond. XLR M to RCA M
g. 3-cond. XLR F to RCA F
h. 3-cond. XLR M to RCA F
i. 2-cond. 1/4" F to RCA M
j. RCA F to 2-cond. 1/4" M
k. 2-cond. 1/4" M to 3-cond. 1/4" F
l. 2-cond. 1/4" M to minijack
m. 2-cond. 1/4" F to miniplug
n. 2-cond. minijack to RCA M
o. RCA F to miniplug
p. 2 minijack to microplug
q. microjack to miniplug
r. 3-cond. XLR F to XLR F
s. 3-cond. XLR M to XLR M
t. 2-cond. 1/4" F to 1/4" F
u. 2-cond. 1/4" M to 1/4" M
v. RCA F to RCA F
w. RCA F to 2-cond. 1/4" F
x. Two 2-cond. 1/4" F to 2-cond. 1/4" M
y. Two RCA F to RCA M
z. Two RCA F to 2-cond. 1/4" M

FIG. 5.1 Adapters from A to Z. It doesn't take a genius to determine the connection problems each adapter solves. Except for the invisible part—electricity—the ins and outs tell the whole story.

Connector Fest

The place to start in understanding audio connections is with the connectors themselves. Four types of audio connectors dominate the typical personal studio environment: 1/4-inch (also known as *phone*), 0.141-inch (also known as *mini, tini,* or—incorrectly—*1/8-inch*), RCA (also known as *phono* or *coaxial*), and 3-pin XLR (also known as *Cannon*). (See the table "Standards, Anyone?" for a rundown of plug types and sizes.) For each type of connector, there is both a male and female version, known as the *plug* and *jack*, respectively. Obviously, it's important to be able to interface among these different connectors.

Standards, Anyone?

Confused by those little stereo plugs that sometimes don't seem to fit well into the jack? You may be surprised to learn that jack tolerances are lax enough that miniplugs and microplugs usually work in 3.5 and 2.5 mm jacks, respectively. There is always the risk, however, of intermittent signal transmission when using the wrong size plug. Here are the specific sizes of each kind of plug, so you can match them to the jacks you use most often.

Type of Plug	Diameter
Phone	0.25"
Mini (aka Tini or 1/8")	0.141"
3.5 mm	0.137"
2.5 mm	0.098"
Micro	0.097"

Note also that 1/4-inch and mini connectors come in two flavors each: unbalanced (*tip-sleeve* or *TS*) and balanced (*tip-ring-sleeve* or *TRS*). For many applications, a TRS connector will work for either balanced or unbalanced connections; however, TS connectors cannot accommodate balanced signals or other three-conductor applications.

Polar Shift

When signals with opposite polarities are combined, a lot of nasty things can occur. Parts of the signals can be canceled (hence, made softer) and other parts reinforced (made louder), causing distortion and generally compromising the sound. That's why it's advisable to maintain consistent polarity throughout the recording/playback system.

Polarity is an expression of phase. Both balanced and unbalanced circuits pass audio through two conductors: a positive (also called *high* or *hot*) conductor and a negative (also called *low* or *cold*) conductor. If these two connections are reversed, the signal's polarity, or phase, is changed by 180 degrees. (Note that polarity is absolute—either "positive" or "negative"—whereas phase changes may occur anywhere between 0 and 360 degrees.)

On the XLR connector for a standard balanced circuit, pins 2 and 3 carry the alternating audio signal. (Pin 1 goes to a shield wire that is connected to ground and carries no signal.) The problem is that manufacturers differ on how they wire pins 2 and 3. Nowadays, most of them wire pin 2 hot and pin 3 cold. This wasn't always the case, however, and even today, some gear comes wired pin 3 hot. Therefore, you should always refer to gear manuals, if only long enough to determine which pin is hot. If the unit is out of phase with the rest of the system and doesn't have a polarity-reverse switch, then you're in the market for an inline device, such as the Whirlwind Phase Reverse (see **Fig. 5.2d**). If you're handy with a soldering iron, you can put together your own: Simply take a three-conductor cable and reverse pins 2 and 3 on one end, and you have a cable for reversing the polarity of a signal. (Be sure to mark the cable so you don't accidentally use it when you don't need it!)

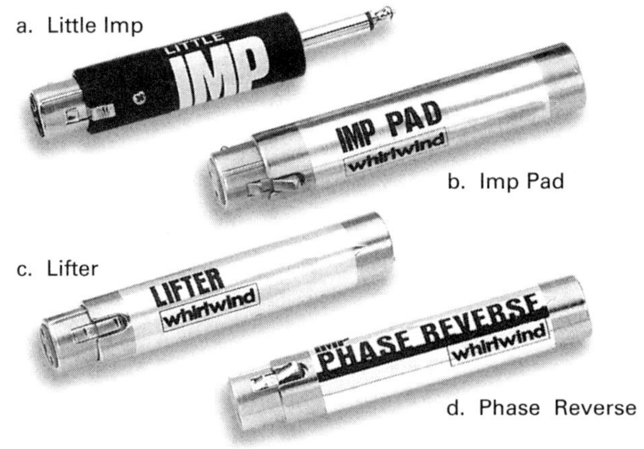

FIG 5.2: Inline transformers.

Figure 5.2 shows four examples of inline transformers that are useful in a personal studio. Whirlwind's Little Imp (a) is used for connecting low-impedance (low-Z) mics to high-Z inputs. The Imp Pad (b) comes in four models (10, 20, 30, and 40 dB) for attenuating balanced low-Z signals. The Lifter (c) lifts the ground by disconnecting pin 1, and the Phase Reverse (d) works by reversing pins 2 and 3.

Keep a Level Head

Signal levels are typically ranked in four categories: mic level, instrument level, line level, and speaker level. These categories are more approximate than precise; sometimes, there is overlapping among them. Think of the levels from weakest to strongest: Mics produce the weakest levels, with passive instrument levels (e.g., from electric guitar or bass) only slightly hotter, line-level signals hotter still, and speaker levels 10 to 100 times as high as line level.

Mic and instrument levels, therefore, are in roughly the same range, usually between –60 dB and –20 dB. A big—and obvious—difference, however, exists between the cables: Most mic cables are three-conductor, carry balanced signals, and terminate in XLR connectors, whereas instrument cables tend to be the unbalanced, two-conductor variety, terminating in 1/4-inch plugs.

This brings up the purpose of direct injection (DI) boxes, commonly called *direct boxes*. Patching an instrument cable into a direct box accomplishes a few things. First, it converts an unbalanced signal to a balanced one, which allows the signal to be sent over greater distances (an important application for the stage) without picking up radio frequency (RF) and other interference. Also, it makes the signal available to a microphone preamp via an XLR male connector, allowing you to increase gain on the instrument signal via the mic preamp's trim pot. This, of course, is a common studio application for recording, say, electric bass direct (i.e., without an amp and speaker cabinet). (See Chapter 16, "Amazing Bass," for more information about using a DI with electric bass.)

Line Level

The standard line level for professional audio equipment is +4 dBu, but for our purposes, we'll consider any signal in a range from, say, –30 dBV to +10 dBV as being line level. Obviously, this includes devices that operate at either –10 dBV or +4 dBu levels (common levels that are referred to as *semipro* and *pro*, respectively), as well as any others in the general vicinity.

This would also include output signals from many "active" instruments, such as electronic keyboards and hybrid acoustic/electric guitars that require batteries. The output from these instruments is considerably hotter than that from a passive instrument. That's why you can typically patch an electronic keyboard directly into an unbalanced, 1/4-inch, line-level jack without having to use a preamp to boost the signal.

Speaker Level

As noted, speaker levels are quite high compared to mic, instrument, and line levels. You may have noticed, for example, that high-quality speaker cable, though thick, isn't usually shielded. That's because it carries so much signal that it masks RF and other interference. Quality mic and instrument cable, on the other hand, is heavily shielded.

The upshot is that we generally seek to increase mic, instrument, and line-level signals to speaker levels only at one or two points in the signal path: at the output of the instrument amplifier (going into the speaker cabinet), or on the combined stereo mix as the system power amp boosts it going to the studio monitors (or P.A.).

Level with Me

Ideally, one would put together studio components that operate at the same level, either pro (+4 dBu) or semipro (–10 dBV). That way, there's less likelihood of incorrectly interfacing mismatched components—a common source of unwanted noise and signal loss in "newbie" studios. In the real world, though, the typical studio sports some mix of pro and semipro gear.

Thankfully, this is far from being a major problem. In fact, much of the quality gear being made for the personal studio market today—from recorders and mixers to effects and dynamics processors—can be operated at either level simply by flipping a switch or using alternative inputs and outputs.

This much, however, remains true: Whether you opt for operating your studio at –10 dBV or +4 dBu levels (the preponderance of gear usually decides the issue), you should definitely choose one or the other and then maintain it throughout the system. That is, any "wrong"-level signals should be converted to match the overall system level using some type of active interface device.

That said, it should also be pointed out that it's wrong to regard devices operating at –10 dBV as inherently inferior to those running at +4 dBu—at least for the reason of their operating levels. Properly set up and gain-staged, a system running at –10 dBV will not have an appreciably higher noise floor than one running at +4 dBu. In many respects, the quality of semipro gear has improved so much in the past few years that distinctions between pro and semipro are becoming meaningless.

The World of Adapters

Basic adapters merely convert one type of connector to another without altering the signal. Most adapters have different connectors on either end, whereas others, called *gender benders* or *couplers*, have the same connector on each end. A female XLR gender bender (see Fig. **5.1r**), for example, when attached to a male XLR connector, reverses the XLR plug's gender (male to female) without altering its type (3-connector XLR).

Other useful adapters include Y-adapters (see **Fig. 5.1 x, y, and z**), which allow you to split signals and send them to two different destinations (or, going in the other direction, to merge two signals into one) and right-angled adapters (see **Fig. 5.3**), which are convenient for navigating tight spaces.

a. RCA F to ¼" M   b. RCA F to miniplug   c. RCA F to RCA M   d. Two RCA F to RCA M   e. Two RCA F to RCA M

FIG 5.3: Right-angled adapters. No room for a straight shot? Right-angled adapters, such as these, let you sneak up from the side.

There are also inline adapters for special applications. These include ground lifters, pads, phase reversers, and impedance transformers. Not only do these devices typically convert one type of connector to another, but they also usually affect the signal in some manner. A pad (see **Fig. 5.2b**), for example, attenuates the signal, and a phase reverser (see **Fig. 5.2d**) reverses its polarity.

Another example familiar to most everyone is the ubiquitous impedance-matching transformer (see **Fig. 5.2a**), commonly used to convert a low-impedance mic signal (terminating in an XLR plug) to a high-impedance signal, while also allowing you to insert the cable directly into, say, a guitar amp via a 1/4-inch plug. Note that this special adapter looks practically identical to the basic adapter depicted in Figure 5.1a, yet the two devices yield different results. Whereas the basic adapter changes only the connector type, the impedance transformer alters the connector type and the signal.

Biology Lesson

The adapter part of making connections requires only basic biological reasoning: Plugs are male, jacks are female, and opposites attract. And here's a good thing to know: If you're missing the straightforward adapter for the job, you can usually jury-rig a makeshift by creatively connecting two or more adapters. For example, from the adapters shown in Figure 5.1, you could connect 5.1b and 5.1r to get the equivalent of adapter 5.1a.

The signal-changing part of making connections is not exactly rocket science. The main thing is to identify which levels are which. Then it's simply a matter of inserting the devices that will make the changes you need. Of course, it's critical that you listen carefully after making a connection. The whole point, after all, is to route the signal without degrading it or adding noise.

Inline Versus Cables

Because in-line adapters can be fitted onto existing cables, they are convenient for keeping in the toolbox to solve connection problems that may arise. However, for certain applications, it may be better to use custom cables.

For example, if a permanently installed processor has special requirements (for example, the unit is wired pin 3 hot and therefore needs its output signal's polarity reversed), it is generally preferable to use prepared cables (in this case, polarity-reverse cables) rather than inline adapters connected to existing cables. Not only does this keep the signal path shorter and cleaner (thanks to fewer connection points), but it also puts less strain on the jack (because an adapter adds both weight and length to the cable).

Cable Care

If you want to avoid problems, keep every cable in your studio (power, audio, digital, speaker, etc.) in good shape. Any time you crease or sharply bend a cable, you increase the chances that the core material will become unstable, leading to intermittent shorts or breakage. For this reason, you should never walk or step on audio cables. This reduces a cable's reliability because each step further compresses the insulation between the center conductor and shield. In addition, never yank or pull on the cable to unplug it. Always grab the connector or plug housing and pull directly outward.

Make sure that delicate fiber-optic cables are well protected. A break, a kink, or even a sharp bend in a fiber-optic cable can mean data loss, dropouts, and distortion. If you have long lengths of these cables between recorders, tie them together loosely with twist ties, being careful not to bind them too tightly.

Avoid storing cables in a box or bin where they will get tangled. The easiest way to store cables is by hanging them over a coat hook. Another solution is to attach a panel of pegboard to a wall and put some tool hangers up on it. That will allow you to keep the various cable types (XLR, ¼-inch, RCA, MIDI) separate from one another, and access them easily without having to untangle them.

Cable care also extends to their use and placement in a recording situation. Because an audio cable can act like an antenna and pick up RFI and other noise, it's important to keep audio cables away from computer monitors, power amps, transformers, and other sources of electromagnetic interference. For the same reason, it's best to avoid bundling power cables and audio cables together. If they have to cross each other, have them pass perpendicular to each other.

Likewise, treat your wall-wart power supplies gently. They can be irreparably damaged if they're dropped. If the power supply has a nonstandard connector or voltage, hunting down a new one can be a major nuisance. If you purchase a device that takes a nonstandard wall-wart power supply, consider purchasing an extra one, especially if you plan on traveling with it. And don't swap wall-wart power supplies between devices without first checking to see whether the power specifications match. Wall warts may look the same, but they can be quite different internally.

Completed Path

It takes some thought to prepare your studio for the myriad connection applications that can crop up in the course of regular audio production. But by studying the adapters shown here and thinking ahead, you should be able to anticipate most of your needs.

A cable tester is an invaluable studio tool. Ebtech's Swizz Army 6-in-1 tester gives you the ability to test the continuity of XLR, balanced and unbalanced 1/4-inch, RCA, tiny telephone (TT), MIDI, and balanced and unbalanced Mini connectors.

A Basic Toolkit for Maintenance

Boy Scouts and recording engineers know the value of being prepared. Technology is fickle, and sometimes sessions are plagued by equipment malfunctions. Often, the demon is something simple that can be cured with a trip to the trusty toolbox. You don't need to be a qualified repair tech to undertake the basic maintenance tips outlined in this chapter, but you do need the following items:

- Set of small- and medium-sized screwdrivers: flat and Phillips head
- Wire cutters
- Small- and medium-size needle-nose pliers

- Tone generator (if your mixer does not have one) with 100 Hz, 1 kHz, and 10 kHz settings
- Glass cleaner
- Soft, clean rag (or paper towels)
- Cleaning alcohol
- Ohmmeter
- Assortment of cotton and foam swabs
- Can of compressed air
- Red duct tape
- Soldering iron and solder

To prevent surprises during important sessions, have your ohmmeter available for testing cables for shorts. Be sure to label bad cables with red tape so you don't confuse them with the good ones. In addition, take some time to learn how to repair and assemble cables, and invest in a quality soldering iron.

CHAPTER 6

Microphones Made Easy

In the world of music technology, where innovations and new products appear almost daily, the microphone hasn't changed much at all. Synthesizers, software, and effects processors are constantly updated and rendered obsolete, but when a recording engineer grabs a microphone, it's as likely to be a model from the 1950s or 1970s as one from last year. Despite this apparent technological languor, the old-fashioned analog microphone remains vital to audio communication.

As noted in Chapter 2, microphones are transducers, devices that convert one kind of energy into another. In this case, microphones convert sound waves into electrical energy that can be stored in a recording device. This conversion frees sound from acoustical limitations, since sound waves are short-lived and travel relatively small distances before falling below the range of human hearing.

Although Alexander Graham Bell is credited with developing the first working microphone in 1876 with his "speaking telegraph" (telephone), British physicist Sir Charles Wheatstone first used the word "microphone" to describe an acoustic device in 1826. Since the earliest carbon microphones (a technology still used in many telephones), a variety of types have been developed. Of these, dynamic and condenser mics are the most common types used by musicians today.

Dynamic Mics

Dynamic, or moving-coil, microphones actually are speakers that work backward. Using a principle called *inductance*, dynamic mics create an electrical signal when air molecules hit a nonmetallic diaphragm attached to a coil of wire that slides back and forth along a magnet (see **Fig. 6.1**). The movement of the coil produces a small electrical voltage that can be amplified through a mixer's microphone preamps and sent down the audio chain. Dynamic mics do not require phantom power or a built-in battery. If phantom power is applied to a dynamic mic, it is simply ignored and won't damage the mic.

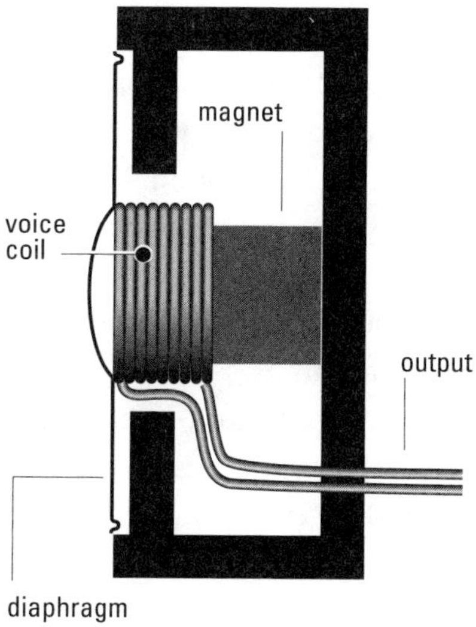

FIG 6.1: In dynamic microphones, air molecules hit a diaphragm attached to a wire coil that slides back and forth along a magnet. The movement of the coil produces a small electrical voltage.

The dynamic mic's reliability and sound quality make it one of the most widely used microphone types. Because its workings are relatively simple, the dynamic microphone is quite rugged. It is often used on drums and electric guitar amps because it can survive high volumes and even physical abuse (such as getting struck by a drum stick).

Because of the mass of a dynamic microphone's diaphragm assembly, the transient response (how accurately the mic reproduces the onset or attack of a sound) is not as true as that of condenser and ribbon mics, because it takes more energy to get the dynamic element moving. This also means that a dynamic mic will not have the transparency and high-frequency response of a condenser or ribbon mic.

Condenser Mics

Unlike the electromagnetic operation of the dynamic microphone, the condenser is a purely electrical system. Separated by a small air chamber, a diaphragm and a conductive back plate are charged by an external power supply to form a capacitor (see **Fig. 6.2**). As the diaphragm reacts to air pressure, voltage fluctuates accordingly on the back plate to produce an electrical "picture" of a sound. However, the charge that reproduces sound is tiny, so the condenser must amplify signals internally.

Some condensers use tube amplifiers, while others utilize solid-state amps. Because of the added electronics, many condensers include built-in equalization (usually in the form of a low-cut filter) and signal-reduction pads. By increasing the signal level, internal amplification optimizes frequency response, minimizes distortion, and maintains signal integrity throughout long cable runs.

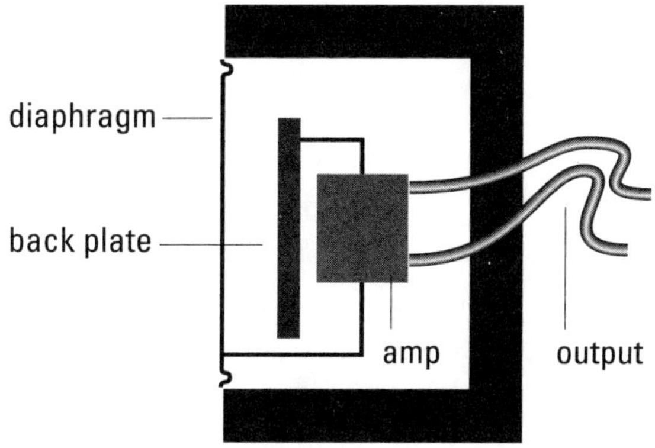

FIG 6.2:
Condenser microphones have an electrically charged diaphragm and conductive back plate, separated by a small air chamber to form a capacitor. As the diaphragm reacts to air pressure, voltage fluctuates on the back plate to produce an electrical picture of the sound.

Condenser microphones require a power source. Although some can run on battery power, phantom power is more commonly used. Phantom power is a DC voltage (usually 48 volts) that travels down the mic cable to the microphone. Mixers and mic preamps generally have phantom power that can be switched on when needed for condenser mics.

Because the condenser's diaphragm is not encumbered with the weight of a voice coil, it responds quickly to musical attacks and signal peaks. Condensers are expensive to manufacture and, because of their complexity, are more fragile than dynamic mics.

A member of the condenser family, the electret microphone utilizes a static charge and typically is powered by an internal transistor amplifier. These microphones can be made very small and often are pressed into service in extreme close-miking situations.

Ribbon Mics

A cousin to the dynamic mic is the ribbon, or velocity, microphone (see **Fig. 6.3**). The ribbon mic shares certain characteristics with the dynamic mic, including a magnet, a moving conductor, and the creation of a signal using the electrical property of inductance. But instead of wrapping the conductor around a magnet, a thin conductive strip (the ribbon) is suspended between two magnetic poles. Like the condenser microphone, ribbon mics have a greater audio transparency than dynamic mics due to the relatively low mass of the ribbon transducer. However, this makes ribbon microphones extremely fragile—for example, a poorly directed cough can shred the conductor.

FIG 6.3: Generally, ribbon mics give you a warmer sound than condenser mics, because they lack the presence peak in the upper frequency range that condensers often have. The Royer R-121, an example of a modern ribbon microphone, is sturdy and can handle high SPLs. Many engineers use the R-121 to record brass instruments and guitar amps.

Ribbon microphones revolutionized broadcast audio in the 1930s by offering smooth frequency response and minimizing vocal "popping." (Bing Crosby reportedly owed his career to the ribbon, since it was the only microphone that properly reproduced his classic croon.) Today, engineers prize ribbon mics for their open, accurate sound.

A word of caution about ribbon mics: They do not require a power source, and if they do receive phantom power, they may be permanently damaged.

Other Mic Types

Although dynamics and condensers are the most common microphone types, other designs enjoy varying degrees of popularity. The piezoelectric microphone is an early design that utilizes a flexible diaphragm and a crystal element. Sound pressure distorts the crystal, generating a corresponding voltage. Also called *crystal* or *ceramic* microphones, piezoelectrics are inexpensive and render sound quality that matches their low cost. Piezoelectric contact mics usually are employed on acoustic instruments (such as acoustic guitar), and they are designed to capture sound from a solid medium, rather than from the air.

Lavalier microphones, tiny elements designed to attach to clothing, are widely used in television broadcasting. Boundary, or pressure-response, microphones are relative newcomers that couple a mic element to a boundary plate. The "pressure zone" principle offers good imaging quality, and the microphone can be mounted to a floor or wall. (The rock group Rush once recorded basic tracks by taping a pressure-response mic to the T-shirted chest of drummer Neil Peart.)

Mic Patterns

Whatever its type, the directional response of a microphone, also called the *polar pattern* or *pickup pattern*, can be plotted graphically to illustrate where it picks up the best sound. There are five main pattern types (see **Fig. 6.4**).

Microphone Polar Patterns Compared

CHARACTERISTIC	OMNI-DIRECTIONAL	CARDIOID	SUPER-CARDIOID	HYPER-CARDIOID	BI-DIRECTIONAL
POLAR RESPONSE PATTERN	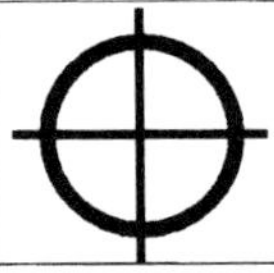	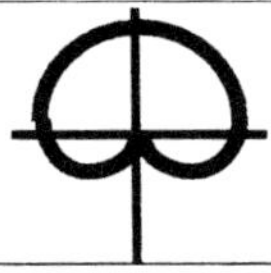	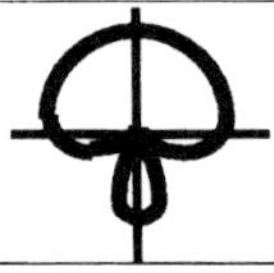	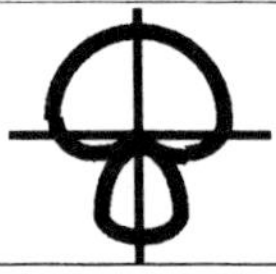	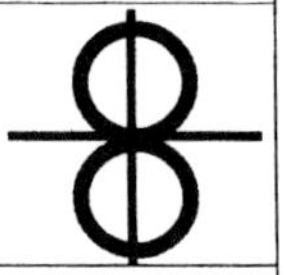
COVERAGE ANGLE	**360°**	**131°**	**115°**	**105°**	**90°**
ANGLE OF MAXIMUM REJECTION (null angle)	—	**180°**	**126°**	**110°**	**90°**
REAR REJECTION (relative to front)	**0**	**25 dB**	**12 dB**	**6 dB**	**0**
AMBIENT SOUND SENSITIVITY (relative to omni)	**100%**	**33%**	**27%**	**25%**	**33%**
DISTANCE FACTOR (relative to omni)	**1**	**1.7**	**1.9**	**2**	**1.7**

FIG 6.4: This figure shows some of the ways in which the five most common microphone pickup patterns can be compared to each other: the angle of coverage, the null angle (the angle of maximum rejection), the level of rear rejection relative to the front, the ambient sound sensitivity, and the distance factor (relative to an omni pattern).

The cardioid pattern resembles a small heart and is more sensitive on the front and sides of the microphone than the back. Cardioid patterns diminish sound "bleed" when miking separate instruments in the same room. This characteristic is called off-axis rejection, because when sounds are outside of the pickup pattern, they are not as loud or as clear as the direct sound.

Hypercardioid and supercardioid microphones are highly sensitive in front and less sensitive at the sides (see **Fig. 6.5**). These patterns diminish the potential for feedback in live situations, since monitor speakers can easily be placed outside the microphone's field of sensitivity. The result of increased side rejection with hypercardioid and supercardioid mics is an increase of sound from directly behind.

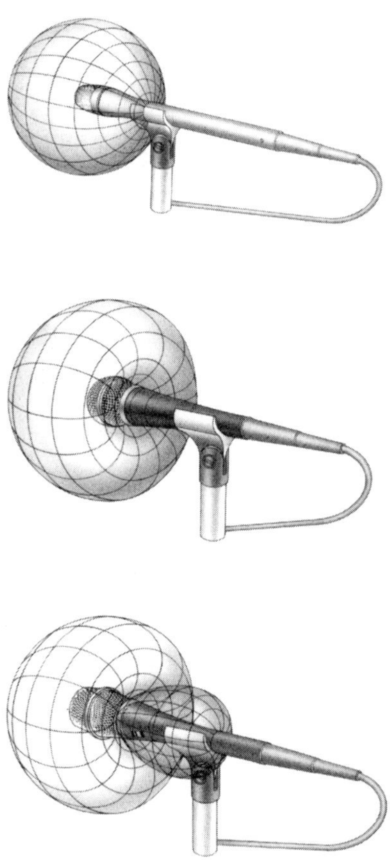

FIG 6.5: Three-dimensional representations of (from top to bottom) omni, cardioid, and supercardioid polar patterns.

A bidirectional, or figure-8, pattern is equally sensitive on the front and back of the microphone, but not as sensitive on the sides. With a bidirectional pattern, you can use a single mic to record two singers who want to face each other while tracking vocals. The majority of ribbon microphones have a figure-8 pattern.

An omnidirectional pattern is equally sensitive to signals from all directions. Omni mics can be used to record an instrument in a good-sounding environment, because the mic will pick up both the instrument and the surrounding room acoustics.

Shotgun microphones are extremely directional and are favored for film location recording, where dialogue must be isolated from environmental sounds.

Some microphones provide two or more polar patterns. Changing patterns can be done a number of ways: by using a switch on the microphone; by replacing the diaphragm capsule with one of a different pickup pattern; or remotely by using a dedicated switcher that connects to the mic with a lead, which is common with high-end condenser microphones.

Mic Characteristics

An ideal microphone reproduces acoustic sounds at the same signal level, no matter where the frequency falls within the 20 Hz to 20 kHz audible range. This is called a "flat" frequency response. However, some microphones are intentionally designed to deviate from a flat response to enhance parts of the frequency spectrum that may define an instrument. For example, vocal microphones typically exhibit a presence peak in the

5 to 8 kHz range, while bass drum mics bump up portions of the lower frequencies.

A microphone's position in relation to the sound source also can affect frequency response. When a directional microphone is placed close to a sound source, low frequencies are boosted. This is called the *proximity effect*. (Because omnidirectional microphones pick up sound from all directions, they do not exhibit this effect.) Off-axis coloration is another characteristic of directional microphones. Sound from outside the microphone's optimum pattern can interfere with the desired sound source, making the overall image ill-defined or muddy.

Diaphragm Discourse

The size and material of the diaphragm help define a mic's characteristics. A small diaphragm is one that is a half inch or less. Midsize diaphragms range from a half to one inch in diameter, and larger diaphragms go up to two or more inches in diameter.

Heavy diaphragms are slower moving than lighter ones. The faster the diaphragm can move, the better it will capture high frequencies and fast transients. In addition, heavy diaphragms have a tendency to resonate or ring at audible frequencies after the initial sound is over.

Address Direction

Where you aim the microphone is another factor. A microphone that has the diaphragm mounted vertically, in line with the body of the mic, is called a *side-address* (or *side-firing*) mic.

The most common side-address mics are the mid- to large - diaphragm mics, such as the AKG C 414 (see **Fig. 6.6**).

FIG 6.6:
The AKG C 414 B-XLS is a large-diaphragm condenser mic that offers five polar patterns, as well as three pad and three bass rolloff settings.

Small-diaphragm mics are commonly front-address (or axial). This means the sound will hit the diaphragm directly when you point the end of the microphone at the source (see **Fig. 6.7**).

FIG 6.7:
Examples of how axial and side-address mics pick up sound.

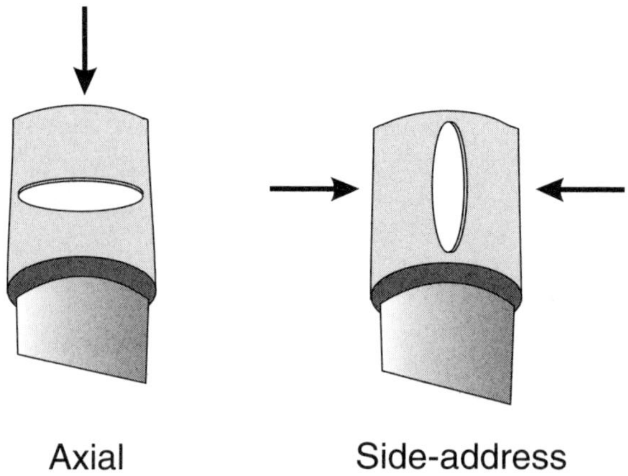

General Microphone Tips

Because each microphone has a distinct personality, deciding which one to use on a particular sound source is an individual choice. There is no proper way to mic anything; if it sounds good, do it. However, keep in mind the microphone's mechanical limits, such as the maximum volume it can handle before it begins distorting or gets damaged, which is indicated by the sound pressure level [SPL] figure in the mic's spec sheet. You don't want to spend $500 on a microphone only to ruin the diaphragm by hitting it with too high an SPL.

As you're finding the right placement for the mic, don't forget to factor in the sound of the room. Listen for any ambient noise, strange hums, bizarre reflections, and reverberation. You may decide to put the microphones closer to the instrument to diminish the environmental interference. This is called *tight*, or *close*, miking. Be sure to bring your ear down to where the microphone is placed to get a perspective of what the microphone hears. To get a better idea of what the mic is hearing, plug one ear and put the other close to the sound source. Just be careful that the volume of the sound source isn't loud enough to damage your hearing when you do this.

The Right Mic for the Job

Every microphone has an intended application; some are meant for use on stage, while others are meant for the studio. The characteristics of a specific microphone (the pickup pattern, diaphragm size, frequency response, etc.) make it better suited for some instruments over others. Even though, theoretically, you can use any mic on any instrument, generally it's best to use the microphone the way it was intended if you are going for accurate reproduction of the instrument.

For example, let's look at a typical recording situation: miking a bass drum. A small-diaphragm condenser microphone would give you less desirable low-end reproduction than a large-diaphragm condenser or dynamic mic would in this application. In addition, specialized bass-drum mics have boosts and cuts in their frequency response that give them an added advantage over mics that have a relatively flat frequency response. The result is that the specialized mic is more likely to give you a useful bass-drum sound that requires less EQ tweaking than a nonspecialized mic.

If you don't have a specialized bass-drum mic, and all you have is a small-diaphragm condenser microphone for that application, then by all means use it. Just take into account the maximum sound pressure level of low frequencies that your microphone can safely handle.

Generally, larger diaphragms sound richer on low- and mid-range frequencies than smaller diaphragms do. For this reason, engineers typically use large diaphragm mics for recording vocals and acoustic instruments that have a wide frequency range (such as the piano, saxophone, or acoustic bass). Small diaphragm mics usually offer an extended frequency response and reproduce fast transients better than most large diaphragm mics. This makes the small diaphragm mic perfect for percussion instruments and plucked strings.

There are exceptions to these rules. For example, the TC30 omnidirectional condenser mic from Earthworks has a small diaphragm, but it boasts an exceptionally flat frequency response that stretches from 9 Hz to 30 kHz (well below and above the range of human hearing). In addition, the TC30 has exceptionally fast transient response. This means that the TC30 can be used on bass or treble instruments successfully (see **Fig. 6.8**). Many large-diaphragm microphones, on the other hand, don't accurately reproduce sounds below 30 or 40 Hz or above 20 kHz.

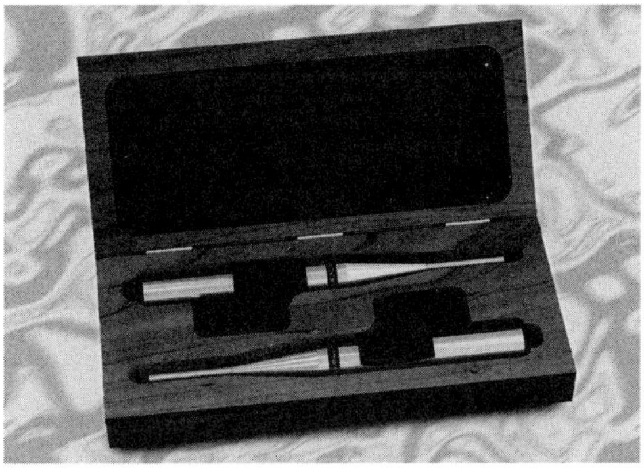

FIG 6.8: The Earthworks TC30 omnidirectional microphone has an unusually wide frequency response and exceptionally fast transient response for a small-diaphragm condenser.

But because the TC30 has an omnidirectional polar pattern, you will hear everything else in the room, which is unsatisfactory if you need separation from other instruments playing at the same time. As you can see, the microphone you choose for a given situation depends on many factors.

Where to Begin?

With so many microphones to choose from, how does a person know which one to buy? You can answer this question for yourself by determining what instruments you will record and how much you wish to spend. The budgetary question is probably the easiest to answer because you know whether you can spend $1,500 for one microphone or can afford only $250. The application question is a little trickier.

Let's look at two scenarios; the solo singer/songwriter and the four-piece ensemble.

As discussed in Chapter 2, a personal studio can get by with as few as one or two microphones. If you're a songwriter who plays acoustic guitar but are planning to record the voice and guitar separately, you can probably get by with one microphone. A good choice in this case would be a condenser with a midsize diaphragm, because it will capture the warmth of the voice, as well as the extended frequency range of the acoustic guitar. A directional mic, such as one with a cardioid or hypercardioid pattern, would be best if you want to capture more direct sound than room tone.

Fortunately, advances in microphone technology (as well as a highly competitive market and overseas manufacturing) have brought down the price of mics with large and midsize diaphragms, so that prices start below $200. Higher-priced mics usually give you quieter electronics, better frequency response, and an overall smoother sound (see **Fig. 6.9**).

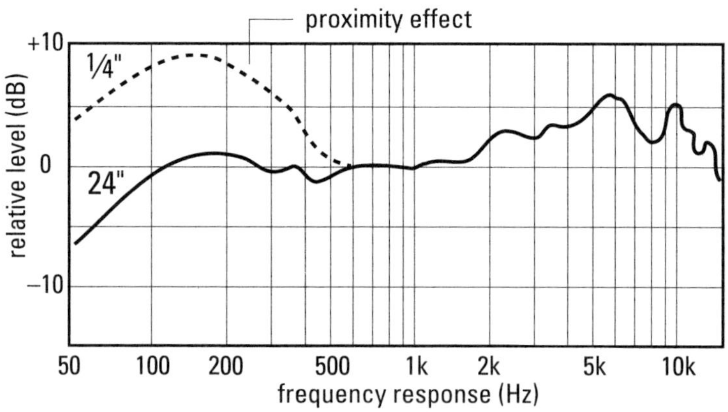

FIG 6.9:
The frequency response of a microphone is depicted in a graph of frequency vs. relative output level. As a sound source approaches a directional mic, the proximity effect boosts the low end. Notice the presence peak between 2 and 10 kHz.

But don't let price be the only factor in choosing a mic. Try out as many mics in your price range as possible, and even some that are out of your price range so that you can gain some perspective. There might be times when a $500 microphone will sound better to you than a microphone costing more than twice that amount.

If you need two mics, you might consider getting one condenser and one dynamic, both with directional pickup patterns. Or, if you plan to record in a quiet, good-sounding room, an omnidirectional condenser would be a good choice for one of the mics. This would allow you to take advantage of the room's acoustics as you record.

At the other extreme, let's say you have a four-piece rock band, which you will be recording live to a multitrack recorder. In this scenario, you are planning to mic a guitar amp, a bass amp, a vocalist, and a drum set. You might consider using seven mics for these sessions: one on each of the amps, one for the singer, and four for the drums. Where to begin?

Let's begin with the drums. The previous scenario allots four mics for the drums: one each for the bass drum and snare drum, and a pair of overheads to get the cymbals and toms. A combination of large- and small-diaphragm dynamic mics, with directional patterns for maximum separation, is a common choice for this setup. A large-diaphragm mic would be best for the bass drum, with small-diaphragm mics for the snare drum and overheads.

For the guitar amp, you can use either a dynamic or condenser mic of almost any size. For the bass amp, on the other hand, you will want to have a midsize- or large-diaphragm condenser or dynamic to catch the lower frequencies of the instrument. Again, both amp mics should be directional to help keep other instruments out of their range. Finally, like the guitarist, the vocalist could choose between a dynamic or condenser mic, and any diaphragm size.

Because the band needs seven mics, price is going to be a big consideration. There are many inexpensive small-diaphragm dynamic mics to choose from, and most will be well suited to the needs of a rock band. Large-diaphragm dynamic mics intended for bass drums would suit the bass guitar as well, and these mics are also priced competitively. Vocal mics are another story altogether.

Vocals are among the hardest things to record well. There are so many different types of voices and vocal styles that it's impossible to use the same microphone and miking technique for everyone, so in both of our scenarios (singer/songwriter and lead vocalist in the band), the singer will want to try a number of microphones to find the one that best fits his voice and style of music. If the singer cannot afford a high-end vocal microphone, such as a Neumann U 87 or AKG C 414, he can still get great sounds from an inexpensive microphone like the Shure SM58. The late Michael Hutchence of INXS once said, "Engineers always use these ridiculously expensive microphones to track my vocals and then spend hours in mixdown trying to make them sound as if they were recorded through an SM58."

Ears Are Everything

Knowing how different microphones work and using your ears help you determine which mic will work best for a particular job. Navigating the unknown may deliver a sound that shakes everyone up. It's great when someone listens to your recording and says, "How did you get that amazing sound?" So, although most microphones deliver optimum sound when used for the application they were designed for, never be afraid to experiment.

CHAPTER 7

Maximizing Your Mixer

In the typical personal studio, the choice of mixer often is dictated by price. Fiscal compromises usually rate the model with just enough features (e.g., no frills) as the winner. For example, MIDI musicians often emphasize quantity of mixer inputs over features such as parametric EQ.

The Yamaha 02R96V2 is a digital mixer that offers 56 channels, 24 100 mm motorized faders, four internal effects processors, and support for 24-bit, 96-kHz audio, and 5.1 surround sound panning and monitoring.

In high-ticket consoles, the money tends to go toward highly refined circuitry for critical functions such as microphone preamps and equalizers, as well as quality connectors and pots. Modern technology allows manufacturers to expand features yet save money by sacrificing circuit sophistication and component quality. Sometimes the most inexpensive console sounds good if pushed to its peak performance. The key is to identify weak spots and find ways to avoid them.

Prime Position

The best place to start is with the placement and connection of your mixer. Avoid putting the mixer near any source that radiates magnetic or radio-frequency waves, such as a power amplifier, speaker, computer, digital signal processor, or video monitor. The most sensitive area of the mixer is near the top of the channel strip where the input preamps are located, as they provide the highest gain.

Be sure your mixer has a solid ground and clean AC power, or you may end up with noise and distortion that can't be eliminated. Neatness counts: Careful wiring and quality cable make a drastic difference in the number of hums, buzzes, and assorted nasty noises a system picks up. Using balanced inputs whenever possible helps avoid these problems and minimize ground loops, too. If you plan to bring an unbalanced signal into the board, use a direct box to make the signal balanced.

Gain Structuring and Noise

Once the mixer is situated and hooked up, the most critical aspect of the sonic performance in virtually any audio chain is gain structuring. Proper gain structuring minimizes the noise and distortion that identifies an amateur recording. A signal passing through a typical mixer traverses at least three gain stages: the preamp, the summing buses, and the output section. Typically, each of these stages offers a level control: a preamp trim (usually found at the top of the channel strip), a channel fader, and a master fader.

The preamp section of the mixer has the most gain, and its behavior largely dictates the gain structure. Some preamps are noisy when turned up near maximum, while others are noisiest when set low. This may be due to a combination of component quality, shielding, grounding, and topology. (Some preamp trims are attenuators that act on the signal before, or even after, a fixed-gain op-amp stage, while others are in the feedback loop of the op-amp, varying the circuit's gain.) The objective is to familiarize yourself with the noise and distortion characteristics of the different stages and find optimal settings.

To get a feel for your system's quiescent noise (the noise level when there's no signal), turn the mixer preamp trim all the way down, leave the EQ flat, and set the channel and master faders at about 70 percent. Listen closely to the noise level as you slowly raise the preamp trim, to see if there is a particular spot where noise takes a jump, as is often the case in the last 10 percent of the pot's rotation. Since this test requires high monitor levels to reveal subtle noise differences, exercise extreme caution. One tiny pop can destroy your speakers (as well as your ears).

Clipping

The most common preventable source of distortion in inexpensive mixers is clipping. This occurs when the circuit runs out of available headroom, so it is important to know the dynamic limits of your mixer's gain stages. Send a signal from a test oscillator, or a simple, steady tone from a synthesizer (a sine wave is ideal), calibrated to the mixer's specified nominal input level (see the manual for this figure), into a channel. Then perform the same exercise used to check quiescent noise levels. As you increase the gain, be careful to lower channel or master fader levels as necessary to avoid overloading any stage other than the one being tested. Listen closely for the first hint of distortion. While listening for distortion, watch the level indicators (channel-overload LEDs and channel or master meters) to get an idea of the correlation between their readings and the aural onset of distortion.

The Mackie Onyx 1220 is a 12-channel, 2-bus analog mixer that offers four mic preamps (with channel inserts) and 3-band EQ. With the optional FireWire card, the mixer can be used to send 14-channels of 24-bit, 96 kHz audio to and from a computer.

A single tone isn't a comprehensive test, as practical use often requires multiple sources to be routed through the mixer simultaneously. While this operation has no effect on the individual preamps, the summing buses are impacted, as each signal contributes noise and reduces headroom. You may need to adjust channel faders, and occasionally even preamp trims, to avoid overloading summing buses and master output stages.

When tracking, less is often more. If your mixer has direct channel outputs, feeding your recorder from those eliminates several stages of electronics and the accompanying noise and distortion.

Equalization

Moving beyond the primary issues of noise and headroom, the next most pressing concern about mixers is the sound of the equalization. Circuit design and component quality are the determinants here. Most inexpensive mixers offer simple EQ, such as fixed 2-band shelving (treble and bass), fixed 3-band (treble, bass shelving, midrange peaking), or 3-band with switchable (or sweepable) midrange. If you are lucky—or paid more for your mixer—you may get switchable/sweepable high or low frequencies, or more bands.

As with gain structuring, you need to learn the characteristics of the EQ to optimize its use. Identify the center frequencies, check the amount of boost and cut available, and find the slope of the shelving and the bandwidth of the peaking filters. One often overlooked concern is that boosting the EQ increases the signal level, which can cause clipping. In most cases, cutting undesired frequencies is preferable to boosting desired ones. Having said that, it is important to note that the equalization of some mixers sounds thin or wimpy when set flat, and it sounds much better when some boost is applied.

Audio Supplements

Another way to get the most out of your mixer is by selectively supplementing it. Many inexpensive mixers sound pretty good except for their mic preamps. Purchasing an inexpensive outboard mic preamp allows for much better sounding vocal or acoustic instrument tracks for an investment of only a few hundred dollars. Similarly, buying one or two parametric EQs will let you treat critical signals more accurately than you can with the limited EQ of your mixer.

Not enough effects sends? Some multi-effects processors have stereo inputs that are summed to mono before processing. You can take advantage of this by routing direct outs from two separate mixer channels into a signal processor and letting the box do the mixing. This little trick also saves your effects sends for more critical applications.

If you plan to get into creative patching, you may find it useful to connect a patch bay to your mixer's ins and outs (see Chapter 8, "The Ins and Outs of Patch Bays"). Although it can be a pain to wire, a patch bay saves wear and tear on the mixer's connectors and eliminates the need to crawl around the back of the mixer. Be sure to construct a patch bay that services all your mixer's inputs and outputs, even if it ends up having a lot of jacks. Doing the job halfway may work fine, but you'll eventually want access to even the most obscure patch points.

Master Fade

Many musicians and engineers recoil at the mere thought of digging into schematics, but all your efforts will be rewarded when you save a brutal mix with some inspired patching. The benefits of learning all these tricks go far beyond the recordings you make now, because the same approach and tricks are used by every engineer on every level of console.

Mixer Maintenance

Keeping your mixer free of dust and dirt is critical, because noisy pots and faders can produce noisy recordings. Use a damp cloth to clean the dust from the board's surfaces and wipe away the grease pencil marks that indicated fader levels during previous mixes. Be careful not to let dust or grease pencil debris fall into the fader slots. The primary cause of noisy faders is all the human hair, dirt, and lunch crumbs that drop between the channel paths and faders. (So don't eat over your mixer, unless you enjoy dancing with tragedy.)

To check if your faders are "slimed," run a pure 1 kHz tone through each input module. While the tone is sounding, slide the fader up and down. Listen for crackles and pops. Be sure to do this test with a pure tone, as a conventional music program may disguise noises.

If you hear pops and crackles, use a commercial cleaner to restore silence. However, don't just squirt the cleaner blindly into the fader. When you hear a noise, mark the fader level with a grease pencil. Then peek inside the fader slot to determine if the circuit board is mounted to the right, left, or bottom of the input module. You must direct the contact cleaner toward the contacts of the circuit board to gain any improvement. After doing so, turn off the tone and slide the fader up and down a few times. Do a final check with the tone generator to make sure the fader is noiseless. If not, repeat the process. It may take a few squirts to completely clean the fader.

Sometimes, hairs or crumbs attach themselves to the metal fader guide, and a blast of compressed air is needed to clear the obstruction. Cans of compressed air are available at electronics and computer stores. Make sure the nozzle can fit into small places and that the chemical propellant is safe for use with electronic equipment.

Now use the 1 kHz tone to systematically check your board, input by input. Listen carefully for scratchy pan posts, aux sends, mute buttons, etc., and then make a list of all problem components.

While it may not be practical (or within your skills) to replace these parts yourself, it's a good practice to map out your console's "problem geography." For instance, if input five has a scratchy pan pot, you'll know to avoid it when returning a track that requires panning changes during mixdown. If you find large numbers of bad pots, call a knowledgeable technician and get them replaced. Don't be lazy; otherwise, audible cracks and pops will become part of your finished mixes.

If your studio is in constant use, it's advisable to leave your mixer (and power amp(s) or powered monitors, for that matter) on. When you switch AC power on, a spike occurs before the power settles down to its normal voltage. While most equipment deals with these spikes just fine, years of constant ons and offs can damage power supplies.

Knowing the ins and outs of your mixing console is critical during troubleshooting, so keep a signal-flow chart handy. Trying to trace mixer problems without this valuable document is like traveling the country's freeways without a map.

CHAPTER 8

The Ins and Outs of Patch Bays

So you've added another signal processor to a rack crammed with effects boxes, all of which are needed for your next mix-down. Unfortunately, too many signals are vying for precious few mixer inputs. Your outboard gear finally has overrun the capabilities of your recording system. Don't get mad—get a patch bay.

A *patch bay* is a sonic traffic controller. Outboard effects and mixer functions (such as input-channel inserts and direct sends) are wired into a mechanical routing system that allows audio signals to be sent from one place to another via cables plugged into the appropriate jacks. Once these patch points are wired and labeled, you can easily route signals to outboard signal processors without climbing behind consoles and effects racks. Obviously, this is a major ergonomic boon to the embattled recording engineer. Patch bays also are useful for tracing signal path problems and providing options for working around them.

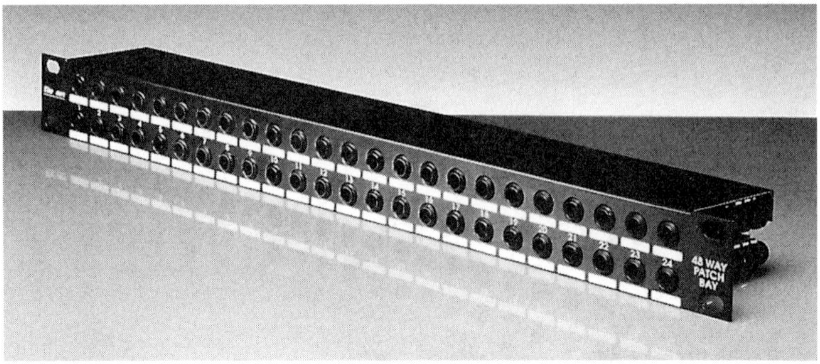

Re'an balanced 1/4-inch patch bay.

System Configurations

We can thank "Ma Bell" for developing the mechanical and electrical switching systems for telephones that are the forerunners of the patch bays used in today's recording studios. (I'm sure you've seen old movies where telephone operators connect calls by plugging cables into a switchboard.)

Several types of patching systems are used for recording. The most common use TT (tiny telephone, also called *Bantam*) or 1/4-inch connectors, but patch bays are available with a wide assortment of military, telephone, and 1/4-inch TRS stereo jacks.

TTs are the small-holed (0.173-inch) patch bays that service large studios, while 1/4-inch systems are considered semiprofessional. The major differences between the formats are size and application. For instance, a 1/4-inch patch bay housed in a single-rackspace configuration can fit 32 to 48 jacks, while a TT system crams 96 jacks into the same space. In a pro studio, where nearly every piece of equipment is wired into the patch bay, the space-saving TT system is essential.

TT jacks can be wired as balanced lines, and it's also possible to find balanced 1/4-inch patch bays. Fortunately, unbalanced systems can be relatively noise free. Balanced lines offer common-mode rejection, where unwanted noise cancels itself out, but a carefully wired unbalanced system (high-quality shielded wire, short cable runs, and so on) can provide reasonable sound quality. In addition, most modern gear conforms to a standard of high-impedance inputs and low-impedance outputs, which diminishes noisy impedance mismatches.

Patch Points

A patch bay has connections on both the front and back. The rear connectors are the permanent links to the various pieces of gear, while the front panel jacks are used for on-the-spot routing changes via the patch points.

Normaled patch bays are wired such that a signal is internally routed from one permanently attached device to a predetermined, permanently attached point without requiring a patch cable (see **Fig. 8.1a**). If a cable is plugged into either front-panel jack (see **Fig. 8.1b**), the internal connection (the "normal" signal path) is interrupted, and the signal goes to the cable instead of following the prewired path. While not a patch bay per se, a console insert point is a good example of a normaled connection.

In patch bays that are not normaled, or denormaled, all signal routing is done at the front panel (see **Fig. 8.1d**). If you want to route a signal from an Aux 2 send to a reverb, you have to use a patch cord to connect the front-panel Aux 2 Out to the Reverb In. Not surprisingly, denormaled patch points are commonly used to access outboard gear, such as noise gates, delays, and reverb units.

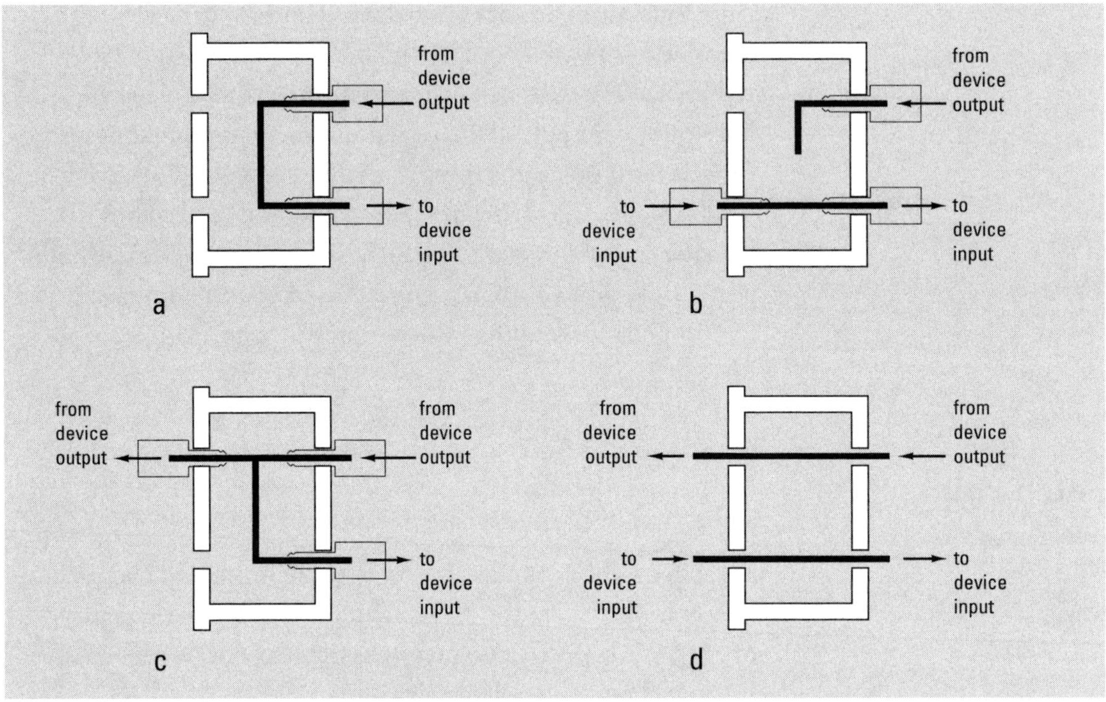

FIG. 8.1: Signal flow in different types of patch bays.

The diagrams in Figure 8.1 illustrate signal flow in normaled (a, b), half-normaled (c), and denormaled (d) patch bays. In a normaled configuration, the rear-panel jacks are internally connected as long as the front-panel jacks are unused (a). When patch cables are inserted into the lower front-panel jack, however, the normal connection is broken (b). A half-normaled configuration splits the incoming rear-panel signal to both the rear- and front-panel outputs (c). In a denormaled setup, the upper and lower jacks are internally disconnected (d).

To simplify personal studio operations, a common practice is to normal (or dedicate) an aux send from the mixer to the input of a reverb unit. This makes mixing easy, since Aux 2 is always Reverb A; for example, no patching is necessary.

During tracking, if you want to feed a guitar directly into Reverb A, simply break the normal on the patch bay with the guitar cord, which will override the connection with the aux send. Without the benefit of a patch bay, the engineer would have to disconnect the aux send cable and replace it with a guitar cord.

If you don't want the signal to disappear when a patch cord is inserted, you can use half-normaled points. These continue to route a signal through the patch bay even when that path is broken by a patch cord (see **Fig. 8.1c**). Half-normaled points are useful because they allow the engineer to "Y" a signal to two different locations.

System Selection

Deciding which patch bay to use for your personal recording system may be a question of how much time you want to spend installing one. Most TT systems are wired via solder lugs or terminal blocks, and these require quite a bit of time to set up. However, one of the advantages of all that work is that you can wire normaled or denormaled patch points wherever you need them.

Cost is another factor. While the price difference between TT and 1/4-inch patch-bay frames is negligible, cable costs are another matter. TT patch cables can cost $10 to $35 dollars each; for a large patch bay, that can mean hundreds of dollars for patch cords alone. (Just count all those signal processors you own!)

Since most semipro recording gear runs at –10 dBV with unbalanced lines, 1/4-inch patch bays offer personal studios a lot of advantages. First, the patch cables are inexpensive and easy to make. The price of one TT cord buys several 1/4-inch cables. On top of that, the rear panels of most 1/4-inch patch bays are prewired with RCA or 1/4-inch jacks. Because 1/4-inch jacks (both balanced and unbalanced) are the standard for most musical instruments, you're already wired and ready to go. You spend less time soldering and more time making music.

Unfortunately, every manufacturer configures its prewired patch bays differently, so exercise care when shopping. For example, some companies make 1/4-inch patch bays in rows of 16 jacks, while others offer a similar frame with rows of 24. In addition, some manufacturers make it easy to switch prewired points between normaled and denormaled, while others make it nearly impossible. So before you buy a prewired model, make sure it offers the flexibility you need.

A final note about 1/4-inch patch bays: They get heavy. When row upon row of cable is connected to the back of the patch bay, the combined weight can pull the plugs right out of the jacks. Make sure that all your cables are bound and secured so that the weight of the cables is off the plugs. This precaution will save you a headache later on. And if your reverb return is mysteriously silent, make sure the patch cable is connected before you tear apart your entire system.

The Case for Normalcy

The next big patch bay decision is which lines should be normaled. The answer depends on how you like to work. If you are a heavy-duty MIDI person, you may want to normal your keyboards (and sound modules) to the line inputs of your mixing board. This means that your analog synth always comes up on Channel 1, your keyboard workstation on Channels 2 and 3, and so on. However, you also have the flexibility (through the patch bay) to route your synth elsewhere, as needed.

For musicians who like to walk into their studios and have everything ready to go, I recommend normaling mixer aux sends to often-used signal processors. It's a joy to simply twist a knob for reverb, instead of repeatedly having to patch cables into effects boxes. Also, because channel inserts are great for putting gates and compressors into the signal patch, it makes sense to have them easily accessible on the patch bay. If you want even more flexibility, patch up your direct outputs.

A Change from Normal

How do you change a patch-bay connection from normaled or half-normaled to denormaled? Depending on the make and model of patch bay, this usually requires removing the circuit board (typically an individual card for each top/bottom set of jacks) and forcibly breaking a designated contact by scratching through it with a knife or screwdriver. Some patch bays, such as those made by Re'an, offer patch points on easily removable reversible cards. To change from half-normaled to denormaled (or vice versa), you simply remove, reverse, and replace the card.

Patched Out

A properly wired and labeled patch bay makes your hours in the studio much more fun and productive. With countless signal-routing options at your fingertips, a patch bay saves time and energy that is better directed toward music-making. After all, most musicians would agree that crawling behind mixers and effects racks is not a creative process.

CHAPTER 9

The Monitoring Milieu

"Penny wise, pound foolish," warns the old adage. That principle certainly applies to personal studio engineers who reference their work on consumer stereo speakers. The sound from those speakers often is a far cry from audio reality. Although there is no law against mixing or recording in an aural fantasy world (some musicians prefer it), you should be aware of the fundamental differences between common hi-fi speakers and professional studio reference monitors.

The basic function of a studio monitor is to reproduce an incoming signal faithfully without adding coloration or changing the character or tonal balance of the sound. On the other hand, the average home-stereo speaker is designed to make music sound as good as possible, often by emphasizing certain frequencies to make them stand out from the rest of the pack (especially during that all-important five-minute audition in the sales showroom). A little zing in the high frequencies and some extra punch in the bass may sell speakers, but these "enhancements" sabotage audio accuracy.

The Dynaudio BM5A is a two-way biamplified monitor with a 6.9-inch woofer and a 1.1-inch tweeter. The BM5A, which has a balanced XLR input jack that accepts +4 dBu signals, offers the transparency and definition needed in a personal studio monitor.

If your speakers don't provide an accurate reproduction of what you have recorded or what's coming out of the console, you'll have difficulty making decisions concerning instrument and patch selection, equalization, and balancing elements during mixdown. In addition, it's essential that your speakers "translate" well to any size system, allowing you to maintain consistent overall instrumental and vocal balances for any commercial playback system, from 3-inch television speakers to elaborate audiophile installations.

Acoustic Perception

Consistent mixes require a critical listening environment. So don't wheel 7-foot, 1,400-pound monster monitors into your studio, stand them against a far wall, and pump up the volume. This live sound-system approach is a bad idea. As the distance from sound source to listener increases, the original gets blended with the acoustical effects of the room. Echoes and reverberations occur as sounds reflect off walls, furniture, floor, and ceiling. This creates psychoacoustic problems, as the listener's brain attempts to sort out the differences between the direct sound and a mixture of unwanted room reflections. Unless your studio budget includes a hefty allotment for studio designers and acousticians, you're stuck creating music in a less-than-perfect environment. An effective and inexpensive solution is listening to monitor speakers in the close field (approximately one meter away), which increases the ratio of direct-to-reflected sound, greatly reducing the effects of poor room acoustics.

Not all studio monitors are practical for close-field applications. For close-up listening, it's important that the combined image of the drivers be coherent at short distances. Systems designed for close-field applications have closely spaced drivers or employ a coaxial-type design, where the high-frequency drivers are located on a concentric axis with the woofers. Another approach employs two small mid- to high-frequency cabinets (satellites), combined with a subwoofer enclosure that is located several feet from the satellites (see **Fig. 9.1**).

FIG. 9.1: The Blue Sky ProDesk 2.1 system combines two powered satellite monitors with a subwoofer.

Monitor Placement

Because close-field reference monitors can reduce unwanted acoustical effects within the listening space, speaker placement is critical. Begin by setting up the monitoring system symmetrically within the room, positioning your speakers with the high-frequency elements at ear level and each monitor aimed slightly inward. The distance between speakers should be the same as the distance from each speaker to your ears, forming an equilateral triangle. This creates a "sweet spot" where the listener is precisely on-axis with each monitor. The most accurate perception of sound is attained from this position, because the sonic character of many speakers changes dramatically when heard off-axis (see Chapter 3, "The Personal Studio Makeover").

To improve the sound quality and imaging of your monitors, it's a good idea to acoustically isolate, or decouple, them from the surface they're on. The typical do-it-yourself solution is to set your monitors on a thick piece of foam or rubber.

Auralex MoPads are a set of inexpensive wedges made of high-density polyurethane foam that not only decouple your monitors from the stand or desktop, but also let you tilt them up or down slightly.

This phenomenon, known as *off-axis coloration*, can be demonstrated by referencing a sound while facing the monitor and comparing that to the sound heard after taking a step to either side of the same monitor. Typical symptoms of off-axis coloration are a loss of high-frequency information or a change in the midrange characteristics. Since low-frequency information is largely nondirectional, bass response generally is unaffected by off-axis listening.

A Look at Monitor Designs

There is any number of ways to mount speakers in a cabinet, but most enclosures designed for music reproduction fall into two basic categories: sealed and vented.

Sealed designs (usually known as *acoustic-suspension types*) have the speaker components mounted on the outside of an airtight cabinet, which prevents the escape of air displaced by the woofer's rearward motion. Increased air pressure within the cabinet acts as a springboard to push the woofer's cone forward.

Vented systems (sometimes called *bass-reflex systems*) have one or more openings that create a small amount of phase cancellation at the woofer's resonant frequency while increasing bass response at a lower frequency. These openings (called *vents* or *ports*) can be on the front or rear of the speaker enclosure. When rear-vented monitors are placed near walls or other sound-reflecting surfaces, the sound waves exiting the port are directed elsewhere in the room. Occasionally, this creates an unpredictable situation in which the direct sound from the woofers reaches the listener's ears a few milliseconds earlier than the reflected signal, often resulting in emphasized bass frequencies. In some instances, the net effect can be a loss of bass response, if the reflected signal is out of phase with the direct sound.

Some speaker manufacturers employ coaxially mounted speakers, usually consisting of a tweeter or other high-frequency unit mounted in the center of a bass reproducer. Coaxial speakers give the impression that sound is coming from a single point source, which improves coherence at close listening distances.

The concept of dividing the load of audio reproduction among many specialized drivers is a good idea. However, each crossover network that routes sound to its respective driver introduces a certain amount of phase error. There is a limit to the number of drivers that can be clustered together to produce a coherent sound image at a close listening distance. Therefore, most compact studio monitors are two- or three-way systems.

Speaker Specs

The most important specification of a loudspeaker system is frequency response, which is the range of frequencies that a loudspeaker can reproduce. Unfortunately, this figure is virtually useless unless combined with some sort of tolerance specification (often expressed as something like ±3 dB). An ideal loudspeaker system offers "flat" response, which occurs when all frequencies can be reproduced at a consistent level.

However, keep in mind that a 3-inch transistor radio speaker theoretically could have a frequency response of 20 Hz to 20 kHz. What's left out is the fact that its actual frequency response could be –100 dB at the extreme ends of the scale. Because every 10 dB of change represents a doubling (or halving) in *perceived* volume, the amount of 20 Hz energy reproduced by the 3-inch speaker is infinitesimally small.

A speaker's overall efficiency is indicated by a sensitivity rating, which is expressed as the sound pressure level (in decibels) that the speaker produces, given 1W input, measured at one meter. Since console-mounted speakers usually are heard from a distance of around one meter, the sensitivity rating is important. Sensitivity ratings for loudspeakers range from about 80 dB to more than 100 dB.

What does this mean for selecting a monitoring system? Take, for example, a monitor with a sensitivity spec of 90 dB. Because each 10 dB volume increase requires ten times more amplifier power, we can determine that this monitor provides 100 dB from a 10W input, or 110 dB from a 100W input. (Because the scale is based on a logarithmic progression, we also know that each volume increase of 3 dB requires a doubling of amplifier power.) By combining this knowledge of sensitivity with a monitor's maximum power-handling capacity, you can tell whether a given monitor is loud enough to suit your needs.

Other Features

Removable front grilles are a plus. While many grille materials are "acoustically transparent," other problems stem from diffraction effects and edge reflections caused by sounds from the high- and mid-frequency drivers bouncing off the wood or plastic grille frame.

On the rear of the speaker, input terminals range from XLR, 1/4-inch, and RCA jacks to screw fasteners and gold-plated, five-way binding posts. The latter accommodates banana plugs, spade lugs, test prods, and bare wires bent to go around the post, but also includes holes in the post itself for inserting various gauges of speaker wire. If you frequently change speakers in your studio, banana, XLR, RCA, and 1/4-inch connectors make a lot of sense, because they provide a solid and easily removable connection.

Computer and video monitors are common in studio, and many reference speakers provide internal magnetic shielding to reduce or eliminate the picture distortion that occurs whenever a large magnetic structure is placed near a video display. The degree of protection varies widely. Some models must be placed three to six inches away to avoid picture degradation, while other speakers can be placed flush against a video or computer monitor without ill effects.

New Directions

High-quality powered monitors have overtaken passive monitors in the personal studio, not only because of the convenience they offer, but because they incorporate state-of-the-art biamplification and active crossovers that precisely match on-board electronics to loudspeaker components for optimum performance. As the technology improves and manufacturing is sent overseas, the quality of powered monitors has improved, and the number of models available has increased, while prices have remained steady (and in some cases dropped).

One noticeable trend is the addition of self-tuning capabilities to the monitoring system. Reasonably priced systems, such as the Genelec 8200 series (see **Fig. 9.2**) and the JBL 4300 series, include a measurement mic and software that can be used to automatically analyze the room and calibrate the monitors to a particular listening environment. You can expect to see continued development in this area, making increasingly sophisticated, yet affordable, monitoring systems available to nearly every level of personal studio.

FIG. 9.2:
The Genelec 8200 series offers bi-amplified active monitors that combine digital signal processing (DSP), Genelec Loudspeaker Manager software, and AutoCal (Automated Calibration) software to create a networked monitoring system that can be quickly set up, measured, and calibrated to any studio environment. The monitors accept analog and digital input.

CHAPTER 10

Gearing Up for Critical Vocals

Part of the allure of the personal studio is low overhead. Rather than pay exorbitant hourly rates at a commercial facility, where the stress of the clock can make it hard to deliver an inspired performance, personal studio owners can relax and take their time while perfecting their parts. The muse, after all, is not a circus animal, ready to jump through hoops at the crack of a whip.

On the other hand, there are definite advantages to recording in a commercial studio. These include great-sounding rooms, a wide selection of premium gear, and—this is important—experienced engineers who know how to get a great sound quickly.

So here's the million-dollar question: Is it possible to get as good a sound in a dinky little home studio as can be achieved in a full-blown commercial facility? Well, it all depends. Obviously, if you're trying to record, say, an orchestra or big band, then probably not. However, many instruments do lend themselves to small-space recording, and the voice is one of them. After all, small, dead-sounding vocal booths are often employed for recording vocals even in major studios, at least for pop applications. And it's relatively easy to construct a dead-sounding space in a closet, garage, or what have you (see Chapter 20, "The House Is Rockin'"). After that detail is taken care of, quality of sound depends on two things: the signal path and your knowledge of recording.

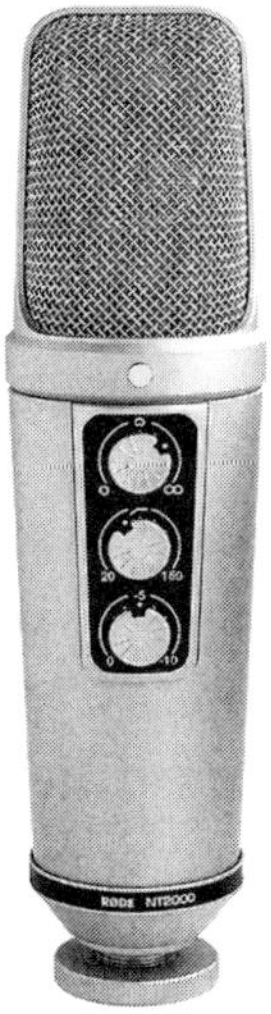

The Rode NT2000 is a large-diaphragm condenser mic that offers three polar patterns (omni, cardioid, and figure-8), a pad, and a highpass filter. All of the controls are continuously variable, giving you an enormous amount of flexibility.

You can use the following test procedures to determine the best signal path for recording a particular vocalist. This is an involved process that is usually reserved for critical vocal tracks only (for example, final tracks destined for a CD), and it is especially enlightening if you've never done it before. It will teach you how each piece of gear affects the final sound, as well as how various components work together—the key information required to ensure an optimal signal path for the application at hand. Each time you perform the test, your knowledge base grows, which ultimately pays off by allowing you to work faster and smarter.

Quality Counts

When you're going to record critical vocal tracks, make every effort to get your hands on the best gear you can. Aside from whatever recording medium you've decided to use, the requisite gear includes a microphone, a mic preamp, a dynamics processor (which may not even be needed), and perhaps a high-quality A/D converter. Those are only a few things, and the fewer the better. In the interests of audio quality, it's wise to keep the signal path as short as possible.

Even among those few items, there are countless products to choose from. Of the four, the microphone is the most critical. However, in the end, the recording chain is only as strong as its weakest link, so it's important to search out quality equipment in each category. What's more, despite the reputation of any particular piece of gear, there's no way of knowing in advance how any two products will sound together, short of giving them a try. Unfortunately, this luxury is seldom available to the personal studio recordist.

So what's a person to do? Scrounge. Borrow. Beg. Rent. Do whatever it takes to amass the gear you need. Try to get at least three different mics, preamps, and dynamics processors to make the tests worthwhile. Then your task is to compare. (I skipped A/D converters, but if you're really fastidious, you may want to compare a few of those, as well.)

The Microphone

Start with the microphones, using the stock mic preamps on your mixer. Your goal is to find the mic that flatters the voice the most—and, ideally, allows you to record with no EQ.

Usually, large-diaphragm condenser mics are best for recording vocals, but not always. Sometimes, a condenser is just too brittle sounding or revealing, especially on a harsh voice. In those cases, a dynamic or ribbon mic may provide the best sound. Again, you never know until you compare.

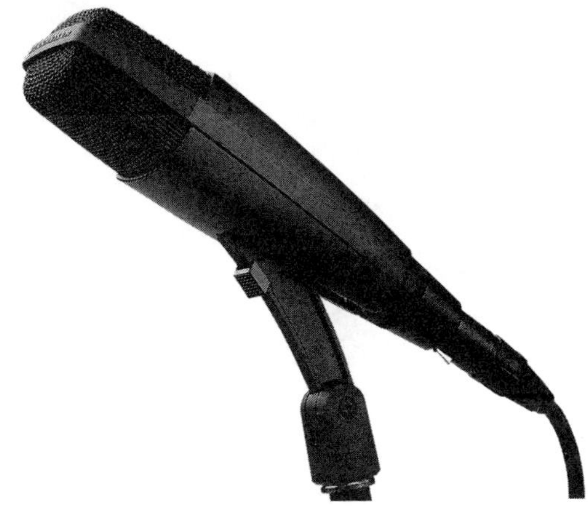

The Sennheiser MD421 dynamic microphone is typically thought of as a tom mic, but it's also an excellent choice for certain vocalists.

Don't fall into the trap of thinking that the most expensive mic is necessarily the best. The choice of mic should always depend on how it sounds on the voice in question (unless, of course, you're using the mic to create a special effect). Bonnie Raitt, who can afford whatever microphone she wants, has been known to use a relatively inexpensive dynamic mic, the Electro-Voice RE20, for her studio vocal tracks.

To compare microphones, set them up in a tight cluster with the capsules aligned on a horizontal plane facing the singer (see **Fig. 10.1**). (Depending on the size of the mics, six is about the most you can group together practically for a test.) Set any multiple-pattern mics to the cardioid position, and disengage all pads and highpass filters. Likewise, on the mixer, make sure all pads, filters, and effects are disengaged for the channels handling the mic signals (both send and return).

The point is to even the playing field so you can hear each mic in its flat, unprocessed state.

FIG. 10.1:
You can easily compare microphones by setting them up in a tight cluster with the capsules aligned on a horizontal plane facing the singer.

Position the singer about two feet back from the mics. This allows enough time and space for the sound to open up so that each mic gets hit with the same information. Next, while the singer rehearses the tune, adjust the gain for each mic preamp until all track levels are the same. This is critical to the process, as even the slightest disparity in levels can skew your perception, possibly leading you to unfairly favor one sound over another.

Now it's time to record a pass and listen to the results. Initially, at least, use studio monitors rather than headphones to listen to the tracks. First, mute all the channels. Then unmute one at a time to compare the signals. Listen to each track both with the music tracks and soloed (to check for mic self-noise, room noise, etc.). I can't tell you how to discern which mic sounds best, of course, but hopefully that will be readily apparent. (In the case of a disagreement between you and a paying client, the client gets the final say.) Once you've selected the microphone, it's time to match it with a preamp.

The FMR Audio RNP 8380 Really Nice Preamp is a two-channel, solid-state Class-A mic preamp that is reasonably priced but offers excellent sound quality and functionality.

The Preamp

The procedure for comparing mic preamps is much the same as for the mic comparison. If you have the resources to split the mic signal and send it through several preamps at once, great. In lieu of that, however, you'll have to record a separate pass for each preamp. (This also means that the singer will have to match his tracks one to another.)

Again, use each preamp in its flat state, with no pads, filters, phase reverse switches, or dynamics processing activated. (You can play with that stuff later, once you've selected the preamp.) Again, be sure to match the levels as closely as possible. If one track is recorded hotter than the rest, you can compensate for the difference by using the faders during playback.

The differences between preamps can be very subtle, so listen carefully. It's often helpful to pan the tracks hard left or right, so you can listen through one speaker only. Things to listen for include openness, airiness, body, clarity, coloration, and detail. Many engineers favor an open, transparent, uncolored sound with good detail (hard, clean edges rather than soft, smeary ones) and full body (plenty of lows and not thin sounding).

Of course, sometimes coloration is what you're after; for example, when matching a solid-state mic with a tube mic pre in hopes of "warming up" the signal. If you're looking for more coloration from a tube mic pre, try a lower-priced unit rather than a high-end one.

The Dynamics Processor

After selecting the mic pre, it's time to compare dynamics processors. Is this starting to sound like a hassle? Well, it is. But I guarantee that if you compare several different compressors head-to-head, you'll hear a surprising amount of variance in the types and amounts of coloration each imparts to the signal.

For vocals, I generally prefer the sound of tube compressors with optical (rather than VCA) control because they tend to sound fatter, fuller, and more luscious than solid-state, VCA-based units. On the other hand, optical compressors may not provide as much precision control as VCA-based models. Again, comparison is the only way to learn what sounds work best for the particular singer, song, and signal path.

Other useful dynamics processes for recording vocals include expansion and peak limiting. Usually, my first approach is to attempt recording without a dynamics control. But often, various factors make this impractical. For example, in a studio plagued by environmental noise (such as big trucks roaring by just outside the door), an expander can keep down the noise between sections. Or, for a song with a big dynamic range, a compressor will allow you to bring up the quieter parts without increasing the loud parts too much.

I do everything possible to avoid peak limiting (including coaching the singer on how to work the mic). However, when recording digitally, it's better to catch overshoots with a peak limiter than to allow an otherwise stellar performance to be ruined by digital distortion.

The Room

In a sense, the recording space is also a part of the signal path, because its ambient sound is critical to recording great-sounding vocal tracks. Even with the best gear in the world, you won't get a good sound in a space that's riddled with unwanted echoes, standing waves, and excessive environmental noise.

Usually, a fairly dead-sounding space is preferable for recording vocals. A vocal booth is ideal, but you can get similar results by deadening a corner of the room with studio foam and then setting up the mic so that the capsule faces into the corner. If you still hear unwanted reflections, position a foam-covered partition in front of the corner, effectively walling it in. If the recording gear is set up in a bedroom, try recording in a clothes-filled closet. Rugs, carpet, padded furniture, and draperies can also be used to help deaden the acoustics of a space.

If house-induced environmental noise is a problem, deal with it. For example, refrigerators, freezers, and telephones can be unplugged temporarily to quiet the recording space. To quell outside noise, close windows tightly and cover them with foam or some other material.

All Together Now

One alternative I haven't discussed is the use of multifeatured, "channel-strip" units, commonly called *voice processors* (see Chapter 11, "The Path of Least Resistance"). These typically comprise a mic preamp, dynamics processor, and EQ section in a single box (see **Fig. 10.2**). Some also contain exciter circuits and A/D converters.

FIG. 10.2:
The Universal Audio LA-610 is a channel-strip that combines a mic preamp with a tube compressor, EQ controls, and a DI input.

Obviously, a voice processor can greatly simplify assembly of the signal path. In my experience, however, a unit with a great-sounding mic preamp doesn't necessarily have the best dynamics section (or vice versa). For that reason, it still pays to compare the individual sections, any of which can usually be bypassed if necessary.

Vocal Ease

Developing your ears is an important part of becoming a good engineer. Even though all of this testing may seem a bit much, the more time you spend on it, the greater the rewards will be.

CHAPTER 11

The Path of Least Resistance

There's no question that direct recording with good gear will give you the cleanest sound. And no instrument reflects the efficiency of direct recording more than the human voice. However, the average vocal signal takes a trip through various gain stages in the mixer's channel strip, through the send/returns to effects (such as compression and EQ), and down the mix bus before hitting the recorder. Electrically speaking, that adds up to quite a distance and can translate into added noise and signal degradation.

The Presonus Eureka is a voice processor that combines a solid-state mic preamp, a compressor (with de-essing capabilities), and a three-band parametric EQ. The device also offers variable input impedance and a saturation control.

To avoid such noise and degradation but still get the effects essential for recording vocals, there are handy devices on the market that minimize the number of parts the signal goes through and thus keep the path from input to output as short as possible. These devices are channel strips and voice processors.

One Voice, One Channel

You will often hear the terms *channel strip* and *voice processor* used interchangeably. That's because both kinds of units have a similar purpose: to get the signal to the recorder as directly as possible. But the two types have significant differences.

Stand-alone channel strips are designed to take the place of a mixer's channel strip. The stand-alone has the same features as the strip on a mixer: a mic preamp, a line-level input, shelving filters, and parametric EQ. Besides the shorter signal path, the big difference is that the stand-alone version contains better components than those in the average personal studio mixer. When you spend $600 per channel, you get components comparable to those in a high-end mixing desk.

Voice processors are also designed for direct recording and contain the same features as a channel strip, but with a few additions. Engineers regularly use dynamics processors when recording vocals because of the voice's wide dynamic range. That means you will want a compressor, limiter, expander, gate, and de-esser in the unit. Of course, these effects work great on other instruments, too, such as electric guitar, bass, and keyboards.

The layout of a voice processor should be as intuitive as that of a channel strip. In a mixer, the signal generally flows from top to bottom. The signal flow in a voice processor is similar, except that you lay the unit sideways so that the signal goes from left to right, entering the input stage at the far left, going through the various effects stages, and ending up at the output on the far right.

Don't limit yourself by using voice processors only for tracking. Using these units during mixdown or for fattening prerecorded tracks can prove equally useful. For this reason, voice processors have a variety of input and output options to maximize their usefulness in the studio.

Generally speaking, voice processors range in price from $499 to around $4,000. Manufacturers have different ideas as to what their direct-recording device should include and how the features should be organized, which usually helps determine the unit's price. For example, a tube unit with Class A components and a wide array of I/O options will probably cost you more than a solid-state unit with a single input and output. Let's review the various features that make up a voice processor.

The Joemeek sixQ is a mono voice processor that features a preamp, an optical compressor, and an EQ. However, the sixQ's compressor is a little more aggressive than most, imparting extra attitude to the sound.

Ins and Outs

When you're looking for the ideal direct-recording solution that is also useful for mixing, the more I/O possibilities you have, the better. Besides a mic input, there should be line- and instrument-level inputs. The ability to tap in and out of the individual effects is a plus. At the other end, having balanced (+4 dBu 1/4-inch TRS or XLR) and unbalanced (–10 dBV 1/4-inch TS) line-level outputs is essential. Let's take a closer look at each section.

Mic preamp. The microphone preamp is one of the most important parts of a voice processor because it sets the stage for your sound. To record with the best signal-to-noise ratio possible, you need to bring up the output level of the microphone (–30 to –60 dBu) needs to be brought up to line level (–10 dBV or +4 dBu).

Usually, this change in level will color the sound somewhat—and in many cases that's good. One of the joys of engineering is tone sculpting, and the mic preamp can have as much to do with this sculpting as the microphone. For example, a tube preamp will have a different character than a solid-state unit. In addition, Class A circuitry (solid-state or tube) will give you superior sound and performance but will often cost a little extra.

Ultimately, the degree of transparency or coloration that you want the preamp to impart depends on your own personal taste and the needs of the music. Other considerations include the recording medium you're using. Engineers with tapeless studios may want a preamp that adds "tube warmth" or that can emulate the effects of tape saturation. On the other hand, analog tape users may want a transparent sound with as little coloration as possible. The call is completely subjective. What sounds harsh and buzzy to one engineer may sound warm and fuzzy to another.

Another consideration is how your collection of mics will sound through the preamp; invariably, some mics will sound better than others. There are no rules that say you can't run a cheap mic through an expensive preamp or vice versa—whatever works best for the style of music you're recording should determine which preamp you choose.

A mic preamp should include a couple of features to make life easier. First, it should have +48V phantom power so that you can power the mics that need it. A phase-reversal (polarity) switch is also useful, to change the phase of the signal by 180 degrees. In addition, preamps often have a –10 or –20 dB pad to attenuate high-output mics and a low-cut filter to remove low-frequency energy such as rumble. Most of the voice processors on the market include many or all of these features.

Instrument input/DI. If you have ever recorded electric guitar or bass, you know how handy it is to have a compressor, gate, and EQ at your disposal. Having access to a tube stage is another plus. You will probably want to plug your instrument into your voice processor and take advantage of these effects. Fortunately, many of these units have a 1/4-inch, instrument-level input jack. The instrument input (or DI) raises the signal from instrument level (–30 to –20 dB) to line level. Keep an eye out for processors with convenient 1/4-inch front-panel jacks.

Line-level input and output. In addition to using a voice processor on mics and guitars, you can use it on keyboards, sound modules, and prerecorded tracks during mixdown. Manufacturers often provide both +4 dBu balanced and –10 dBV unbalanced line-level inputs to facilitate this type of use.

Voice processors also typically have both a –10 dBV and a +4 dBu output. Depending on your studio situation, having the option of both output levels means that the device will have upward compatibility if you're moving from so-called semipro gear (which typically operates at –10) to professional gear (operating at +4).

Compressor/limiter. The dynamic range of the voice goes beyond what the average recorder can handle, so engineers routinely use compression when tracking vocals. The type of compressor and how well it operates can impact how the signal sounds after the fact. Consequently, take great care when choosing and using a compressor.

With a dedicated compressor, you will usually have control over threshold level, attack and release times, ratio selection, and gain makeup, as well as the choice between *hard* and *soft knee* (that is, how suddenly compression begins).

Limiting is at the extreme end of compression, when the ratio is 10:1 and beyond. Limiting effectively inhibits any increase in output level, no matter how far the signal goes above the threshold.

Compressors and limiters have three common designs: photo-optical, VCA, and variable mu. Photo-optical compressors (also called *photoelectric* or just plain *opto*) differ in several ways from compressors governed by a voltage-controlled amplifier (VCA). Opto compressors use a photosensitive resistor controlled by light-emitting diodes that are triggered by the input signal. Opto units compress over a narrower range (with less extreme compression ratios) and impart a livelier sound to the signal. Because of their simple user interface, they lend themselves to tweaking by ear.

VCA units, on the other hand, are far more predictable and easier to use, have greater ratios, and allow for more flexibility and precision with attack and release times. Variable-mu compressors (*mu*, in this case, means *gain*) use a vacuum tube as a variable resistor to control the signal level.

Expanders and gates. Downward expanders and gates are processors used to reduce noise. Expanders create a greater dynamic range by progressively attenuating sounds that fall below a specified threshold; in other words, they make the quiet sounds quieter. You can think of an expander as the opposite of a compressor, which brings up the level of the quieter sounds.

A full-featured expander gives you control over the threshold where the processing begins, the ratio of expansion, and the speed of the processing. Expanders are used primarily for eliminating extraneous sounds, such as bleed from headphones, lip smacks, and clothing noises. Used more often during mixing than recording, the expander is often placed after the compressor to reduce the low-level noise that compression brings out. Many voice processors, however, locate the expander ahead of the compressor, giving you the opportunity to reduce noise before the compression stage.

At the extreme end of downward expansion is gating. Rather than simply reducing the signal level when it drops below the threshold, a gate will shut the level off completely. Gating is used as much to shape the envelope of signals as it is to remove unwanted noise. For example, gates are used to fatten up drum sounds by quickly attenuating the instrument's natural decay. You can also use a gate to keep the buzz of an amp from passing through the unit when a guitarist isn't playing. Typical gate parameters include threshold and rate.

EQ and filters. Direct control over the timbral aspects of the signal is always welcome. Whether you use EQ to enhance the signal, remove unwanted anomalies, or repair damage caused by compression, you will want a band or two of parametric EQ as well as high- and low-shelving filters.

A parametric EQ lets you control three essential parameters: the exact frequency that you want to effect; the bandwidth, or Q, which is the range of frequencies around the center frequency; and the volume for cutting or boosting.

For those of us with a limited number of mics, parametric EQ supplies the tools with which to expand the sonic palette. EQ is also a must when tracking instruments such as electric guitar. Ranges in which the guitar can often use help include the lower-mid range, around 500 Hz; between 3 to 6 kHz for added bite; and from 8 to 10 kHz for sparkle. Unlike a graphic EQ, a parametric EQ enables you to locate the exact frequencies that need attention.

Shelving filters allow you to modify the extreme ends of the signal and are usually found in the input section of the voice processors. The most common is the highpass filter (also called a *low-cut filter*), which attenuates everything below a specific frequency. This is especially useful for removing rumble and mic-handling noise. Because the human voice doesn't go below 80 Hz, a typical cutoff frequency for a highpass filter is 75 Hz. Some units give you variable control over the cut frequency, sometimes ranging from 15 to 320 Hz. At the other end of the spectrum is the lowpass (or high-cut) filter, which affects everything above a specific high frequency, such as hiss.

De-esser. De-essing is a form of frequency-dependent compression used to remove sibilants when recording vocals. Sibilants, which include "s" and "sh" sounds, have a high-frequency concentration between 3 and 8 kHz. Traditional de-essing is done by splitting the vocal signal, sending one side through the compressor's audio input, and the other side to an EQ patched into the compressor's sidechain input. The exact sibilant frequencies are boosted on the EQ, which makes the compressor more sensitive to them. The EQ-enhanced signal causes the compressor to attenuate the sibilants in the direct signal. Meanwhile, the signal going into the sidechain is not heard.

A de-esser increases the usability of a voice processor. However, a poorly implemented de-esser can sound more like a lowpass filter than a frequency-dependent compressor.

Insert and sidechain. As with a mixing console, an insert lets you introduce an additional outboard processor into the signal path. It also gives you an extra output point before the main output stage.

The sidechain input, a common item on dedicated dynamics processors, lets you control the compressor with an external signal. This is useful for ducking and frequency-dependent compression.

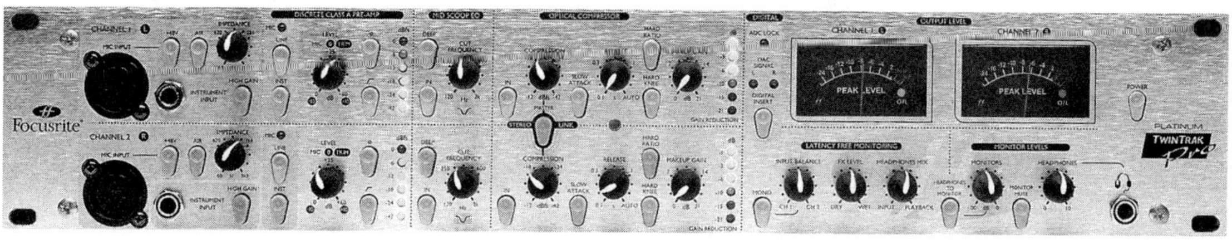

The Focusrite TwinTrak Pro offers two channels of preamplification, for dual mono or stereo tracking. Each channel includes an EQ section and optical compressor, and the compressors can be linked for stereo operation. The A/D converter card is optional.

Implementation

In designing a product such as a voice processor, manufacturers make assumptions about how recording engineers like to work and the kinds of features that they need most. For example, whether the de-esser comes before or after the compressor determines how useful the device will be in certain applications. The advantage of having the de-esser before the compressor is that you can remove the sibilant peaks that are causing unwanted compression. On the other hand, having the de-esser last in the chain is useful for removing increased sibilant frequencies caused by extreme compression. You may want to consider purchasing a product that allows you to switch the order of the de-esser and compressor in the signal chain.

I/O. A very useful setup for the personal studio owner is having a mic preamp and other effects that can be used independently, so you can simultaneously track a vocal while processing another signal. A unit like the LA Audio PS-1 has a separate input and output for each section: dynamics processor, EQ, and preamp (see **Fig. 11.1**). All this I/O flexibility means that you can further shorten the path to the recorder by using the preamp's 1/4-inch line output, use the different effects independently, or reorder the effects in the signal chain.

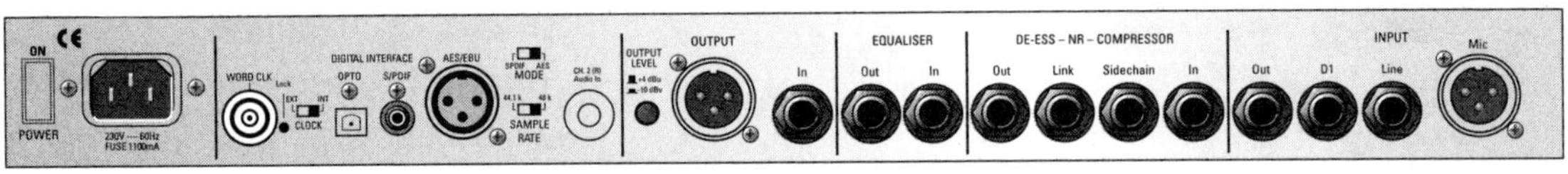

FIG. 11.1: On the rear panel of the LA Audio PS-1, each section has its own input and output, so you can use the sections independently or repatch the signal flow.

Stereo Linkage. A question you will need to ask yourself is this: Will I ever use two of these processors together in stereo? If the answer is yes, then the unit you buy should have a way to be linked to another one. Usually, this can be done by connecting the two units with a cable via a link jack on the back panel. Stereo linkage will allow the dynamics processing of the two units to be synchronized so that there are no phase anomalies between the two channels.

A/D Converter. Many voice processors have room for an optional analog-to-digital converter card. This feature lets you go directly from the voice processor into a digital recorder. Some A/D cards include a second analog input, so you can use two voice processors with only one A/D card, which saves you from buying another card for your second voice processor.

Balancing Act

As with any piece of gear you use, a voice processor will have to match your style of working. Deciding on which features you need the most, as well as how they're implemented, will help you pick the processor that's right for you. If you prefer quick-and-easy results over flexibility, a unit with one or two buttons per effect will do the trick. If you're the kind of person who likes to tweak, then features and knobs may beckon you.

By using a single-channel voice processor, rather than a mixer channel, you get the shortest distance from source to recorder and the best signal-to-noise ratio possible. And because it can be used for mixing as well as recording, the flexibility of a voice processor gives you maximum versatility for your money.

Part II

Recording Techniques

CHAPTER 12

Multitracking Fundamentals

Multitracking is a recording method that allows you to record the various parts of a song one at a time. When you're finished recording, all of the parts are combined to simulate the sound of a group of musicians playing together. Similarly, a group of musicians can use a multitrack recorder to record their parts individually or simultaneously with other group members.

Multitrack equipment lets you record each instrument on a separate track. Each track can be recorded or played back by itself or together with other tracks. This gives you the flexibility to replace, add, or modify individual parts of a musical composition without directly affecting the parts that should remain unchanged. When you are finished recording the tracks you want, they are mixed down, either to stereo or to a surround format.

Until the mid-1970s, the professional studio was the only place a musician could access multitrack recording gear, and studio time was not cheap. Today, however, multitrack recording can be done on the desktop using a personal computer. As you record and overdub, you'll be using a process that dates back almost 60 years. Although technology has affected recording tools, (primarily by greatly improving multitrack recorders), the basic techniques remain unchanged.

Preproduction Plan

Before pushing the Record button, think about the final product. How do you want the results to sound? How many instruments are required? Begin your project by developing a preproduction plan so you know how best to utilize your equipment to accomplish your goals.

Let's say you want to record a standard rock tune with a six-piece band: drums, bass, rhythm guitar, lead guitar, lead vocal, and keyboards. First, determine how many people will play at the same time. Next, determine how many tracks each instrument requires. Will you record a stereo keyboard track? Does the guitarist use a stereo rig? How many drum tracks do you want?

Some of the answers will be determined by your choice of recorder, the number of mics and recording inputs you have, and the number of simultaneous tracks your recorder supports. If you plan to record all six musicians, but your recorder supports only eight channels of simultaneous recording, you may not have enough inputs for all the drum mics you want. However, if the rhythm section is able to play through the song without the lead instruments, you can make use of the extra inputs for the drums and track the other parts later.

Basic Tracking

Basic tracks, or *basics*, are just that—the musical building blocks upon which a song is built. In most situations, basics consist of the rhythm section parts, such as the drums, bass, rhythm guitar, and keyboard in our previous example. Recording these parts at the same time, but on separate tracks, helps you capture that elusive quality of real-time musical interaction.

On the other hand, if you're working solo, you will record each part on its own, often while listening to a click track or drum-machine pattern. The trick for the solo artist is to create the illusion of group interaction.

If you plan to record more than one instrument at a time, or one instrument and vocals, it is important to acoustically isolate each instrument as much as possible to minimize microphone bleed (one mic picking up the sound of another mic's sound source). By maintaining this separation, you can rerecord and fix mistakes on the individual tracks without requiring all the parts to be played again. Isolation can be achieved by putting different instruments in different rooms, putting baffles in front of amps and speakers, or plugging instruments such as electric guitars, basses, and keyboards straight into the mixer. (In many cases, you will want to use a direct box for this last technique.) The better your isolation, the more flexibility you will have later.

Whether you're a solo artist or in a band, you might begin by creating a template for the song. Often, this is in the form of a sequenced "scratch" keyboard part that outlines the entire arrangement. This part can be erased later or replaced by other parts after the basics are done.

Headphones are essential if you are using a click track or synchronized synth parts, have musicians in different rooms, or have the musicians in the same room as the engineer. Most portable multitrack mixers offer a direct headphone output, which can be connected to a headphone splitter so that several musicians and the engineer can all use headphones.

Environmental Concerns

No matter how pristine your signal chain is, an open mic is always susceptible to environmental noise. Beware of unintended ambient sounds creeping into the background of a track. If traffic noise is a problem and room modification is not an option, you have two choices: Use EQ and noise gating, or record things that are less sensitive to the unwanted noise. For example, the rumble of traffic may be acceptably masked by loud drums, distorted guitars, and aggressive electric bass playing.

If traffic noise does end up in your track, a highpass filter can be used to reduce the rumble. Use a parametric equalizer to cut the signal below 100 Hz to diminish low-end mud. You can also use the EQ to reduce audible hiss by rolling off some high frequencies. But take care not to thin out the overall sound of the track when using an equalizer.

Noise-gating can clean up unwanted sounds by shutting down the signal when an instrument is not playing. This approach works best on removing residual hiss from a guitar amp. Even sounds that are input directly (without using a microphone or amp) are subject to unwanted noise, especially from unshielded bass or guitar pickups. EQ and gating work well in these situations. Another approach to diminish pickup hum is to have the bassist or guitarist rotate until the quietest position is found, and ask him to play without moving from that spot.

Overdubbing

Overdubbing is the process in which additional parts are recorded after the basics are finished. You can do anything from adding lead and background vocals to rerecording parts of the basics. For example, you might record a drum machine during the basic tracking for reference, and then replace it with a live drummer during overdubs.

Once again, headphones are necessary because you need to hear the basic tracks to play along with them. One of the most important things to remember about overdubs is that noise from other instruments and sound sources should be kept to a minimum. Consequently, don't let the headphones get so loud that they bleed into a nearby microphone. Noise gates and downward expanders can be used to minimize the effects of headphone bleed into mics.

During basics and overdubs, keep the recording level as hot as possible without letting distortion occur. This keeps the signal-to-noise ratio as high as possible, resulting in a clean, noise-free sound. It will take some experimentation to determine the right recording levels for your equipment, but good results are definitely worth the trouble.

A useful piece of outboard gear for both basics and overdubs is a dynamics processor. These devices provide such functions as compression, expanding, gating, and limiting of audio signals, which can help reduce the noise level and prevent distortion (see Chapter 21, "Dynamics Processors").

Mixing

Mixing is the final process that combines all the recorded tracks into a stereo master, and it can make or break a song. A good mix has a nice stereo image (left to right) and a sense of depth (front to back). Aspects of mixing are covered extensively in Chapter 25, "Creating the Ultimate Mix," but for the time being, let's have a quick look at what's involved in a mix.

For a first, or rough mix of a tune, it's best to start from the bottom and build up. Begin with the rhythm section and quickly put together a mix of all the basic tracks. Then add the main instrument into the mix (usually the lead vocal or lead guitar), and make sure everything else supports it. Remember, you are mixing a song, not trying to create the perfect snare or guitar sound, so listen to the overall mix and don't get hung up on any one part for too long. Once all the elements are in place, with approximate relative levels and stereo placement, you can go back and fine-tune things (such as changing the reverb on the lead vocal, equalizing drums or guitars, etc.).

The stereo placement of each instrument depends on the musical arrangement and type of music you're doing, but there are a few rules that apply to nearly every mix. Be careful not to place two instruments in exactly the same spot in the stereo field. Subtle panning can prevent instruments from piling up at the same location and creating a muddy and unfocused mix. Typically, the bass, kick drum, and lead vocal are near the center. Stereo instruments, such as synths, should be panned left and right to preserve their stereo image. Front-to-back placement is determined primarily by the volume and reverb level of each part. Loud, dry instruments, with little or no reverb, sound up front and in your face; instruments at a lower volume, with more reverb, will get pushed back in a mix.

Equalization is best applied by cutting rather than boosting. If the sound of an instrument is too dull, cut the low end instead of boosting the high end. This avoids increasing the level of hiss in the sound. Conversely, if the sound is too bright, cut the high end rather than adding bass. For some reason, many people add bass to everything; try to avoid this temptation.

As you mix, consult professionally recorded CDs as references. Listening to other mixes is one of the best ways to learn how close you are to a really great sound. Another helpful technique is to audition your finished mix on different playback systems and in different environments, to see how well it holds up in terms of energy, timbral balance, and dimensionality.

End Session

Although the studio tools we use are continually being upgraded and improved, the fundamentals of multitracking remain the same. At the rate studio technologies change, it's nice to know that you won't have to relearn the basics of recording year after year.

CHAPTER 13

Keeper Vocal Tracks

A common strategy for folks producing their own records is to record scratch vocal tracks first, as a reference for other musicians and future overdubs, and then, once all the instruments are recorded, to rerecord the vocals. The advantage of this approach is that vocalists get to sing their parts over a fully realized, and hopefully grooving, arrangement of the song, giving them heightened inspiration and a sense of realism.

The disadvantage is the pressure. Once the other tracks are perfected—perhaps after many thousands of dollars' worth of musician and studio fees—the singer is on the spot. Vocalists not only expect the most of themselves, but they also expect the engineer to deliver the best possible recording of their voices.

Ultimately, the quality of the performance distinguishes a "keeper" track from a scratch. But woe unto the engineer who records a magical performance, only to discover upon playback that the sound is screwed up. To avert that awful fate, let's look at techniques and considerations for recording premium vocal tracks.

Positions, Please

Chapter 10, "Gearing Up for Critical Vocals," details a procedure for determining the best-sounding signal path for recording a specific vocalist. Although painstaking—it is largely trial and error—it enables you to sort out which gear to use on a critical vocal session.

Of course, after you've selected the most complementary components of the signal path (and rendered the recording space sufficiently quiet and dead-sounding for recording), there's still plenty of room for error. Even the best gear in the world can be used badly, resulting in lame-sounding tracks. Fortunately, good recording technique goes far in compensating for less-than-premium equipment or compromised recording environments.

One important element of getting a great sound is mic placement. You have two issues to consider, either of which can affect the sound considerably. One is the position of the mic in the room. (I will assume that, when you were treating the room's acoustics, you also figured out the best part of the room to record in.) The other is the position of the mic relative to the singer.

Regarding the second issue, two primary factors affect the sound. One is the distance between the mic and the singer, and the other is the angle of the mic capsule relative to the singer. With a mic in cardioid pattern (the most commonly used pattern for recording lead vocals), the closer the singer is to the mic, the more the bass frequencies are enhanced. This is called *proximity effect*, and experienced studio singers often use it to their advantage by moving closer to or farther from the mic, depending on the mood of the passage.

Close to You

A good starting position for a singer using a cardioid condenser mic is six to eight inches from the capsule. From there, if the voice sounds too thin, bright, or frail, have the singer move closer to the mic. But be careful, because moving in only two or three inches will increase bass response and fullness of sound dramatically. Conversely, if the sound is too big or warm, have the singer move back a bit.

If the mic is omnidirectional (or is set to the omni pattern), there will be no proximity effect. That is, bass frequencies will not be enhanced as the singer moves closer to the mic, although the mic will still register the sense of distance from the capsule. This is the most natural-sounding polar pattern, and it could be the right choice if the room is quiet and the acoustics fit the song.

An omni pattern is especially useful for singers who move around a great deal as they perform, or for inexperienced studio singers who can't seem to stand still. However, because an omni mic hears all parts of the room equally, it is not always a viable option, particularly in one-room studios filled with noisy gear (not to mention a living, breathing engineer hunched over the board). Just the same, thorough preparation includes auditioning each polar pattern available on the mic you've selected.

Right Angle

The other factor that affects the sound is the angle of the mic in relation to the singer. This varies from mic to mic, of course, and also depends on the type of mic. Condenser mics, for example, sound brighter and harsher when the capsule is positioned directly on-axis with the singer's mouth (see **Fig. 13.1a**). As the capsule is tilted forward (see **Fig. 13.1b**), the sound tends to get warmer, darker, and less strident. This is because the sound hits the capsule less directly and the capsule captures more of the singer's chest resonance. (To attenuate harshness and highs without increasing chest voice, tilt the capsule slightly to one side or toward the ceiling.) An off-axis tilt can also help reduce sibilance and popping caused by plosives. You can further minimize popping and sibilance by positioning the mic slightly above or below the singer's mouth.

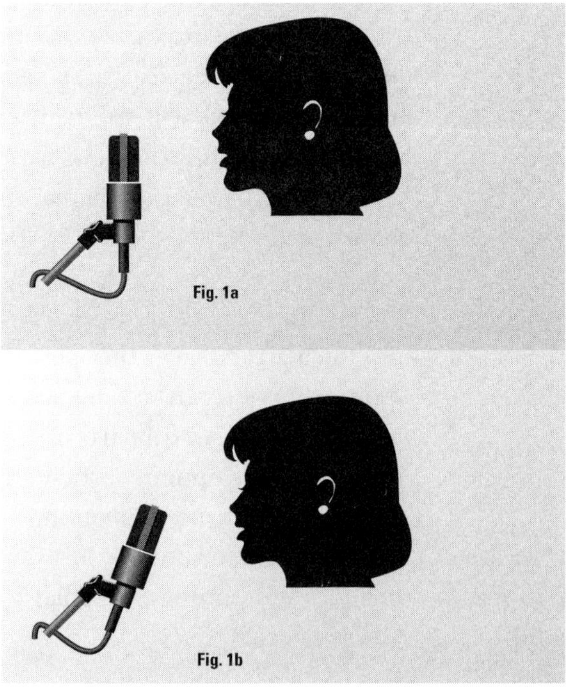

*FIG. 13.1: A large-diaphragm condenser mic positioned with the capsule pointed directly toward the singer's mouth (***13.1a***) will tend to yield the brightest, most focused sound, but it may sound a bit harsh and "spitty." Usually, a slight downward tilt will make the same mic sound warmer, darker, and smoother (***13.1b***), while also reducing susceptibility to plosives.*

For dynamic mics (at least those with cardioid patterns), the opposite is usually true: On-axis response is warmer and fuller, whereas off-axis response tends to sound thinner and less articulate. For that reason, when recording vocals with a cardioid dynamic mic, have the vocalist sing directly into the mic.

Armed with this information, and assuming that you have selected a complementary mic for the singer, you should be able to get the sound you want without resorting to EQ. Indeed, let your mantra be "No EQ whenever possible."

Finally, be aware that the slightest change in the position of the mic or singer can alter the sound drastically. This fact becomes very obvious as soon as you start punching in. Therefore, when tracking vocals (especially with a directional mic), ask the singer to make a mental note of his distance and position relative to the mic, and then to maintain that position. For an additional reference, put a strip of tape on the floor just at the edge of the singer's toes.

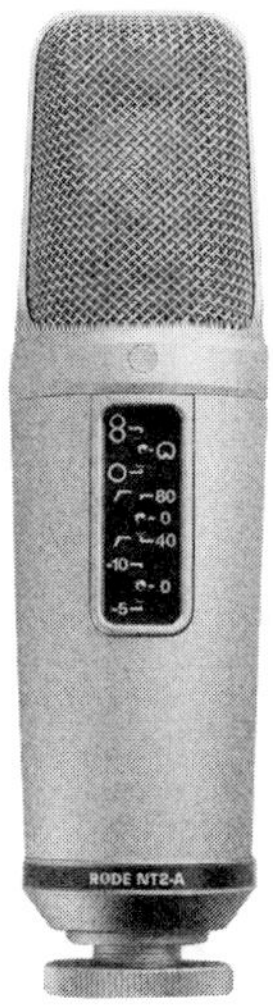

Large-diaphragm condenser mics, such as the Australian-made RØDE NT2-A, work well for recording vocalists. The NT2-A includes a number of useful features—three polar patterns (cardioid, omni, and figure-8), a low-cut switch, and a pad switch—that increase its versatility in the studio, making it a great value.

Les Accoutrements

One of the most helpful tools for recording vocals is a pop filter, so-called because it helps filter out pops or plosives. This is one item you can't do without. All it takes is one mic pop (usually caused by a word beginning with a p or b) to ruin an otherwise perfect take. Once recorded, a pop is virtually impossible to get rid of; usually, the only solution (short of digital waveform editing) is to rerecord the section that contains it.

A foam windscreen can also be useful when recording vocals, both for taming plosives and for attenuating sibilance, although it is less effective than a pop filter for reducing plosives. Furthermore, a foam windscreen can reduce high-end response significantly, sometimes to the point of making the mic sound muffled. Try to avoid using windscreens in the studio (where, after all, there is no wind).

Other helpful accoutrements for studio-vocal recording include a sturdy boom stand and a shock mount for the microphone. When mounting a heavy microphone on a lightweight, tripod-base boom stand, position the mic directly over one of the legs to increase stability. If you have only a round-base stand, stabilize it by slipping one or more barbell weights over the base.

Why are studio vocal mics commonly positioned hanging upside down, bat-style, in front of the singer? One reason is to make room for music stands and lyric sheets. Depending on the mic and shock mount, it can make positioning easier.

Gremlins

Any number of little things can spoil a vocal recording, such as the early reflections from a music stand positioned close to the mic. For this reason, whenever a music stand is required, I opt for the cheap, foldable type rather than an orchestra stand with a solid metal back. If you use the latter, angle the stand so the reflections bounce away from the mic. You can also place a towel over the metal to reduce reflections.

Noisy jewelry or clothing can ruin a great take, so watch out for those, too. For a singer who doesn't want to remove an armful of bracelets (or for bracelets that simply won't come off), wrap a towel around the noisy arm and tape it there. In case someone happens to wear a noisy (as opposed to loud) shirt to the session, I keep a few clean T-shirts nearby. This happens more often than you might think. It's also a good idea to have a pitcher of drinking water nearby to help minimize lip smacking and other unwanted mouth noise.

The Mindprint En-Voice MK II is a channel strip that provides three-band EQ, compression, tube-saturation, and A/D conversion. It even has a front-panel instrument input so it can serve double-duty in the studio as a DI.

Keep It Hot

Now that everything's set up and ready to go, it's time to adjust levels. But first, here's some good advice: Push the Record button from the get-go, even if you're still setting levels and the singer thinks it's just a practice run. Sometimes, those first takes are the best. (And invariably they are, if you don't have the Record button on!)

First, set the gain control on the mic preamp. Then, if necessary, apply dynamics control. Be gentle, though. For a compressor, start with a 1.5:1 or 2:1 ratio. In general, avoid going higher than 4:1, with no more than 8 or 10 dB of gain reduction on the loud passages. You can always compress more, if necessary, at mixdown. Also, engage the soft-knee setting if the compressor offers it, as soft-knee compression is generally smoother sounding on vocals than hard-knee.

If you use an expander to keep down unwanted noise, set the threshold low enough so that no words or breaths get muffled. And if you must use a peak limiter (not advisable, but sometimes necessary for digital recording), set it at the highest possible level before you start to get digital distortion.

Finalizing settings for a particular song should take one or two passes, at most; from then on, resist the urge to change them. That way, if the singer has to punch in, the new part will sound consistent with the rest of the track, and composite tracks will be easier to assemble.

Daily Monitor

Full-enclosure headphones are typically best for vocal tracking because they minimize leakage; however, some folks have a hard time singing in tune when using them. That's why you'll sometimes see musicians with one headphone on and the other off. If your singer is having difficulty keeping the pitch, suggest that he remove one headphone. Then pan the mix to the ear that's still in the can and make sure the other headphone is positioned snugly against the singer's head to quell leakage of any signal that remains in the unused headphone.

The quality of the monitor mix can greatly affect how well the singer performs. Singers don't always realize that the mix can be customized to their tastes, so take an active role and ask specific questions such as, "Do you want more vocal? Or less? Is that enough guitar? Bass? Kick drum? Snare drum? Is the overall mix too loud? Not loud enough?" Don't be alarmed if the mix that works for the singer doesn't sound optimal to you. After all, you're not the one performing.

Although most singers will want to hear some vocal reverb or delay in their monitor mix, be careful not to overdo it. Too much processing can negatively affect the singer's pitch and even timing.

Progress Report

After the levels are properly set and you've recorded a track or two, listen to the recording. If you're tracking in one room, turn on the monitors and listen through speakers rather than headphones. (Remember to mute the mic first.) Solo the vocal track and listen for any problems. This is the time to make any final tweaks to the microphone position, the compressor, or some other link in the recording chain. Again, actively solicit the singer's opinion, especially if he is the reticent type.

Once you've got your sound, don't be afraid to tweak it, if need be. Although you should strive to find the path that lets you record the sound you want without EQ, you shouldn't hold back if, say, boosting the highs clearly improves the sound going to disk. Ultimately, there are no absolutes; rather, do whatever it takes to get the best sound you can.

Doppelgänger

The old trick of double-tracking can increase the appeal of a vocal part, making it sound fuller, richer, and more powerful. The success of this technique, however, depends largely on the singer's skill.

If you are fortunate enough to work with someone who can double his part well, a neat trick is to vary the singer's distance from the mic with each successive pass. For example, if the first track is recorded six inches from the mic, record the second one at 12 inches, making sure to increase the preamp gain so the track levels are the same. Got another track? Then try a third pass two feet away. When combined at mixdown, the tracks will create a magical sense of depth. The extra tracks also provide more creative options for the mix engineer, who might, for instance, choose to process them differently.

Best of Both Worlds

When all is "sung and done," of course, it's the performance—not the quality of the gear or perfection of the recording—that makes a vocal track worth keeping. George Benson's vocal on "This Masquerade" (from the album *Breezin'*, Warner, 1976), for example, was recorded with an inexpensive, handheld-style dynamic mic. Yet the song earned him a Grammy award for Best Jazz Vocalist of the year and stayed at number 10 on the Billboard Top 40 chart for 11 weeks. The vocal track, a live first-take, was intended to be a scratch. "But when we listened back," explains engineer Al Schmitt, "it felt so good that we just left it."

Hopefully, the tips and techniques detailed in this chapter will help ensure that any killer takes you record are keepers, too. After all, art is only enhanced when it coincides with good technique and technology.

How the Pros Approach a Lead Vocal Track

Whitney Houston—Lead Vocals, *The Bodyguard* soundtrack (Arista Records); David Frazer—engineer

"With Whitney, you basically push Record, and you've got half the track. If you're not set up, you're in trouble. She is incredibly fast at getting her performances down and can ad lib very naturally. Her vibrato is like a little flutter—sometimes you don't even realize it's there—and it really energizes a vocal track. She also can double [her vocal performance] very well. She's so precise that when her doubled tracks are mixed together, it sounds like one voice, only fuller.

"To record the song 'I'm Every Woman,' I set up an AKG C 414 with a wind-screen in a small room at Ocean Way Studios in Los Angeles. Before we started recording, I worked up some basic EQ and compression settings based on the vocal register Whitney was in. I used a Focusrite equalizer as a mic preamp—it sounds good and acts as a consistent entity from one studio to another—and limited the signal through a Neve stereo compressor.

"We have a pretty consistent system for tracking vocals, and this method was employed on 'I'm Every Woman.' Narada Michael Walden [the track's producer] works singers pretty hard to find the right attitude and phrasing, so we'll typically record 10 to 12 vocal tracks for each section of the song: the verse, chorus, and bridge. The final vocal performance is assembled from bits and pieces of these multiple takes. Of course, with Whitney, any of these takes could be the final track. But Narada always looks for that perfect expression of feeling, which may be more pronounced on one take over another [for a particular section of phrase].

"We usually give Whitney two tracks to run down the song before Narada starts critically directing her performance. Much of the final track is often composed of these 'run-down' takes, because they're fresh and spontaneous. Narada like to nail the entire vocal track on the first day. Then he'll check the tracks the next day and decide whether to rerecord a few sections.

"When Narada approves the final composite vocal track, I'll re-EQ and recompress it slightly to get a blend between the various performances. We'll go from beginning to end to get a good sound, which is sometimes difficult because vocalists sing a little differently from day to day. To make the combined performances sound natural, we often have to match vocal EQ settings line by line, and sometimes we're changing EQ on syllables. All of this probably sounds pretty crazy, but the real trick is matching the song to the singer. If that's right, you just can't mess it up."

CHAPTER 14

Glorious Acoustic Guitars

Recording superlative acoustic-guitar sounds is not a simple step-by-step procedure like changing the oil in your car. In fact, the acoustic guitar is one of the most challenging instruments to record well, because it produces a wide range of timbres, tones, and frequencies. Documenting that sonic rainbow requires not only good gear but also good ears, good technique, and on occasion, the patience of Job.

Let's assume that your session is blessed with a talented musician and a good-sounding guitar. The first challenge you'll face is finding the ideal room, because where you record the performance may be as important as how you record it. To really nail the nuances of an acoustic guitar, you should match the recording environment to the artist's performance style.

For example, when recording a classical guitarist, independent producer/engineer Jeff Saltzman booked time at San Jose's Lick Observatory, a cavernous, perfectly hemispheric room. He stereo-miked the nylon-string guitar with his favorite mics for recording acoustic guitar: two Neumann KM 84s fitted with KM 83 omnidirectional capsules. "I pulled the mics about six feet back," says Saltzman. "It's amazing what the room did for the sound. It was like having the most expensive Lexicon reverb with all the diffusion and predelay perfectly dialed in, only better."

At the other end of the spectrum, an acoustically dead room is usually better for tracking guitar parts that are destined for a crowded mix or intense signal-processing. Too much room sound in these applications may cause the acoustic guitar to appear diffuse or "washy" and effectively destroy any contribution the guitar was supposed to make to the audio spectrum. In addition, putting effects on a track that already includes a room sound means that both the room and source sounds will be affected. Saltzman, who has worked extensively in Francis Ford Coppola's movie studio, American Zoetrope, solves these dilemmas by recording the acoustic guitar in a padded isolation booth.

"I sometimes go for the classic 1970s AM-radio acoustic guitar sound, which requires a lot of compression," he explains. "And that sound also requires doubling the guitar part. Therefore, if I were to record the guitarist in a reverberant space, the compressor would increase the volume of the low-level room sound. Then, when the player doubled the part, all the different reflections in the two performances would make the guitar sound really 'comb filtery.'"

If your goal is to capture a realistic, natural-sounding portrait of the acoustic guitar, your best bet is to record in a natural-sounding room. That's because, in the real world, people listen to guitars in ordinary rooms, not iso booths or observatories. When it comes to recording unsullied, organic acoustic guitar tracks, one recognized master of the genre is Nashville veteran Bil VornDick. Originally chief engineer for country-music legend Marty Robbins, the award-winning VornDick has recorded countless artists, including James Taylor, Doc Watson, Chet Atkins, Rickey Skaggs, Tony Rice, and Alison Krause. "I like a medium-sized, neutral-sounding room, not overly dead or live," says VornDick. "And it needs to have a hardwood floor to get some natural reflections."

If you don't have a wood floor or are forced to record in an acoustically dead space, you can liven up the sound by placing a large wooden board on the floor beneath the guitarist. Consider keeping several boards on hand for this purpose because you can also erect them vertically on either side of the guitarist to create reflections.

Mics and Placement

Second in importance only to the quality and musicality of the sound being made in the studio is the choice and placement of microphones. Three parameters should govern your miking strategy: the type of microphone best suited for the job, which polar pattern is most appropriate, and whether you are recording a source sound in a monaural or stereo perspective.

The choice of mic usually comes down to dynamic or condenser, and due to the complexity of the sound emanating from an acoustic guitar, a condenser is almost always the better choice because it is more sensitive. However, for aggressive rock or film-score tracks, a dynamic mic can be used to produce a strong midrange tone that will cut through almost anything. Depending on the mic used, the dynamic also may not reproduce the low-frequency rumble of the guitar as well as a condenser would—and this can be a good thing when the acoustic is adding mud to a track.

Polar Considerations

The two most commonly used polar patterns are cardioid and omnidirectional. Obviously, the cardioid pattern is useful if you're recording other instruments in the same room simultaneously because the pattern's rear rejection minimizes bleed from nonsource sounds. However, if there is no interference from other instruments, be sure to audition an omni mic. The omnidirectional pattern typically gives a bigger picture of the sound, which can be especially desirable if you're miking the guitar with a single microphone.

Opinions vary about the use of cardioid versus omnidirectional mics. Saltzman feels that using a cardioid pattern on an acoustic instrument produces a "pinched" sound, so he prefers to use omni mics. "A mic capsule is naturally omnidirectional," he explains. "To make the mic cardioid, a manufacturer has to add acoustical porting and other modifications. So a cardioid mic is basically a crippled omni. A cardioid doesn't capture all the sound coming from an acoustic guitar. When I put a mic on an acoustic, I want to pick up as much sound as possible, so I go with an omni."

Another advantage of omnidirectional mics is their lack of proximity effect, which means bass frequencies won't increase as the mic gets closer to the sound source. This attribute lets you position the mic closer to the sound hole without increasing boominess. A corollary benefit (for small-diaphragm models only, because they employ a single capsule that does not "hear" behind itself as well as a dual-capsule, large-diaphragm condenser) is the inverse relationship to ambient sound: The closer the mic is to the guitar, the less room sound it hears. This is an important consideration if the only place you have to work is a bad-sounding room.

Two on One

The issue of whether to record a monaural or stereo perspective of an acoustic guitar is typically decided by aesthetic considerations and available tracks. Let's discuss tracking in stereo first, because although it offers more tonal and spatial options than mono, it is at least twice as hard to get right. For one thing, the addition of another mic introduces potential phase-cancellation problems. If you detect the hollow or thin sound that accompanies phase cancellation, you have two options: activate the mic preamp's phase-reversal switch for one of the input channels to alleviate the problem, or reposition the mics farther away from each other until you hear a full-bodied tone. Of course, if phase cancellation is responsible for a strange but wonderful tone, go with it.

One advantage of stereo miking an acoustic guitar is that you can position one mic to capture the instrument's treble qualities and the other its bass. In this case, you're listening for two sweet spots, each with a different character. In fact, you can further emphasize the different tonalities by using unmatched mics. For example, you could train a small-diaphragm condenser near the strings and a large-diaphragm near the bridge or sound hole, or vice versa.

When recording acoustic guitars, VornDick swears by stereo miking. "It gives the sound dimension," he says. He aims one mic, pointing downward, at the sound board between the top of the guitar and the bridge, and positions the mic so that it's about the same distance from the guitar as the player's right ear (assuming the guitarist is right-handed). "In essence, this mic picks up what the player hears," says VornDick. "Of course, I then move the mic around until I find the sweet spot.

"The other mic," continues VornDick, "is aimed about three or four inches below the neck, between the sound hole and where the neck joins the body, but not pointing at the strings. It's about five to seven inches away from the guitar. With this mic, I'm trying to capture the high side of the instrument's ambient structure without emphasizing the sound of the strings on the fretboard. Naturally, the positions may change depending on the guitar."

In the mix, VornDick pans the stereo tracks in a V. "I never pan them hard left and right," he explains. "That would sound too spread out. The widest I would get is one track at nine o'clock and the other at three o'clock—and then only if it is a guitar-based song. As more instruments are added to the mix, the size of the V gets smaller."

Another way to mic an acoustic guitar in stereo is with one mic up close and the other five or six feet back, positioned as an overhead looking down on the guitar. Again, you can use a matched pair of mics, or two different mics, if you want to broaden the tonal picture (see **Fig. 14.1**). The two signals can then be blended to taste in the final mix. This is an excellent application for a guitar-based song with little or no other instrumentation, because it creates a spacious stereo image.

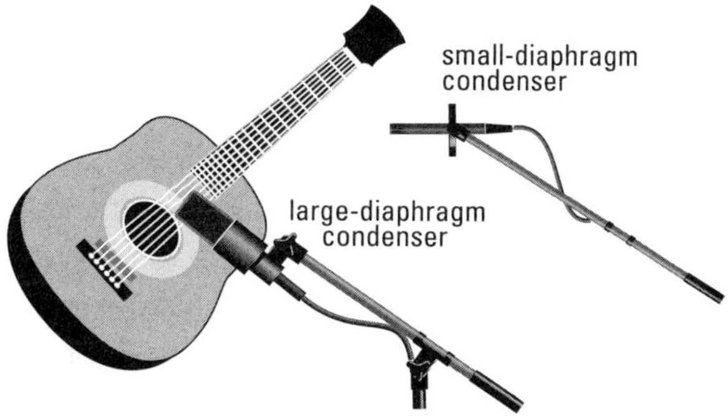

FIG. 14.1:
You can create a more complex stereo picture of the acoustic guitar by using two different mics. In this figure, a large-diaphragm condenser is slightly off-axis to the guitar's sound hole, and a small-diaphragm condenser is up near the fretboard.

One on One

For monaural recordings of an acoustic guitar, try to find the spot with the best balance of low- and high-end frequencies. This is usually somewhere between the sound hole and upper frets, with the mic far enough back—6 to 12 inches—to capture a blend of warmth from the sound hole and zing from the strings (see **Fig. 14.2**). If the guitar sounds thin, angle the mic toward the sound hole; if the tone is boomy, angle the mic more toward the strings. Also, move the mic up and down. Try several positions, and keep in mind that the slightest difference in mic placement can cause a big change in sound.

FIG. 14.2:
A RØDE Classic tube condenser microphone set to the omnidirectional pattern is positioned to capture a blend of warmth (from the sound hole) and high end (from the strings) of a Gibson J-160E.

Legendary producer George Martin used to listen for the sweet spot by putting a hand over one ear to simulate the perspective of a single mic. In fact, whether you're tracking in monaural or stereo, there's no better way to position a mic than by first listening to the instrument with the unaided ear. However, because a microphone invariably hears differently than the human ear, be sure to audition mic placement by listening through your monitors (or headphones) as well, to home in on what the mic perceives as the instrument's sweet spot.

Slim-line, acoustic-electric guitars can sound huge if you position a condenser microphone approximately six feet above the guitar to capture a lush mix of source sound and room ambience. Use the guitar's direct (electric) sound to maintain articulation.

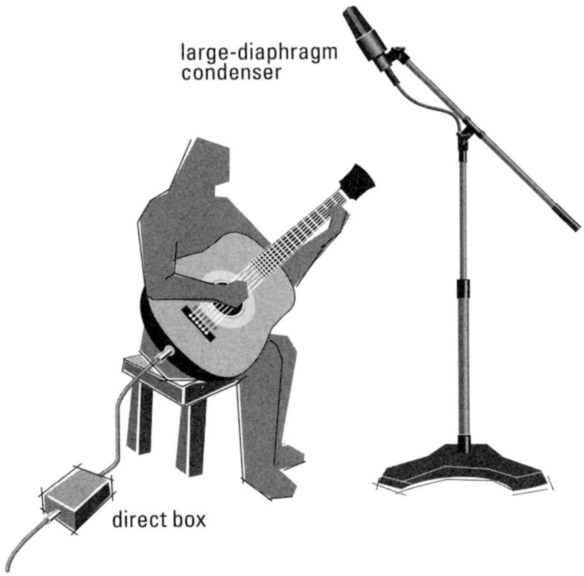

Tweak City

Compression is the most common and useful type of signal processing for acoustic guitar, as it can enhance the impact of the guitar while still maintaining a natural sound. Although you can compress while tracking, while mixing, or both, engineers have different opinions about what works best. Saltzman, who likes using a UREI 1176 or 1178 for acoustic guitar, says that he usually avoids compressing while tracking. "When you close-mic an acoustic guitar," he explains, "you're going to pick up a lot of low-end frequencies, which can drive a compressor crazy. The compressor will be pumping and breathing while trying to hold back the low end. But in the mix, you can dial out excessive low end and make any other necessary EQ adjustments before compressing. That way, the compressor is only reacting to the final sound."

VornDick, on the other hand, prefers to compress while tracking. "But I only use the compressor as a catch-all," he clarifies. "I don't try to squish the sound. Usually, a very light setting, around 2:1, is sufficient." VornDick, who favors the Aphex Compellor and Rane MC 22 compressors for acoustic guitar, also tweaks the EQ a bit while tracking. "Martin guitars," he explains, "often have a muddy bottom. So I'll use a highpass filter to roll off everything below 80 or 90 Hz. Or if the boom is really drastic, I'll switch microphones until I find one that de-emphasizes the problematic frequencies."

Bay Area independent producer-engineer Tom Luekens, formerly Booker T. Jones's engineer, often compresses lightly while tracking and then again in the mix. "The denser the mix—and the more instruments there are in the same tonal range as the guitar that are playing similar rhythms—the more I'll compress," says Luekens. "But I rarely go above a 4:1 ratio for acoustic guitar because it starts sounding funny."

Luekens has been getting good results with the Focusrite Red 3 compressor. "The Red 3 is great. I typically set the attack and release controls on automatic, which works just fine for most applications. But if I do adjust the parameters manually, I usually like a medium to fast attack and release. If you have the release set too long, the compressor tends to pump because the next thing coming down the audio stream catches the tail end of the compression from the previous note."

Unfortunately, compression can't cure all ills. For example, a performance that features both fingerpicking and strumming can present problems due to varying dynamic levels. A compressor can level out the dynamic range to some extent, but not always enough to optimize the nuances of each style. Saltzman has another solution (see **Fig. 14.3**): "I try to persuade the musician to perform the two sections on separate tracks. That way I can close-mic the fingerpicking for a wonderfully dramatic effect and then pull the mic back enough to get the strong, rhythmic impact of the strumming."

FIG. 14.3:
To ensure near-perfect documentation of each style, engineer Jeff Saltzman recommends recording fingerpicked and strummed performances in two passes, on two separate tracks. Here, songwriter Mike Lawson strums his Gibson J-30C, miked with a pair of Earthworks OM1 omnidirectional condensers.

If you're looking to forge beyond au naturel acoustic-guitar tracks, a wealth of effects and studio tricks is at your disposal. Most multieffects processors contain a number of preprogrammed patches—typically chorus-based—designed to enhance the acoustic guitar. Or you can always experiment and develop your own processing tricks.

On an album by Japanese artist Jun Hirose, for example, Luekens and producer Scott Mathews created a bizarre-sounding acoustic guitar track by running the signal through a Leslie speaker cabinet. They documented the swirling sound with three mics: a pair of AKG C 414s positioned toward the top of the cabinet to capture a stereo perspective of the Leslie's rotating horns and an AKG D 112 placed near the speaker bottom to grab some bass frequencies. In the final mix, Luekens panned the two top mics hard left and right and the bottom mic in the center. "It sounded really strange and wonderful."

Lifesavers

But how do you get a great acoustic guitar sound if you aren't blessed with an excellent player and a superb guitar? Here are some techniques you can use to salvage a third-rate performance on a bum axe.

For example, the sound of dead strings can be brought back to life with some compression and EQ. Start with a 2:1 compression ratio to raise low-level signals and smooth out the sound. Then, depending on the tempo of the song, experiment with a medium-to-slow release to add sustain. Watch out for bass signals, which are likely to increase disproportionately as you add compression. (It may be necessary to dial out troublesome low frequencies with console EQ.) You can also increase sparkle by boosting mid and high frequencies a few decibels somewhere between 5 kHz and 10 kHz, depending on the instrument.

A de-esser is another useful device for salvaging acoustic guitar tracks. This device is designed to attenuate sibilance on vocal tracks, but it can also be set to diminish annoying fret buzzes. Finger squeaks are difficult to tame, although an outboard graphic equalizer may be able to notch out some of these distractions. Remember, reverb can emphasize squeaks and buzzes, so go extremely light on the effect sends during the mixdown. To a limited extent, it's possible to use chorus and pitch-shifting effects to correct bad intonation or out-of-tune notes, but these tricks should be used as a last resort, because the results on acoustic instruments rarely sound natural.

The Nashville Thing

Ever wonder how Nashville engineers create the wonderfully crisp acoustic-guitar tone that has become a classic element of country music productions? You can approximate that sound by dialing out a lot of low end, but it takes more than that to get the real thing.

"For the classic country rhythm-guitar sound," explains VornDick, "you double the part with a high-strung guitar. A high-strung guitar has the three bass strings tuned an octave higher than standard tuning. You need to use thinner-gauge strings on the E, A, and D strings to do this. Then the guitar is recorded with a single mic positioned above the player and shooting down at the sound hole. At the board, the engineer cuts out the bottom end, boosts the top, and slams the signal [compresses it extremely hard].

"The goal is to have the tone of the acoustic match the hi-hat," continues VornDick. "You're going more for a rhythmic 'ching' than the full-bodied sound of the instrument. Country engineers also do this trick to clear a space for the piano, because the guitar and piano are so alike in their overtone structures."

Let It Ring

The only foolproof recipe for great acoustic guitar tracks is this: a great guitar, a great guitarist, a great-sounding room, one or two great mics, a great set of ears (yours), and a clean signal path. Throw in a great compressor, and you're in business. But even with less-than-perfect ingredients—such as a poor guitarist flailing away on a balsa-wood acoustic—you can produce a palatable track by employing the same care and sonic sense that you'd bring to an ideal session. Just listen carefully, be open to experimentation, and do whatever it takes to make the track jangle and sparkle.

CHAPTER 15

Ultimate Electric Guitar

Just like tracking acoustic guitar, recording the ultimate electric guitar tone requires good ears, ingenuity, and the ability to concentrate on minute nuances of sound. If you use an amplifier, mic placement will be a major factor in the sound you get. The closer you get to your idealized sound through mic placement, the less you'll rely on equalization and signal processing. The result is a cleaner signal with maximum impact.

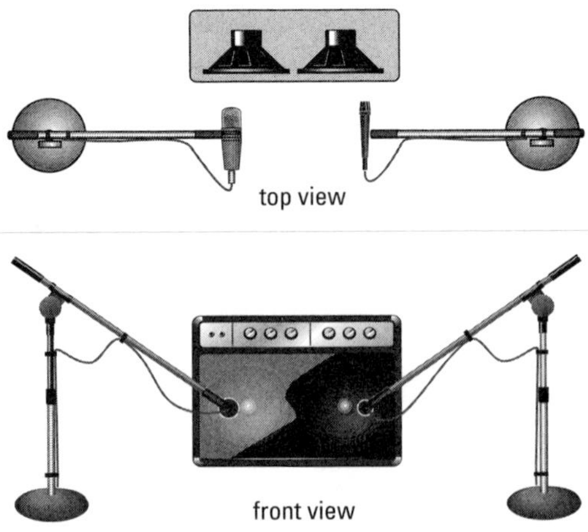

You can create a monstrous sound in the mix by using two different mic models on a twin-speaker amp. Make sure that the two microphones are the same distance from the amp, positioned at the same angle relative to the speakers.

Good mic placement requires cognitive hearing. The trick is to imagine yourself as a microphone, using your ears to sense what tones the transducer will pick up. Just be careful not to get too close to loud sound sources (such as amps turned up to 10) that may damage your hearing.

Point and Shoot

The classic rock and blues miking position is simply a single dynamic mic pointed dead center at one guitar speaker (see **Fig. 15.1**). This position accurately represents the sound of the guitar and amp, because the on-axis orientations and close proximity of the mic to the speaker eliminate much of the personality of the room.

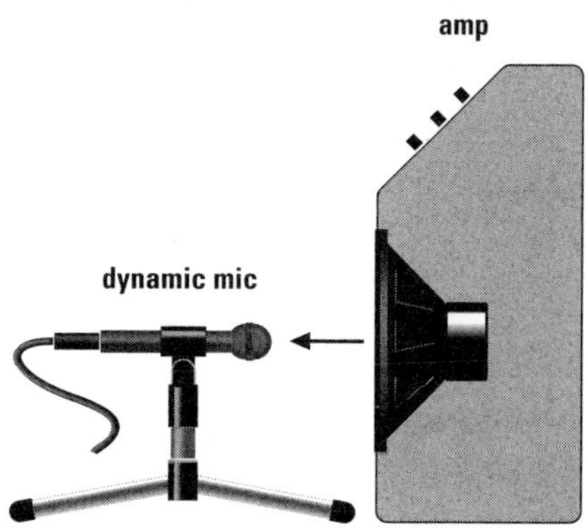

FIG. 15.1:
The classic team of a dynamic microphone and a tube amp is hard to beat when seeking the ultimate electric guitar sound.

The mid-'80s revival of funk music popularized an interesting turn on the single-mic technique: The off-axis position (see **Fig. 15.2**) accentuates the sparkling tones of a clean, undistorted guitar while still producing a sharp, aggressive sound. Condenser microphones work well for off-axis applications because they tend to emphasize the brighter timbres.

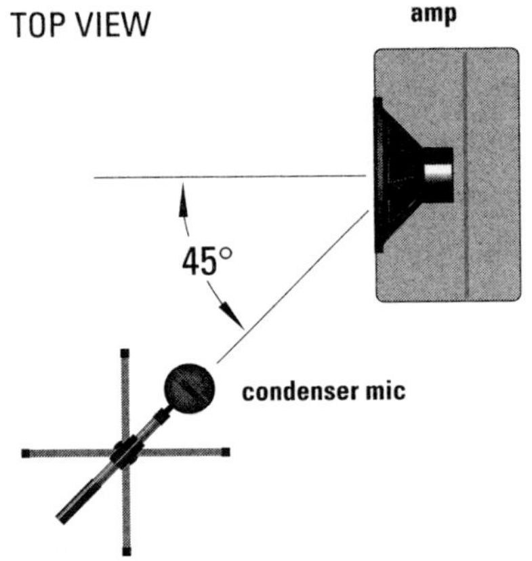

FIG. 15.2:
Off-axis mic positions favor the crystalline tones popularized during the late-'80s funk revival.

The classic room-mic setup (see **Fig. 15.3**) is the simplest way to mix the acoustic environment with the source sound. But, of course, the sky is the limit. In an extreme example, you could have both speakers of a 2-by-12-inch, open-back cabinet close-miked front and back, stereo room mics positioned behind and in front of the amp, and stereo mics mounted on the ceiling. (See Chapter 20, "The House Is Rockin'," for further tips on mic placement.)

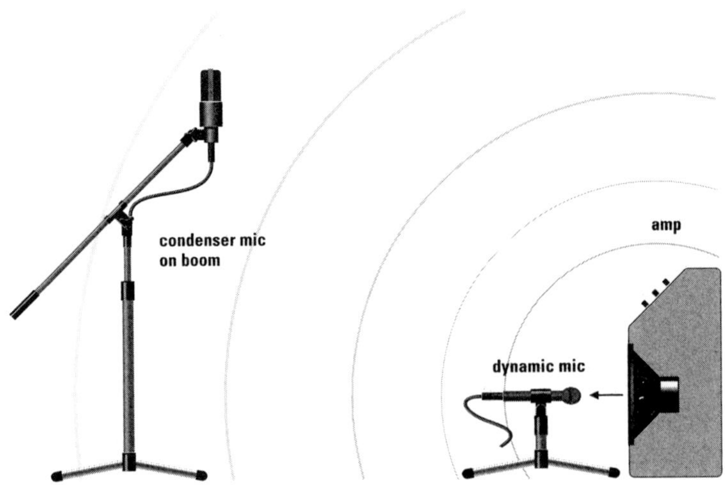

FIG. 15.3:
Expansive guitar sounds are captured by positioning a condenser mic to record the room environment, while a conventional close-miked perspective handles the amp timbres.

Garbage In, Garbage Out

Microphones are not magic wands. Inspired miking of a poor guitar/amp combination only serves to record a bad sound exceptionally well. Too many musicians and engineers, seduced by the methodology of recording (such as mic selection, mic placement, gain stages, equalization, and signal processing), forget to scrutinize the sound that is being recorded until it's too late.

For starters, pay close attention to room acoustics and how they are affecting the sound of the instrument. However, acoustics aren't the only sonic booby traps awaiting the recordist. Be sure to check for anomalies haunting the guitar itself: fret buzzes, dead strings, poor intonation, and so on. The easiest way to fix a crummy guitar is to beg, borrow, or buy a good one. However, if you're stuck with a dud, remedies are available.

Lifeless strings can be punched up by compressing the guitar during recording. This raises the levels of weak signals to produce a smoother, more robust sound. Start with a basic setting of a –10 dB input threshold at a 2:1 ratio, and continue to tweak the compression parameters until the strings sound tight and even. You may have to adjust the EQ on the board to compensate for increased bass response. (The relative level of low frequencies often increases when a signal is compressed.) It doesn't hurt to add a little sparkle by boosting the upper mid-range frequencies; just take care not to increase audible hiss.

Amp and guitar combos sometimes produce a symphony of hisses, hums, rattles, and buzzes. Luckily, this sonic hullabaloo usually is masked by the sound of the guitar. However, a noise gate is a wonderful tool to help clean up unwanted noise during passages in which the guitarist is not playing. Simply set the gate's input threshold to shut down the guitar signal when it's not being played. (Be careful that the gate isn't set to cut out the player's softer dynamics.) If there is hiss so strong that it is audible during a performance, try using a noise-reduction device in addition to the noise gate.

Axing the Amp

When there are space and volume limitations in the personal studio, speaker simulators, amp emulators, and rackmount preamps are handy replacements for the amplifier rig. A good amp or speaker simulator makes it possible to record loud guitar sounds directly, avoiding the hassles of mic placement and amp noise.

If you want to continue using your amp head, speaker emulators let you route the amp signal directly to the mixer. Once the speaker output of an amp head is plugged into such a unit, the signal is brought down to line level, and impedance is tracked like a real loudspeaker. The result is a direct sound that emulates the timbre of your amp close-miked through a quality microphone. There's no room environment, of course, because you've eliminated the room sound along with the mic. A little reverb is all that's needed to replace the missing ambience.

On the amp emulation front, devices like Tech 21's versatile SansAmp (available as a floor pedal or rackmount) are favorites of home recordists. The SansAmp allows you to emulate the sound of various classic amplifiers with the flick of a switch or parameter knob.

Line 6 has pioneered products that physically model not only the sound of classic amps, but also their response. The PODxt models dozens of amplifiers, including Fenders, Marshalls, Voxes, Mesa Boogies, Soldanos, and even a Matchless Chieftain (see **Fig. 15.4**). Physical modeling captures not only the sound of each amp, but also the way the amp behaves, right down to how the knob settings affect amp performance. The feel of modeled amps is far more realistic than previous amp emulators because the physical models react to produce the same range of tones that the real amps do.

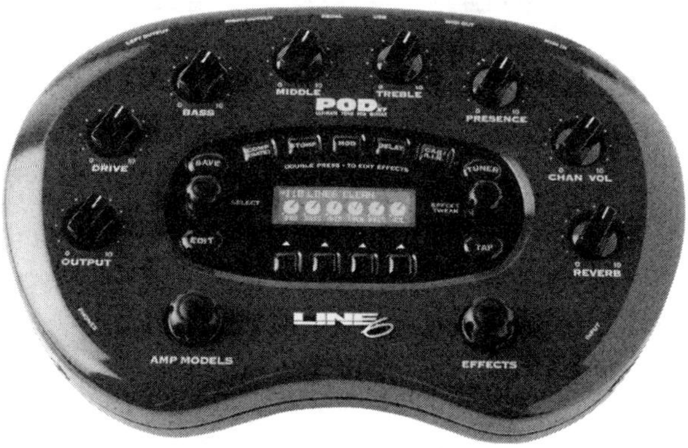

FIG. 15.4:
For guitarists with volume and space restrictions, a specialized DI box is essential. PODxt, by Line 6, physically models dozens of famous amps, right down to how the tone and volume knobs affect the sound.

With each amplifier, PODxt gives you a choice of effects, such as spring reverb, flanging, and delay. With the optional pedal controller, you get access to variable effects, such as physically modeled wah-wahs.

Success rates vary with less expensive amp and speaker simulators, but most of them at least approach a professional sound. Almost any model is fine for demo use. However, if you plan to cut guitar tracks worthy of a master recording, audition these devices with a critical ear.

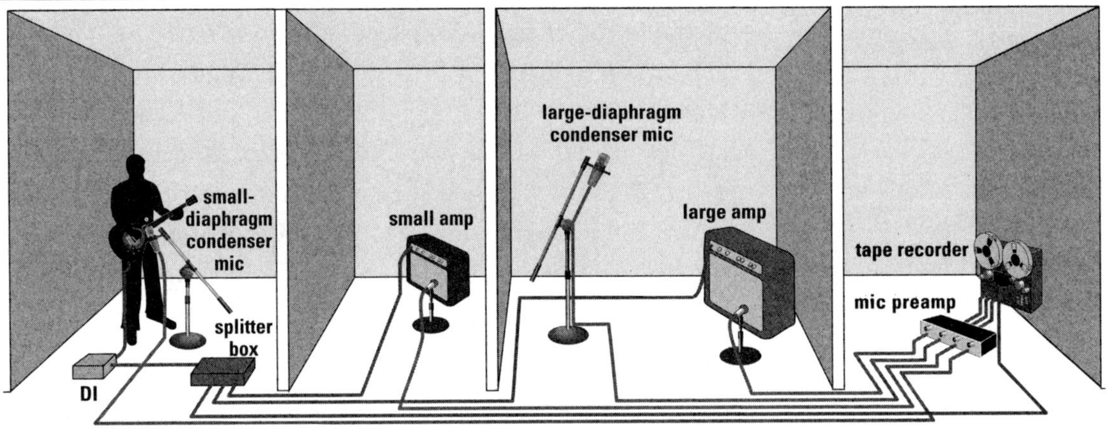

For huge guitar sounds and any number of processing options, use an air mic on the guitar itself and split the guitar output, sending one signal direct to your recorder and the others to amps located in separate rooms, each miked differently.

Play It Again

It takes more than the right gear to get a monster guitar tone. One of the quickest ways to get a huge sound is by layering. Guitar legend Ted Nugent once noted that the lead melodies of his songs were usually made up of no fewer than a dozen tracks of the same line layered and mixed together. Just as vocalists sometimes double their performances by recording a second track identical to the first, electric guitarists have been doubling, tripling, and quadrupling both rhythm and lead parts since the earliest days of multitrack recording.

Obviously, you can simulate this technique using delays and other effects processing. But nothing beats doing it the old-fashioned way if you have the extra tracks and the guts to overdub and submix.

Before the advent of modern multitrack recording, Les Paul recorded his fabulous multiguitar pieces using the sound-on-sound method: Record one track, and then play the tape back while recording the next track directly on top of the first. Each time he recorded a new track, the previous track would automatically drop a few decibels. But Paul didn't let this stop him. He arranged the sessions so that the background parts were recorded first and the leads last. That way, the lead lines were always at the hottest level and the rhythm parts were well in the background (mixed automatically, you could say). It was not uncommon for him to record as many as 37 overdubs to get all of the parts to tape.

You don't need to layer the same sound over and over again to fatten a track. Consider doing each track differently. For example, you can play the second part in a different octave, change pickups, change amp settings, and even record at a different tape speed (if you're working in the analog domain) to get a completely new timbre. Jimmy Page has gone as far as lowering a microphone into a bucket in front of the amp to get the best sound for a track. No technique is too weird if it sounds right in the mix.

CHAPTER 16

Amazing Bass

In most genres, the bass defines the music as much as the beat does—not only by what the bassist plays but also with the instrument's sound. Yet, when it comes time for tracking, the beginning recordist often takes the electric bass for granted (unless he is the bass player). The overall sound of the rhythm section can be just as important as its performance, and a wimpy bass tone can sabotage the impact of any beat.

A well-rounded engineer should be aware of the sonic demands of different types of music. A hardcore punk band might want the bass sound to be a low-end rumble, while a funk bassist might ask for a heavily articulated midrange. Getting a great bass sound is a challenge, but you already have the tools to succeed in doing it.

The Direct Route

The easiest way to record an electric bass is through a direct connection to the recording console. If you're running a –10 dB unbalanced system, you can plug the 1/4-inch cable from the bass right into a mixer line input. However, a more robust signal can be achieved by utilizing a direct box—an essential tool for interfacing with +4 dB balanced systems—to run through a microphone input. (Mic inputs typically provide more gain than line inputs.)

For demo projects, the "naked" direct method provides a good enough sound to document sonic and musical arrangements. However, the tight, visceral punch of professional bass tracks is difficult to achieve without compression. There are many great compressors on the market. Some of the more popular ones for personal studios include the dbx 166, the Symetrix 425, and the UREI 1176. In addition, many bass amplifiers have built-in compressors and line outputs to facilitate direct recording.

In the absence of an amp, speaker, and room environment, direct recording tends to highlight performance blemishes, revealing fret noise and sloppy dynamics. Therefore, it's important to match compression parameters to the sonic demands of both the track and the bassist's technique. Doing this well requires critical listening and intuitive processing. However, there are some basic settings that can be used as starting points.

If a player has excellent tone and technique, you may need only to tame the odd dynamic peak with a –10 dB compression threshold at a 2:1 ratio. Midlevel bassists usually require more help to achieve a smooth, round tone, so the settings are upgraded to a –15 dB threshold at a 4:1 ratio. Seamlessly tight bass lines (or technically deficient players) can be recorded by crushing the signal under a –20 dB threshold at a 12:1 ratio. However, be careful with the high numbers: Heavy compression often emphasizes low frequencies. If overcompression turns your signal into mud, you can retrieve some snap with your console EQ by cutting at least 3 dB at 100 Hz.

Many dedicated bass preamps allow controlled direct recording. These units are not as plentiful as guitar-oriented devices, but who says you can't run a bass through a guitar preamp?

Getting Amped

One thing direct recording can't deliver is the sound of an 18-inch speaker pumping bass into a room. Documenting an amplified performance requires a good amp and speaker combination, as well as good microphones.

A typical personal studio setup (see **Fig. 16.1**) utilizes an enclosed room or isolation booth as a "bass trap" to prevent low frequencies from dissipating in an open acoustic environment. Position a large-diaphragm dynamic microphone (such as an Electro-Voice RE20 or Sennheiser MD421) approximately six inches from the center of the bass speaker cone. If the speaker enclosure has midfrequency horns, move the mic farther back from the bass speaker to get a mix of low-frequency boom and midrange articulation.

To record the bass-enhanced room tone, position a medium- to large-diaphragm condenser mic ten feet away from the amp at a height of about seven feet. The close-miked and room sounds can be routed to separate mixer input channels and submixed to a mono bass track, or recorded onto two individual tracks for stereo imaging.

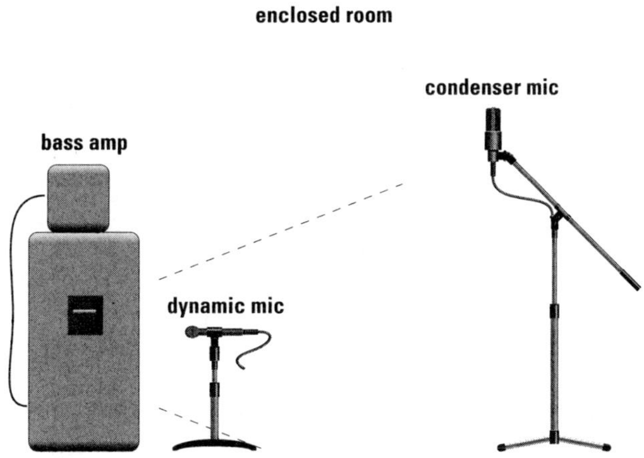

FIG. 16.1: Mammoth bass tones can be recorded by enclosing an amplifier in a sealed room. Combining a close mic and a room mic gives recordists the option of using two diverse sounds in the mix.

Home recordists can transform an enclosed closet into a neighbor-friendly bass trap. First, purchase enough three-inch-thick foam to cover the closet's rear and sidewalls to a height of approximately four feet. The foam needn't be permanently attached; you can lean it against the walls or tape it in place. Leave your clothes on their hangers to provide additional sound absorption, but remove belts and other accessories that may rattle during tracking.

Now place a small "practice" bass amp or guitar amp—a compact model with a single 12- or 15-inch speaker is perfect—inside the foam room, with the speaker facing the closet door. Position a mic directly in front of the speaker and close the door. You shouldn't need a lot of amp volume to create a "boom room." A few tweaks of the amp's tone controls often is all that's required to evoke a punchy bass track. (See Chapter 20, "The House Is Rockin'," for more tips on recording electric bass at home.)

Combination Plate

Sometimes, a direct or amp sound alone doesn't cut it. Direct bass signals can sound a tad sterile, and amp tones often venture into the muddy side of the sonic spectrum. Luckily, a simple direct box is the key to accentuating the positive attributes of the two sound sources (see **Fig. 16.2**).

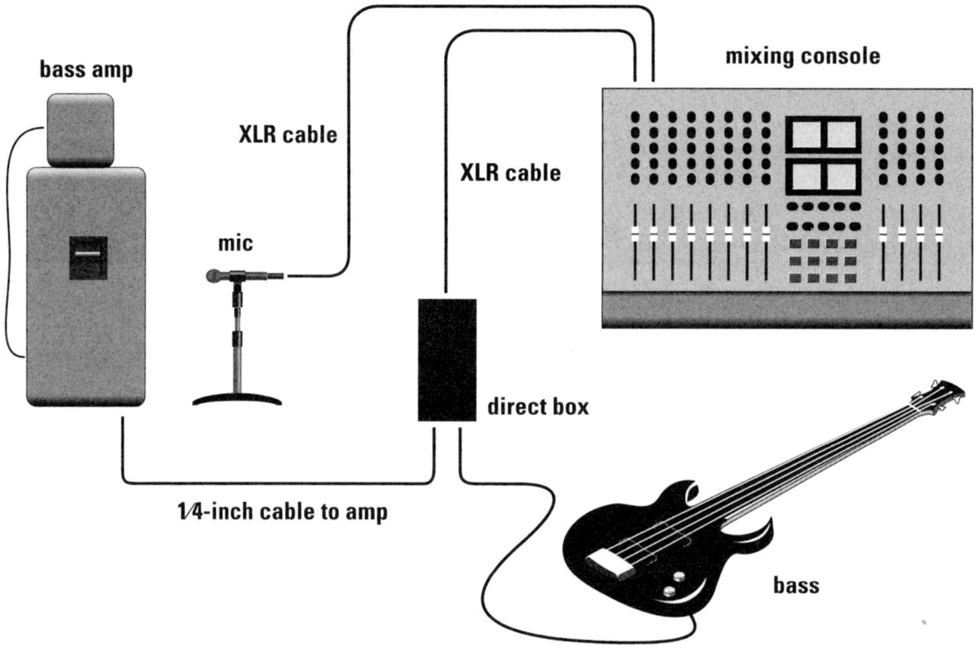

FIG. 16.2: Combining a clean, direct sound with the sonic impact of an amplifier often energizes a bass track.

Plug the bass into the 1/4-inch instrument jack of the direct box (the normal connection for direct recording) and connect a balanced XLR cable from the direct box to your mixer. Then run a 1/4-inch cord from the amp jack of the direct box into your amplifier's input jack. Now, position a microphone in front of the amp's speaker cabinet and route the mic cable to another input on your mixer. Voilà! You have two sound sources on two separate mixer inputs. You can submix two sounds to a mono track or record both bass tracks and postpone sonic decisions until the final mix. The two tracks also can be mixed in a stereo spread.

Basic Impact

Ugly bass tones spring from compromised signals. Classic instruments, such as the Fender Precision and the Hofner "Beatle bass," often have poorly shielded electronics that add annoying hums and radio-frequency (RF) waves to the signal. However, if the audible level of the malady is discreet, the unwanted noise may be hidden in the sonic wash of the overall mix. There's no sense in obsessing over a minute detail that is fated for obliteration under 10 tracks of distorted guitars.

For instance, audible hiss seldom is an issue, because the critical frequencies for meaty bass tones lie far below the hiss strata. Simply use your console EQ to cut frequencies above 10 kHz, and the hiss should disappear without compromising the fundamental bass sound.

RF waves are more problematic, because they can be as audible as the bass signal. Noise gates or manual signal muting can't eradicate RF whines if the anomaly can still be heard when the instrument is playing. (Obviously, muting the RF signal also kills the bass signal.) Positioning often is the only cure. The idea is to find a spot where the instrument is less effective as an RF antenna. Have the bassist turn his body in different directions while holding the bass until the RF noises stop. Tape the floor to identify the "safe zone" as a reminder during the heat of performance. If RF waves invade every position, find a bass that is better shielded.

Home Bass

According to *Rock on the Road* (a British book about the music industry, published in the 1970s), the genius of glam-rock band Slade was that their records were produced to feature the bass lines when the tracks were played at loud volumes. Supposedly, the enhanced bass made Slade records a hot commodity in discos.

Of course, even a James Taylor record played at dance-club volumes will produce deep bass tones, because the human ear's sensitivity to bass frequencies increases with volume. But the point is that the perception of a driving bass tone is crucial to the rhythmic ideals of rock, rap, dance, salsa, and other popular music styles. Slade's historian knew this, even if he did mistake physics for audio wizardry.

What does this anecdote teach us about bass tracks? Well, besides the fact that a music critic should never understand more about the magic of making records than you, it shows that cool records always have great-sounding bass lines. The pop graveyard is chock-full of lifeless rhythm sections, so don't spare the intensity as you struggle to produce a killer bass tone.

Combination Saves the Day

Combining an amp and direct sound can revitalize lackluster bass tracks. This approach literally saved the rhythm tracks during my production of a label-development demo for San Francisco's Bolshoi Rodeo, an alternative country act. The group's bassist had great musical ideas, but her tentative technique produced an indistinct and dynamically erratic signal.

I was loath to hire a session player, because Bolshoi's bassist was also the lead vocalist and obviously had a special understanding of the band's material. As a last chance, I tried using a direct signal with an amp miked in the bass-trap configuration, with close and room mics. For maximum effect, I treated each of the three signals differently: The direct signal was flat (no EQ); the close mic was cut at the low-mids and boosted at 100 Hz; and the room mic was drastically cut at 10 kHz, left flat along the low-mids, and boosted at 100 Hz.

The three signals were submixed to mono, with a compressor inline at the subgroup insert point. Fader levels for the direct and room mic signals were almost equal (favoring the room sound), with the speaker mic mixed in to add subtle midrange frequencies. The compressor was set to ruthlessly tame dynamic levels, posting a –25 dB threshold with a slow release at a ratio of 10:1.

What resulted from all this trouble was a huge, booming rumble devoid of (noticeable) fret squeaks, yet punchy enough to articulate harmonic movement. The thick bass sound complemented the sharp attack of the drums and provided a perfect foil for the band's acoustic guitars and delicate vocals.

— Michael Molenda

CHAPTER 17

Supreme Drum Strategies

During the early years of the Beatles, legendary drummer Ringo Starr was recorded with nothing but one mic on his kick drum and one mic hanging over his head. Two microphones captured the beat that drove the band that changed rock 'n' roll. Today, some engineers use two mics just to record a snare drum. Was Ringo robbed?

Hardly. The Beatles' primary recording engineers, Norman Smith and Geoff Emerick, had the ears and imagination to wring one heck of a boom-boom-snap from two microphones. Home and project-studio owners should be inspired by the fact that the limitations of early pop recording didn't prevent Smith and Emerick from laying down a timeless thump.

For the recordist tracking drums in a personal studio, a multiple-mic setup may not be practical, due to the number of mixer or interface inputs or the number of mics available. Therefore, it's very handy to know a few tricks for getting a good drum sound using one, two, or three mics. Good ears, decent microphones, and a little bit of forethought empower virtually anyone to record rockin' drum tracks.

Prepping the Drum Kit

Drums can take forever to record, because even basic kits contain a jungle of hardware that creaks, rattles, and groans. Microphones record every sonic blemish, so pristine drum tracking requires the taming of mechanical noises.

When the drums are set up, check the kit for loose connections. If cymbal or tom stands rattle, wrap some foam around the noisy joints and tape everything down with heavy-duty vent tape. Whining kick-drum pedals may be silenced by spraying the moving parts with a lubricant such as WD-40. (See the sidebar "Drum Survival Kit".)

Once everything is battened down, have the drummer play a simple beat, occasionally throwing in tom-tom fills and cymbal crashes. If everything sounds great, you're blessed with incredible luck. Most likely, you'll hear a symphony of obnoxious drum overtones, a paper-thin snare, and more creaks and rattles.

Don't drive yourself crazy tracing minute problems. Go for the big ones. Find the new rattles exposed by the drummer's performance and tape them down. If overtones are excessive, have the drummer retune the offending drums until they produce a clean, full-bodied sound. Be prepared to jump in and help, because some drummers aren't skilled at tuning their own drums. If you don't know how to tune drums, get a lesson from a professional drummer. It'll be well worth the money.

If tuning and retuning won't kill the offensive overtones, place two fingers on the drum head, approximately a half inch in from the rim, and move them in a circle around the head until you find a position where the overtones are muted. Cover this "hot spot" with a single piece of vent tape. Although this is an oversimplified remedy, the tape should muffle the unwanted overtones. Some drummers use commercial "ring killers," homemade muting templates cut from old drum heads, or even facial tissue taped to the drum head to diminish unwanted overtones.

Be careful not to use so much tape that the drum begins to sound like a telephone book when struck (unless, of course, that's the sound you want). In even the best cases, muting a drum's overtones compromises the natural tonality of the instrument. If the ring cannot be tuned out of the drum, and you must resort to taping heads, be prepared to make some concessions between the overtones and the pure tone of the drum.

There's a reason for all this toil and trouble: Drum kits that sound great acoustically usually retain that quality under the bitter scrutiny of microphones. You will appreciate the energy spent hunting down noises and overtones if you decide to mic individual drums.

Drum Survival Kit

A good engineer is always prepared to combat the unknown. If you want to survive acoustic drum sessions, here are some indispensable supplies:

- Drum key
- Duct tape
- Adjustable wrenches, screwdrivers, and heavy pliers
- WD-40 or other lubricant
- Cymbal felts and sleeves
- Assorted blankets, pillows, and towels
- Roll of strong twine (for securing snares)
- Assorted pieces of cloth, felt, and foam rubber

One Mic, Many Drums

The easiest way to record a drummer is with one strategically placed microphone. The type of mic you use and how you use it will largely determine the mix of the instruments that you record. Because you're using only one mic, you are committing yourself to a mono drum track. But that's not necessarily a bad thing. Many hit records were made using a single mic on the drums, in situations not much different than your own.

Another thing to understand about the one-mic approach is that you will have no control over individual drum sounds during mixdown. If you decide to EQ the bass drum, the EQ settings will affect the sound of all the drums. That means that mic placement is of the utmost importance when using one mic.

Begin by putting a condenser mic 8 to 10 feet in front of, and pointing toward, the drums (see **Fig. 17.1**). You can use either a cardioid or omni pattern. The omni will get more of the room sound, while the drums will be more present with the cardioid pattern. Adjust the exact position and height of the microphone until you get a good balance of the drums and cymbals.

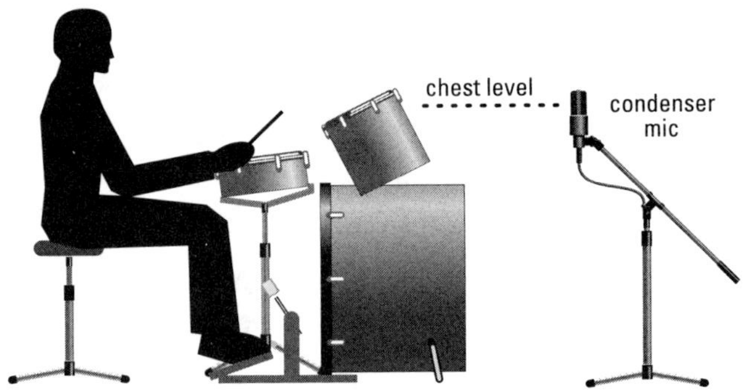

FIG. 17.1: A single, large-diaphragm condenser mic placed at chest level about ten feet in front of the drum kit produces a sonic snapshot of the drum/room environment.

You can also experiment with positioning the mic over the drummer's head. This works with the mic raised to a height of six feet from the floor. Using a cardioid pattern, place the mic stand in front of the bass drum and raise the mic over the kit, pointing down toward the drums. You can also try this from behind the drummer to get his perspective; put the mic stand behind the drummer, raise the mic about six feet from the ground, and point it toward the instruments.

Two-Mic Techniques

Using two mics on a drum kit gives you more control over timbre and volume than the one-mic technique. The position of each mic depends as much on the style of the music as on the way the drummer plays.

Let's begin by expanding on the one-mic setup. Begin with one mic over the drummer's head, pointing down at the instruments. This microphone will pick up cymbals, hi-hat, toms, and snare drum very well. By adding a kick drum mic, you gain control over the instrument that provides the punch in a mix. Some large-diaphragm dynamic mics intended for bass drums will also subtly pick up other portions of the kit, most notably the snare drum. However, with the two-mic method, this shouldn't be a problem. Check for phase problems by summing the two tracks to mono and listening for any noticeable changes in the sound.

If you are more interested in emphasizing the snare drum, point your second mic (this time a dynamic cardioid) at the snare drum, with the mic approximately an inch from the head. Either use the overhead mic or mic the kit from the front to get more of the bass drum.

One other method is to use two mics in a stereo pair from overhead (see **Fig. 17.2**). This configuration documents the spatial characteristics of a drummer's personal kit configuration. This perspective is as important to the drummer as a guitar/amp combination is to the guitarist. One of the classic overhead positions consists of two condenser mics on boom stands placed three to five feet over the drummer's head. Use either a spaced pair or XY configuration, with the microphones pointing down at the instruments.

FIG. 17.2:
Two condenser mics placed in a crossed pattern over the drummer's head provide an alternative to traditional overhead mic placement. This drummer's perspective offers sharp cymbal timbres and robust tom sounds with just two microphones.

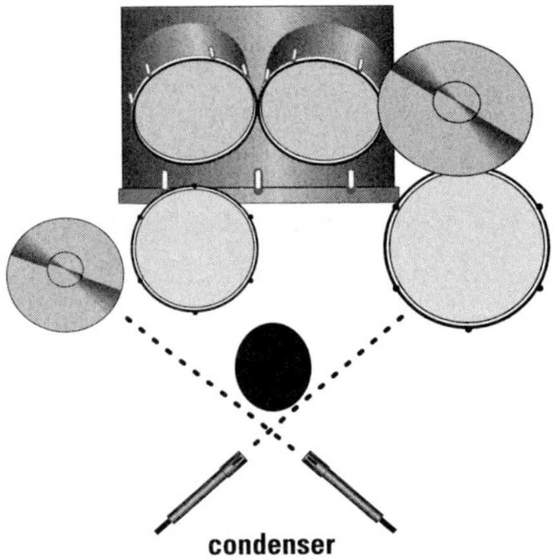

Again, the mix you get depends on the exact placement of the mics in relation to the drums. Therefore, it's wise to spend a little extra time recording different positions and listening back to hear which one has the balance that best suits the music.

Three Mics

You will gain even greater control over the drum sound by dividing the kit with three mics. The most common way is to use one mic on the bass drum, one on the snare drum, and the third as an overhead to cover the cymbals and toms. For better isolation, position the overhead mic so that it doesn't point directly at the snare or kick drum.

Another three-mic method is to use two mics in the stereo overhead configuration and reserve the third mic for the bass drum. This will give you a natural stereo spread for the upper instruments while giving you an isolated bass drum track to work with in the mix. This method works well with any type of music that calls for a more natural drum mix.

Individual Voices

Whether you plan to use two, three, or a dozen mics, knowing the common ways to mic the individual drums is important. The tips that follow are just beginning reference points; always listen and experiment with mic placement to get the sound that works best for the music.

Snare drum. The classic snare-miking technique involves positioning a dynamic mic an inch or two in from the snare rim opposite the drummer and an inch above the snare drum head. A favorite snare mic among engineers is the Shure SM57, because it records the impact of stick to drum without accentuating overtones. Your style may favor broader timbres, so be sure to experiment with different microphones.

Snare EQ Repairs

Sound	EQ Tweak
More sizzle	Boost 10 kHz
More snap	Boost 5 kHz
More crack	Boost 3 kHz
More pop	Boost 1 kHz
More meat	Boost 200 Hz
Less meat	Cut 200 Hz

Some engineers also mic the bottom head to capture the rattle of the snare. You can use another dynamic mic for this position, or even experiment with a condenser. (Be sure to pad the mic input at least –10 dB to avoid problems caused by high sound-pressure levels.)

Bass drum. Getting a solid kick-drum sound requires a large-diaphragm dynamic mic, such as an AKG D112, an Electro-Voice RE20, or a Sennheiser MD 421. Several manufacturers make mics specifically for use on bass drums. Each has a completely different sound that favors some frequencies over others. For example, a bass-drum mic may have a pronounced lower midrange, as well as a bump in the upper frequencies to get the "tick" of the beater hitting the head. A mic like this may also pick up other instruments in the same range, such as the hi-hat or snare drum. If you have a chance to borrow bass drum mics from fellow recordists, it's worth an afternoon comparing a couple to see which meets your needs.

There are almost as many ways to mic a bass drum as there are styles of music. Deciding if the drum should have one or two heads is only the first decision. For tight, dry bass-drum sounds, remove the front head and place the mic inside the drum, pointing at the batter head (see **Fig. 17.3**). How far into the drum the mic should be placed depends on the kind of sound you're going for. The closer to the batter head you get, the more impact and the less shell resonance you will get. Having a foam pad or blanket resting in the shell of the drum helps dampen unwanted reflections.

For starters, try positioning the mic approximately five inches inside the drum and tilting slightly toward the floor tom. This position records a clear, tight kick with a robust low end. The off-axis position helps you avoid the "woof" caused by air exploding directly into the mic.

FIG. 17.3:
Many engineers go for a tight, dry bass-drum sound by removing the front head, placing a pillow or towel inside the drum, and pointing the microphone slightly off-axis of the spot where the beater hits the head.

For a large, live sound, use a double-headed bass drum. This sound is far richer with overtones, so good drum tuning is essential. Some drummers put a cloth strip across each of the heads to help dampen the overtones a little without killing the resonant boominess of the drum. For a double headed kick, try using a condenser mic two feet in front of the kick drum, pointing at the center of the head. Don't forget to set the pad on the mic to keep it from overloading.

Some drummers cut a hole in the front head to facilitate miking. The mic can be aimed into the hole from the outside, or positioned slightly inside the hole. The problem with this method is that the front head may have an annoying ring to it. You can solve this problem by laying a blanket or foam pad against part of the front head to remove the unwanted ring without disturbing the overall drum tone.

To increase the intensity of the kick drum as it's recorded, compress the signal –10 dB at a ratio of 2:1 and boost the EQ at 100 Hz. Then run it through a noise gate to shut down the boom a few milliseconds after the initial impact. This will give your bass drum a well-defined punch that is irresistible.

Quick Kick EQ Tricks

Sound	EQ Tweak
More boom	Boost 80 Hz
Less boom	Cut 80 Hz
More click	Boost 12 kHz
More attack	Boost 5 kHz
More thud	Boost 1 kHz
More wallop	Boost 220 Hz
Less wallop	Cut 220 Hz

Toms. To mic a tom-tom, place either a cardioid dynamic or condenser mic two to four inches over the top drum head, listening critically for a harmonious blend of drum tone and percussive impact. To achieve maximum tonal control and articulation, you will need to mic each tom individually. If you don't have enough mics or channel inputs on your mixer, you can use one mic to record the rack toms and another to record the floor tom (or toms). Position the rack-tom mic between the two toms, approximately four inches above the top rims and one foot back. The floor-tom mic should be placed closer, approximately two inches above the outside rim of the head. If the drummer uses two floor toms, try to position the mic between the drums, more than four inches above the top heads.

To intensify the impact of the toms, compress them as you record. Assign the individual tom tracks to a left/right subgroup and use a dual (stereo) compressor to process the submix. The processed tom submix is recorded on two separate tracks to maintain stereo imaging. Subtle compression settings usually work the best, as severe compression can cause cymbal hits that leak into the tom mics and sound like high-end splatters. During mixdown, run the tom submix through a stereo expander to wipe out snare and cymbal bleed. Remember, the cleaner the tom tracks, the more punch they'll have in the mix.

Hi-hats. Since the hi-hat often is the linear timekeeper in popular music, it's important that it be crisp and articulate. A small-diaphragm condenser mic is commonly used, positioned three inches from the top cymbal at a 45-degree angle. Moving the mic a few feet away from the hi-hat provides a blend of the hi-hat with the other cymbals, which you can use instead of an overhead mic if you're short on microphones or mixer inputs.

Drum Roll, Please

Drums are such an integral component of rock music that scores of anecdotes exist regarding bizarre recording techniques. Elvis's drummer, J.D. Fontana, once remarked that he cut many classic tracks by slapping cardboard boxes. New-wave godfather Nick Lowe expressed an affinity for the "telephone book" snare. And, according to a Dick Clark biography, when the drums were too loud during the session for "The Monster Mash," the engineers simply moved the kit away from the sole microphone and draped blankets over the toms, kick, and snare. (Back in those days, vocals and instruments were recorded through a single microphone.)

Once again, practical examples prove that there is no right or wrong way to record a drum kit. The key issue of drum tracking is finding out what it takes to drive the song. If you keep your creative options open, you'll find that most limitations are merely challenges. After all, if you can't get a good tone from a battered snare, you can always pound on the local *Yellow Pages*.

CHAPTER 18

Perfect Piano

Of all the acoustic instruments you are likely to record in a personal studio, the piano has the greatest frequency range. As a result, it's important to think about how the piano will fit into the music before you press Record, so you can make sure it has a tonal quality that supports the arrangement rather than muddies it up by obscuring other instruments.

If the arrangement calls for voice and piano, or if it's a solo piano instrumental, the timbre you strive for will be different than if the piano will be part of a rock arrangement that includes guitars, horns, bass, and drums. In the former scenario, you will strive for the most realistic piano sound you can get. In the latter, you will record a piano track that doesn't necessarily sound realistic on its own, but it fits nicely into a busy mix.

Prepared Piano

There are a number of things you should think about when preparing for the session. First, consider the overall condition of the piano you will be using. Is it in good working order? Do the pedals squeak or make other noises? Is the timbre uniform across the instrument? Are any strings missing?

The pianist should play the instrument to see if the action is suitable and to find out if there are any problems that are not obvious at a glance. If you will be playing the piano yourself, and you are going to record on an unfamiliar instrument, it's a good idea to have another pianist play the instrument—preferably a piece similar to what you will perform—while you listen for any problems with the instrument.

While you're listening, move around the recording space and find the places where the instrument sounds particularly good, because these will be areas to consider for distance mics: either mark the floor with a piece of tape or write down the location in a notebook.

It's also important for the piano to be in tune. If the instrument is continually in use, it should be tuned as close to when the session begins as possible. If you're playing an unfamiliar instrument, it's a good idea to check that the overall tuning hasn't lowered. A battery-powered tuner with a built-in mic can be used for this. Occasionally, you will find that the pitches on an older piano that hasn't been tuned frequently will be too low to be safely corrected in one tuning session. For example, if you play middle C, but the tuner says the actual pitch is closer to a B-flat, you should consult a piano tuner before setting the date of the recording session.

One of the most important considerations in recording a piano is the room. If you have a great piano and an acoustically interesting room, you will have plenty of timbral options. The kind of music you will be recording will help you determine whether the room is right for your music. For example, for a solo piano piece where you want plenty of natural reverb, you will want to record in a church or concert hall rather than a carpeted living room. On the other hand, if you are looking for an aggressive, in-your-face, rock-piano sound, the room will be less important because you will get that edgy sound through close-miking.

Grand Tone

A basic approach to recording a piano in stereo is to mic the bass and treble strings separately from inside the piano, with each mic assigned to its own track. Begin by placing a pair of cardioid condenser mics between 6 to 12 inches above the strings. The mics should be slightly behind the area where the hammers strike, with one mic pointing toward the bass strings and the other mic pointing toward the treble strings (see **Fig. 18.1**). To get less of a percussive sound, tilt the mics slightly away from where the hammers hit the strings.

The trick with miking a grand piano in this manner is to get an even sound, both in timbre and volume, as you play from the lowest note to the highest. You may find that you have to reposition the mics slightly after you do some test recordings to achieve the right balance. In addition, both mics should be the same model if you want a consistent sound across the instrument.

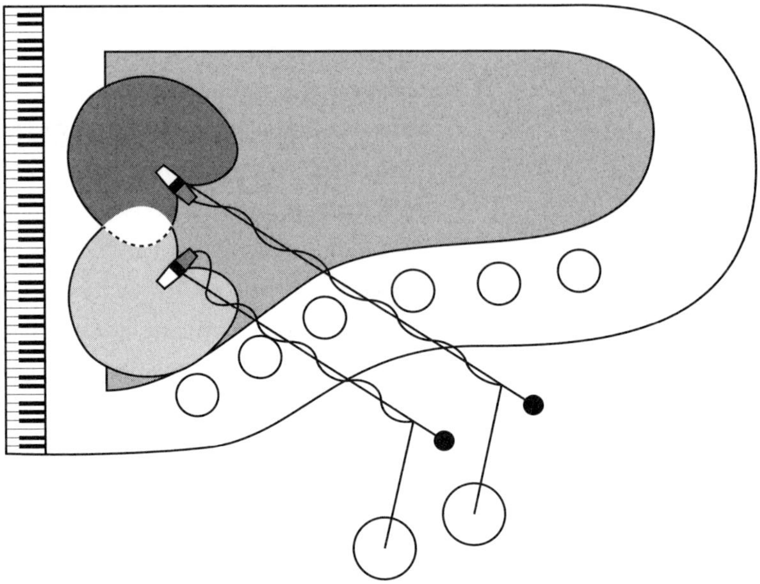

Fig. 18.1:
To get a wide stereo sound, place a pair of cardioid mics inside a grand piano, behind where the hammers strike, between 6 and 12 inches above the strings. One mic should point toward the lower strings, while the other points at the higher strings.

Be sure to check for phase anomalies when you listen back to the test recordings by panning the mics to the center and listening for any drops in level or strange sound coloration. If you can keep the mics 10 inches or more away from each other, your chances of phase problems will be lower.

The Major Third

Professional engineers will often augment the close pair of mics with another mic farther away but still inside the piano. The mic of choice usually has an omnidirectional or figure-8 pattern to capture a blend of the high and low strings. The best choice for this application is a high-quality large-diaphragm condenser or ribbon mic.

A common mic position is at the same height over the strings as the stereo pair, but placed just beyond the midway point of the strings. An alternative is to position the mic equidistant from the piano lid and the strings. The success of this position depends on how good the blend is between the sound reflecting off the lid and the sound of the strings.

The pattern of the mic will also be a major influence on the sound. For example, the back of a figure-8 mic will receive sound reflecting directly off of the lid, while rejecting sound that hits the off-axis null points. An omni, on the other hand, is sensitive to sound coming from all directions, and close proximity to the lid may not be an issue.

Many engineers will place the third mic near the curved edge of the piano, but still slightly inside and under the lid. Depending on its position, the mic will capture a bit of the room sound.

There are two distinct ways to mix a three-mic setup. The most intuitive is to simply pan the close mics hard left and right and place the third mic in the center, bringing up its volume to round out the sound. Another approach is to begin with a warm, blended piano sound from the third mic, and then add just a bit of the closer mics to subtly increase the stereo image and add articulation.

Au Naturale

Another common stereo technique for recording a grand piano is to use a pair of mics two or three feet outside of the instrument, but pointing toward the strings. One of the mics should point toward the treble strings, while the other points toward the bass strings. In a good room, this technique gives you a natural sound that is good for classical and jazz styles.

With this mic setup, it's good to remember the 3-to-1 rule to avoid phase problems: For every unit of distance between a mic and the sound source, there should be at least three times that distance between the mics themselves. For example, if your treble mic is two feet from the piano, your bass mic should be at least six feet from the treble mic.

The Cover-Up

Up to this point, the miking techniques have been based on the assumption that the piano is being recorded on its own, or that we don't mind other instruments in the room bleeding into the piano mics. However, if you want the piano to be completely isolated from any external sound—including the voice of the pianist—you have to acoustically contain it, as well as the mics within.

Putting the other musicians in a separate room is your best bet for total isolation. However, depending on the configuration of your studio, that may not be a practical solution.

Marginal isolation can be achieved by putting sound absorbing baffles around the piano to minimize bleed from other instruments. You can also put baffling around the other instruments to isolate their mics from the piano sound.

Greater isolation can be achieved by covering the piano with a thick blanket. Depending on mic placement, you may have to keep the lid completely open using the full length of the stick. If this is the case, you will need a large blanket to cover the entire area. The heavier the blanket, the better the isolation will be.

To keep the pianist's vocals and the piano interior acoustically separate, create a barrier between the vocal mic and the mics inside the piano. One way is to lean a large sheet of cardboard against the music stand toward the open lid of the piano. Be sure to cover the cardboard with the blanket to mitigate unwanted vocal reflections from its surface.

Nice and Roomy

You can add depth to your recordings by placing a couple of mics at a distance from the piano and taking advantage of the natural reverberance of the room. The farther away the mic is from the piano, the more of the room reflections you will hear. When it comes time to mix, adding just a tiny bit of this sound will help make your piano tracks come alive.

Again, be careful to check for phase problems when using distance mics. If you bring up the level of a room mic, and the stereo image from your close mics suddenly skews to one side, you know there is a phase issue between the mics.

Tracking an Upright

The most common, and often best sounding, way to record an upright piano is by opening the upper lid and pointing a pair of directional mics toward the interior from a distance (see **Fig. 18.2**). To increase the stereo spread, point the mics farther away from each other in an x/y pattern. The height of the mics above the piano will depend on how much of the room sound you want to capture and how loud the pianist plays.

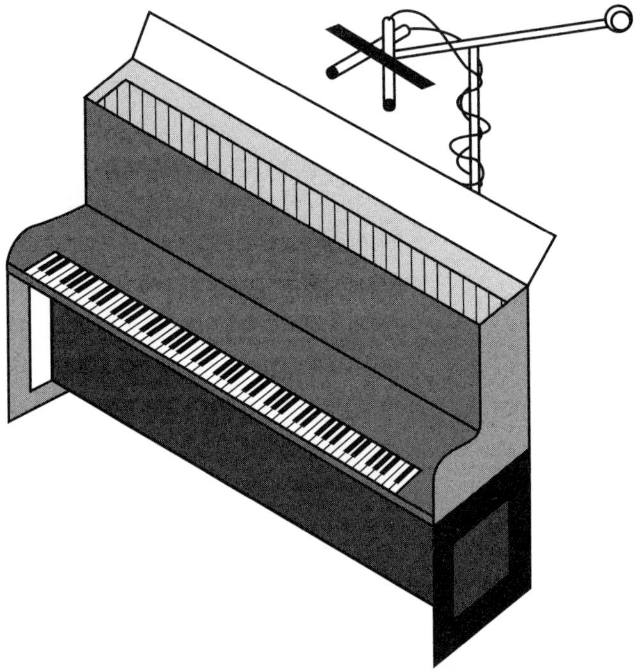

Fig. 18.2: The classic way to record an upright piano is from above, with the lid open. In this figure, a pair of small-diaphragm cardioid condensers are mounted on a stereo bar and pointed directly into the piano.

It is often recommended that you move an upright piano away from the wall before recording, to capture more of the instrument's natural resonance. However, if the piano isn't a very good instrument, or it's not very loud, the wall can be used to reflect and amplify the sound. If that doesn't help you get a better tone, try moving the piano next to a glass door or a large window if they are available.

The Right Combination

When it comes to recording piano, nothing beats a beautiful instrument in a great sounding room. If your studio is too dry or your own piano is a clunker, look for an alternate place that has a good instrument in an acoustically flattering space.

Churches and school auditoriums should be the first places you visit. Often, these spaces are available for community use, and they can usually be rented for a fraction of the cost of a professional studio.

CHAPTER 19

Tracking Killer Synths

Recordings that are compromised by noisy tracks smack of an amateur effort, and even a modern digital synth can add unwanted noise if recorded improperly. Capturing the great sounds of a hardware synthesizer is not difficult; it just takes imagination and careful attention to gain stages.

Most digital synthesizers produce a strong enough output signal to be plugged directly into a line input on a mixing console or digital interface. However, some synthesizers (especially older analog models) have weak signals that require more kick to deliver optimum levels. This can be accomplished by routing the signal through a direct box and plugging into the mixer's microphone preamp. Depending on the mixer, you will typically get 20 to 30 dB more gain than you would get by using the line inputs. Some engineers prefer to use microphone preamps for all keyboards and synth modules, as they tend to produce a warmer sound.

Be sure to listen critically to all the gain stages between the synthesizer and mixer to protect against unwanted noise. This includes the volume control on the synth; some instruments sound terrible if run at full volume. It pays to experiment with synthesizer and mixer fader levels to ensure a clean signal.

Delicate EQ

One of the most important things to remember about analog signals is the less you do, the cleaner the signal. Musicians love tweaking equalization, but tonal bliss attained this way often comes with a surcharge of increased hiss. If a string patch isn't "intense" enough, change to a brighter program (or adapt the synthesizer's internal parameters), instead of boosting 10 kHz toward a wash of noise.

If you must change the EQ of the synth sound, you are always better off cutting rather than boosting frequencies. For example, if your electric piano patch is too mushy, try cutting some of the bottom end and increasing the overall gain.

Dynamics

A problem frequently encountered when recording synthesizers is the extreme dynamic range of the instrument. Analog tape hates large differences in signal level, and you have to be careful of "overs" when tracking to digital recorders. Setting an optimum recording level for one section of a song may risk distortion on another section where the synth really kicks in. If you're firing sound modules from a keyboard or sequencer, this is remedied by adjusting sensitivity and volume parameters to prevent sudden dynamic changes.

Obviously, you want to record the instrument as hot as possible to attain the best signal-to-noise ratio. Setting an overall lower recording level to protect against "surprise" peaks is undesirable, because soft synthesizer passages will be recorded too low, inviting unwanted tape hiss on analog machines or quantization distortion on digital recorders. However, it's madness to track level changes by constantly adjusting the mixer's input faders. The easiest solution is to run the synthesizer through a compressor.

A compressor will limit the instrument's dynamic range and allow you to record a stronger level without distortion. Try starting out with an input threshold of –10 dB, with a fast attack and a 2:1 ratio. From there, tweak the compression parameters until all performance levels are "smoothed out" enough to permit setting a safe and reasonable recording level. Don't forget to check that the compressor hasn't added any dirt to your synth signal. Also, compression tends to bring up a signal's bass frequencies, so you may want to audition the processed tone to ensure that it's what you want.

Noise Gates

Sometimes, audible hiss enters the signal path, regardless of how much care you exercise. In these instances, noise gates become essential studio tools because they can shut down any signals below a user-set threshold. Since audible hiss usually is at a softer level than the actual synthesizer sound, the noise gate can eliminate hiss whenever the instrument stops playing. (Hopefully, the hiss is masked when the synthesizer is playing. If not, try cutting some of the high-frequency EQ.)

The importance of keeping tracks clean when a particular instrument is silent cannot be stressed enough. If you're running 10 ungated synthesizers that pop in and out of a composition at different times, the audible hiss produced by "silent" modules can be high enough to compromise overall quality.

In addition, a gated synth appears in the soundscape with more apparent dynamic punch than an ungated synth that must rise from the muck of constant audible hiss. If you submix multiple synthesizer sounds (playing the same part) for textural emphasis, remember to insert the noise gate at the appropriate subgroup of your mixing console so that all sounds are gated at the same time.

Track Stacks

There is more to a great synthesizer sound than cleanliness. If you really want to construct masterful timbres, you have to stack two or more different sound modules. While stacking synth sounds via a MIDI sequencer is great for creating pads and solo sounds, many keyboard players and producers have gone back to old-fashioned performance stacking. This is where a keyboardist plays each part two or more times onto separate tracks. The engineer then submixes these tracks either to a mono track or to two tracks for a stereo (left/right) split.

The reason this organic method is popular is the difference in sound between programmed (and quantized) MIDI stacking and stacked performance tracks. Individually performed tracks will have minor differences in timing, and these anomalies often fatten up the overall sound.

Another stacking trick is to use different sounds for each pass. Because most manufacturers provide two or three varieties of the same sound ("Strings," for instance), it makes sense to mix and match timbres to create thicker and more vibrant textures.

If you mix sequenced virtual tracks with live-performance tracks, try using different synthesizers for stereo images, rather than internal stereo patches. Because it is easy to find similar sounds from many different manufacturers, a more intense stereo image can be gained simply by placing one manufacturer's synthesizer on the left side and a different synthesizer model on the right side.

Effectations

A common engineering and production concern is whether it's practical to record effects along with the synth sound. From an engineering standpoint, this is risky, because the processed sound cannot be changed once it is recorded. (Considering how often musicians change their minds, it's a big risk.) On the other hand, if the amount of effects is sparse and you really can commit to a particular sound, it makes sense to save mixing aggravation by recording the processed sound. After all, the worst-case scenario is that you'd have to replay the part in question.

Signal processing also can bestow stereo imaging upon old analog synthesizers with mono outputs. Simply route the synth's mono signal into a delay processor and set the delay time to approximately 30 milliseconds. This timing will essentially "clone" the original synth sound. Then pan the original signal to the left and return the delayed signal to an available input channel or effects return. Pan the delayed signal to the right, and there you have it: a faux stereo image from a mono signal. Also, you can play with longer delay times to create interesting "ping-pong" images that headphone listeners will love.

If you are uncomfortable diving into synth sound programming, signal processing allows another path to unique sound construction. Many sound mutations can be enacted by simply running the synth signal through a chorus or pitch shifter. Experiment with multiple-pedal configurations; you never know when you will stumble across an unbeatable combination.

CHAPTER 20

The House Is Rockin'

If you think the thundering sound of John Bonham's drums on Led Zeppelin's legendary fourth album is the result of slick signal processing, think again. Three elements are responsible for that sound: the way Bonzo tuned his drums (he used, for example, a double-headed 24-inch kick drum with no muffling); the way he played (slammin'!); and the acoustic properties of the room he was recorded in. In this case, the drum room was a stone hallway at Headley Grange, the country house in Hampshire where most of the album's tracks were cut. Had Jimmy Page and engineer Andy Johns not thought to put the drums in that hallway, the awesome intros to "Rock and Roll" and "When the Levee Breaks" may not have exploded their way into rock 'n' roll history.

That kind of experimentation is what makes recording as much an art as a science. The only problem is that we tend to be creatures of habit—and habit is the nemesis of art. For example, it is easy, once you've found a reverb that works nicely on vocals, to get in the rut of relying on it for all your vocal tracks. Ditto for miking—after discovering the "best" way to record a cello, we tend to do it the same way forever. That's a shame, though, because a different mic or mic position might yield a tonal quality more suitable to a particular piece of music.

But that is not the only reason to break old recording habits. Even if you're no Luddite, there's a healthy pleasure to be had in sidestepping digital effects processors and other technological contrivances in favor of seeking out and documenting new, organic soundscapes. After all, where's the sense of adventure in turning knobs and pushing buttons? Once you've blown through the bells and whistles on a black box, the thrill is gone.

The fact is, even the finest effects processor on the planet is still a wannabe. That's because it's filled not with real spaces, but with algorithms attempting to replicate the sound of real spaces. Of course, having a gazillion acoustic environments at your fingertips is a great convenience. But why settle for an approximation when the real thing is as close as your kitchen? You may not have a concert hall in the back of your house, but you do have several other sonically distinctive rooms. Making use of those spaces not only will expand your sonic palette, but also may get your creative juices flowing. With a little experimentation and luck, you'll end up with some sounds not available in that rack full of gear.

Kitchen Kudos

If you need a more spacious sound but still want plenty of ambient reflections, stay in the kitchen. The combination of linoleum floor, wood cabinets, smooth walls, and glass windows (as well as glass or metal doors on the oven, dishwasher, etc.) makes a perfect antidote to the dampened acoustics you struggled to achieve in your studio proper.

I documented an authentic Chicago-style blues-harp sound simply by putting the harp amp on my kitchen table and miking it with two mics: a Shure SM57 up close, angled off-axis; and an AKG C 414 (in the omni mode) positioned as a room mic about 20 feet back. Of course, it helped that I played a Shure 520D "Green Bullet" mic through a small, vintage tube amp (an Airline model by Montgomery Ward) with the volume cranked nearly to 10. The reflective fury of the kitchen perfectly complemented the gutsy distortion of the diminutive, overdriven amp. Talk about a shredding tone! —Brian Knave

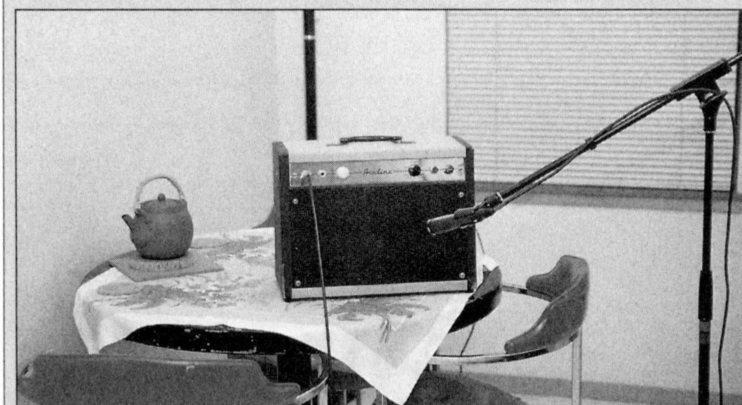

FIG. 20.1: The number of reflective surfaces in a kitchen lends reverb to the sputtering chaos of an overdriven tube amp.

That Familiar Ambience

For the purposes of this chapter, we'll be referring to four different types of acoustic spaces found in almost any house or apartment: small dry rooms (such as closets), small ambient rooms (bathrooms typically), large dry rooms (usually bedrooms), and large ambient rooms (such as garages and living rooms).

Of course, every home is different, and you may have to adapt some of the following recording techniques to your own situation. If, say, your living room is carpeted and your spare bedroom has a wooden floor, the roles of these rooms might be reversed. On the other hand, if your bathroom is carpeted, you'd be better off using a wood-floored closet or a tiled foyer as your small ambient space.

The first thing to do is to assess the acoustic properties of the various rooms in your home and determine which category each fits into. In general, think of carpeted rooms as dry and those without carpeting as ambient. This is not an ironclad rule, of course: A carpeted living room with 15-foot ceilings and brick walls might be more suitable as an ambient space.

The bottom line is that different instruments sound best when played—and recorded—in particular acoustical environments. For example, I'd be hard-pressed to recommend recording an electric bass-guitar amp anywhere other than in a dry room. But certain instruments can be recorded in either dry or ambient spaces, with very different but equally usable results. An acoustic guitar recorded in a bathroom, for instance, yields a much more lush tone than one recorded in a walk-in closet. A drier sound, however, may be just what you are trying to achieve for a particular song. Obviously, it comes down to knowing how you want the final product to sound. Therefore, it is imperative that you think ahead, always keeping the final mix in mind.

In addition, you have to decide how much of each room's ambience you want to capture—that is, how close to the sound source are you going to place the microphone? In general, the closer the mic is to the source, the less room ambience it will pick up and the drier the recording will be. But no matter how close you position the mic, you'll inevitably hear some room ambience. So even with close-miked instruments, selecting the proper recording room (and the proper mic) remains a critical consideration.

It's also important to remember that, although ambience can be added with an effects processor, it cannot be removed from a track. Therefore, you must be very sure of what you're doing if ambient sound is part of your plan. Again, a strong sense of the final mix is most helpful.

Don't think that because you live in a small apartment, there are no spaces large enough to be useful. A spacious delay, after all, is not the only effect in the book. There are many usable enclosures and "subspaces" in the average home, each with a unique sonic signature. Recording within these spaces can alter the sound of a voice or other instrument in strange and sometimes wonderful ways. And if you still desire a big double delay, you can always add it digitally, afterward.

Getting Started

It is simple to utilize your home's acoustic spaces in your recordings. Aside from the usual gear, all you need are cables long enough to reach from the source to the recording console. (Due to potential signal degradation, it's better to buy 50- or 100-foot cables than to connect a bunch of shorter ones.) First, play the instrument you intend to record in different parts of the room or space. The goal is to determine the position that maximizes the particular quality of sound that attracted you to the room in the first place. Then simply position a microphone or two to capture the sound. You can monitor the results with headphones. (Of course, it always helps to have a friend acting as your engineer.)

But before we get into specifics, let us reflect on the Number 1 rule of recording: There are no rules. The purpose of this chapter is not just to suggest alternative, organic means of creating new sounds for your recordings, but also to cultivate your creativity and listening skills to stretch your recording chops.

Morning Warbler

Have you ever wondered why people are inclined to sing in the shower rather than in walk-in closets? It's because of the ambience. A tiled shower stall produces rich reverberations similar to those generated by the reverb chambers used in the early days of recording. In fact, the bathroom is typically the personal studio owner's best space for capturing natural reverb.

Obviously, vocals are a prime choice for recording in this ambient environment. Take care, though, to position the vocalist and the mic carefully. Otherwise, you might end up capturing more reflections than direct signal. The first step is to remove the shower curtain. (If your shower has a sliding door, you're out of luck; for this application, you need a complete opening.) Next, position the singer close to the rear wall and centered in the shower stall or tub (see **Fig. 20.2**). Although any mic will capture the distinctive sound of singing in the shower, a large-diaphragm condenser mic set to the omnidirectional polar pattern will best document the effect.

FIG. 20.2: Recording vocals in a shower stall requires proper mic placement. Here the singer stands in the center of the tub. The blanket behind him will dampen excessive reflections.

The microphone should be positioned about 8 to 12 inches in front of the vocalist and about 6 to 8 inches above his head, with the capsule directed downward toward the singer's mouth at roughly a 30-degree angle. You may need to move the microphone around a bit before you find the sweet spot, so monitor through a pair of headphones while positioning the mic. If, after adjusting the mic's position, you're still picking up too many reflections, try hanging a blanket or another absorbent fabric on the rear wall of the shower (behind the singer), on the opposite wall (in front of the singer), or on both walls. This should eliminate any unwanted reflections.

Acoustic guitars also sound great in the bathroom. Try positioning the player on a stool in the center of the tub, sitting in the same position as outlined for the vocalist above. Position the mic from below at a slightly upward angle about two or three inches from the guitar. (Angling the mic downward from above the guitar will usually pick up too many reflections from the shower floor.)

Sometimes, you may need to record acoustic guitar and vocals simultaneously—say, if you're working with an artist who can't do the parts well separately. In this situation, you'll probably get the best results using two mics, one for voice and one for the guitar (see **Fig. 20.3**). Putting a small baffle between the two mics—for example, a piece of cardboard or plastic mounted on the mic stand—helps to isolate the sound sources.

FIG. 20.3: Here's one way to record acoustic guitar and vocals simultaneously. The small baffle between the two mics helps to minimize bleed, especially in ultra-ambient environments like this shower stall.

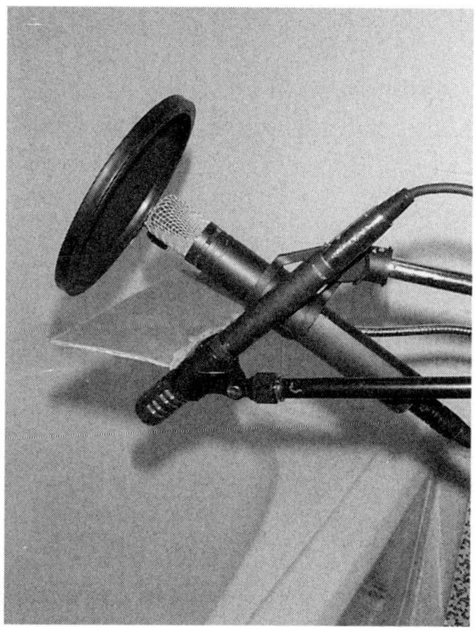

One application that's practically guaranteed to rouse the neighbors is an electric guitar amp played loudly in the bathroom. Done right, it will produce an absolutely huge guitar sound. Place the amp on the bathroom floor against a wall and face it toward the center of the room. Consider using two mics: a dynamic about an inch away from one speaker cone, and a condenser placed about three feet back from the amp. Record the signals to two separate tracks so that they can be blended in the mix.

For an even bigger sound, use two ambient mics in a coincident pair placed on the opposite side of the room and pointing downward toward the amp at a 45-degree angle. This picks up a nice stereo image of the room that can later be blended with the dynamic mic to fatten up the sound. Be sure to listen for phase cancellation by summing the tracks to mono (either with a mono switch or by panning each track to the same position in the stereo field).

Another interesting technique involves positioning the guitar amp in the bathtub (see **Fig. 20.4**). The smooth, sloping, porcelain contours of a bathtub are even more reflective than walls of tile—and if your bathtub and shower are built together, you'll get the reflective benefits of both. This trick can do wonders to bolster the already searing tone of a cranked-up tube amp. Use an omnidirectional polar pattern for this application to capture the whole gamut of reflections. Also, position the mic far enough back to emphasize the ambient sound further. It also helps to place a towel or some other kind of padding under the amplifier to prevent annoying amp vibrations that can soil the sound with rattles, screeches, and hums.

FIG. 20.4:
The sound of a cranked-up Supro tube amp is given a dose of attitude and reverb by being recorded in a bathtub.

Of course, vocals and guitars aren't the only things to record in the tub or shower stall. Any of the wind instruments can benefit from the acoustical reflections of a tiled-in space. Try flute, saxophone, trumpet, harmonica, or recorder. Even an accordion can sound good in a shower stall. Finally, if you really love what the tile is doing for your sound, but you don't always have the time or inclination to set up in the bathroom, you can bring a similar sound into your studio by building some tile gobos. Simply lay tile on a 4-by-4-foot (or larger) sheet of plywood and fit it with sturdy legs. With three or four such gobos, you can quickly erect a reflective tile booth wherever it's most convenient.

Porcelain Perks

If you want to record vocals with the bright, reflective sound that comes with porcelain but you happen to live in an older-style house or apartment that has a bathtub but no shower stall, you can get similar results using a good-sized kitchen sink. Simply position the mic so that it is down inside the sink, facing up toward the ceiling (see **Fig. 20.5**). The resulting sound is less bassy and reverberant than what you get in the tub or shower, but it's still pretty dramatic.

FIG. 20.5: To create naturally bright backup vocal tracks, try miking the reflections produced in the kitchen sink.

Obviously, this application requires that you sing down into the sink. Audition the cardioid, omnidirectional, and figure-8 polar patterns to determine which sound is most appropriate to the song. And be sure to push the faucet away from the sink so you don't accidentally drip water onto the mic.

Cook and Clean

The kitchen sink is not the only distinctive-sounding acoustical enclosure in your dwelling. You can cook up an exceedingly bright, metallic, resonant tone in the oven (see **Fig. 20.6**). Practically any mic will work for this application because the glassy coloration imparted by the oven's metal interior is anything but subtle. Simply position the mic so that it's approximately in the middle of the oven with the capsule facing out. Naturally, to capture the full effect, this requires that the musician sing or play into the oven—a feat most easily accomplished with the performer sitting on a low stool or chair.

FIG. 20.6: Recording from inside an oven will provide a glassy, reverberant tone sharp enough to cut through the toughest sonic grime.

Because the enclosure exaggerates the high end yet imparts some reverberation as well, it is especially well suited to recording bassoon, oboe, and other low-midrange wind instruments—that is, if you can persuade a classical bassoonist to perform while bending over an oven! You can also get cool results tracking vocals, harmonica, kazoo, shaker, and claves this way.

For a warmer, surprisingly intimate sound, position the mic the same way inside a dishwasher (see **Fig. 20.7**). You can remove the rubber-coated dish trays to get a brighter, more reverberant sound, or you can leave them in place for some diffusion. Also, experiment with how far back you position the source sound. For example, you could record a trumpet (with the bell aimed at the mic) 10 or 15 feet back and still retain the coloration imparted by the dishwasher.

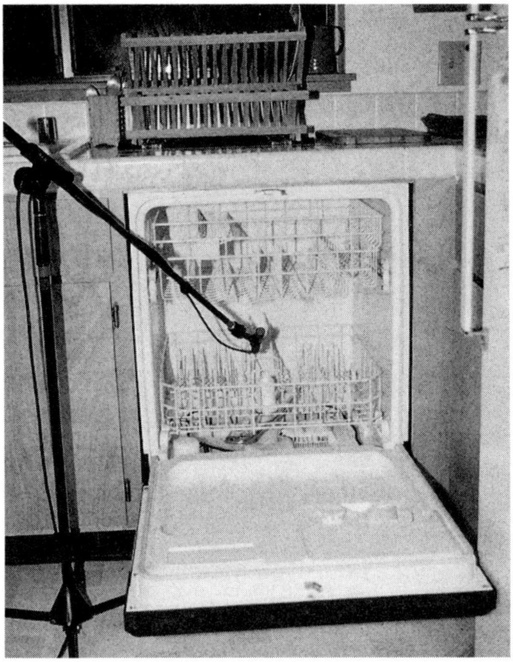

FIG. 20.7:
The plastic walls and rubber-coated dish trays inside a dishwasher add a surprisingly warm and intimate sound to a vocal track.

Living Large

As great as the bathroom and kitchen are for certain ambient applications, for others it doesn't provide a large enough work area. For example, a drum kit would be difficult to fit into most bathrooms. But if you're lucky, you have a fairly large living room with wood floors and a high ceiling. If not, perhaps you have a garage or other large space that isn't filled with too many absorbent materials. (The smaller the room, the more that such absorbent materials will dampen the ambience.) Whatever your situation, use your largest ambient space and turn it into a temporary live room.

Behind Closed Doors

I must confess that some of the best drum tracks I've ever recorded were captured in bedrooms—without close-miking the entire kit. There's something about a small, dry room that makes for killer drum sounds. In fact, I generally prefer to record drums in a dry room. They tend to be among the more difficult instruments to blend well in a mix, and the drier tracks give me more flexibility at mixdown.

Here's my typical approach. Put the drums against a wall in a carpeted room (preferably one with relatively low ceilings). Place a mic on the kick and another on the snare, and position two overheads above the drum kit as a spaced pair. Make sure the overheads aren't too high, or you won't pick up the full sustain of the toms. Conversely, if the overheads are too low, you may get a phasing effect when the cymbals are hit. That's about it. Not only will the drums sound fat and powerful with this setup, but you'll also have a lot of room to tweak the tracks in the mix.

I sometimes employ an approach that's really unorthodox: using only three mics to record a drum kit—one in the kick drum and a stereo pair facing the kit from the middle of the room. I came across this technique by accident. I had miked a kit using the previous setup outlined (snare, kick, and two overheads), but I decided to throw a pair of room mics up, too. Well, I forgot to connect the cables for the snare and overhead mics, so all I got on tape was the kick and the room mics. But when I listened back to those three tracks, I was amazed at the detail from the kit. Granted, the two room mics needed to be delayed a bit so that they matched the kick. But after I had time-aligned the tracks, the kit sounded really fat. The moral? Don't be afraid to experiment—except on your client's time, of course!—Jeff Casey

A great way to capture a group vocal performance involves using an L-shaped corner sofa in a living room. Sitting on the sofa not only makes the singers feel comfortable, but its shape also helps tighten the sound and absorb stray reflections. To capture a nice stereo image, seat the loudest vocalists toward the center of the sofa and farthest from the mics, and set up a spaced pair of condenser mics five feet in front of the sofa, with each mic aimed at a point just behind the center singer. Fit as many people as you can on the sofa.

This technique also works well for recording acoustic ensembles of various types and sizes. If you're working with two singer-guitarists, for example, place them on either side of the sofa (using the same mic setup outlined in the previous paragraph). For a three-piece band with two guitarists and a singer, again place both guitarists on the sides of the sofa and put the singer in the middle (see **Fig. 20.8**). There are dozens of ways to set this up, as long as you keep the stereo image nicely balanced.

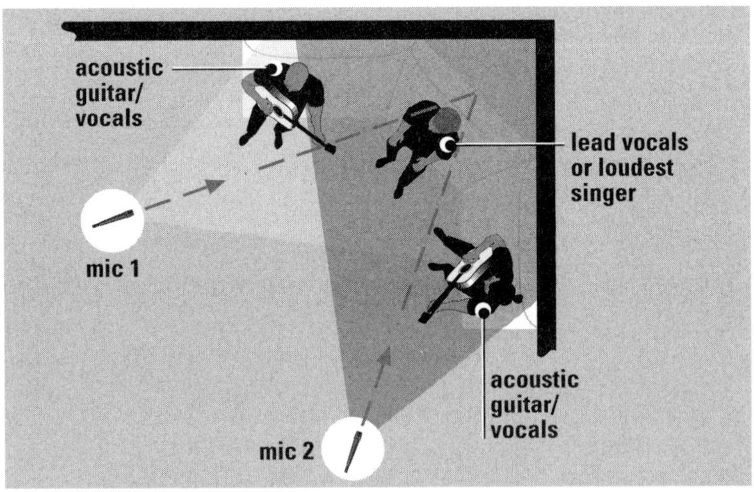

FIG. 20.8: To capture a group performance in a living room, the artists sit on an L-shaped sofa, which provides comfort while helping to contain the sound by absorbing early reflections.

An engineer who worked on some of Santana's early recordings once noted that the band recorded its percussion sections in gymnasiums. Well, if Santana did that, then the rest of us should record our percussion in the largest rooms we can find, too! Single instruments—shakers, congas, and the like—will probably sound best close-miked with condensers. If you're recording a percussion section, though, it's good to employ some ambient mics as well.

A great way to record a large percussion setup is to capture the performance from above. It's common for engineers to suspend a stereo pair of mics as high above the players as possible. If the ceiling of your space has exposed support beams, this is fairly easy to do: Simply drape the mic cables over one of the beams. If you don't have exposed beams, secure the mic cable to the ceiling with duct tape, allowing the microphone to hang down at the desired level. Keep in mind the 3-to-1 rule: For every unit of distance (inches, feet, or meters) between a mic and its source, a nearby mic should be separated by at least three times that unit of distance. In other words, the farther away the microphones are from the sound source, the farther apart they must be to maintain a good stereo image and to be free of unwanted phase effects.

A drum set can be recorded well with this setup, too, especially if you're looking to capture a huge "John Bonham–esque" sound. First, position the drums against a wall facing the center of the room; then tape a blanket on the wall behind them. How you mic the kit will depend on the size of the room you're working in. In a larger acoustic space, consider close-miking each drum with its own microphone and employ two pairs of condensers: a spaced pair over the kit and a coincident pair on the opposite side of the room. Set up the coincident pair about a foot above the tallest cymbal and pointed down at the kit, with the mics positioned so that they form an equilateral triangle with the drums.

When working in a smaller space, four mics will often suffice—one on the kick drum, another on the snare, and a pair of overheads. You might also try putting up a pair of room mics. Done properly, this type of recording should make you feel as though you're right there in the room with the drums when you play it back with your eyes closed.

You can also use a large ambient space to create natural reverb for an electric guitar. This technique is similar to that for miking an amp in the bathroom. Place the amp in a corner of the room with a dynamic microphone situated in front of the speaker. Then put up a coincident pair of condensers in front of the amp to capture some room ambience. If possible, clear the room of furniture or anything else that might dampen desired reflections.

Down the Hall

A long hallway—preferably with a wood floor—makes a great reverb chamber. In fact, this is just the trick producer Tony Visconti employed to create the multiple-reverb effect on David Bowie's song "Heroes." Visconti set up three mics for the vocal track: one directly in front of Bowie, another halfway down the hall, and a third at the very end of the hall. The second and third mics were gated with settings that required a medium-loud note to open the gate on the second mic and a full-volume note to open the gate on the farthest mic.

The recorded effect is extremely cool. As Bowie sings quietly during the verses, we hear his voice—warm and dry—solely from the perspective of the close mic. As he increases volume during the initial choruses, the gate on the second mic opens up, creating a bigger, mildly delayed vocal sound. By the end of the song, as Bowie belts, "We can be heroes just for one day," the gate on the far mic opens as well, resulting in a spacious, triple-miked vocal sound.

The Real McCoy

With the present-day glut of digital effects processors on the market, it's easy to forget that, originally, all recording studios had separate rooms called *echo chambers* that were used to generate natural reverb and echo. But just because the echo chamber is antiquated doesn't mean it is an inferior technology. Remember, the best digital reverbs and delays attempt to replicate the complex sonic attributes of real spaces. However, they never entirely succeed, a fact that becomes evident when you record a musical performance in an acoustically first-rate concert hall.

But even without a concert hall, you can devise a true echo chamber in your own home if you have a room that's large and reflective enough. A big bathroom—or even one that is long and narrow—can work splendidly. Other good candidates are large basements, washrooms, garages, attics, or even a deep stairwell. Simply go from room to room alternately singing and clapping your hands in each space. What you're listening for is at least one discrete echo or a rich, reverberant quality to the sound. (Reverb is the result of thousands upon thousands of tiny echoes, each with slightly different delay times that intermingle in a complex wash of sound.)

If you're lucky enough to have a workable space, you'll need an extra speaker and enough cable to run it from the console to the echo chamber. Set up the speaker at one end of the room, facing the farthest wall, and place two mics (or just one if a mono signal is sufficient for your needs) at the other end. Aim the two mics at opposite corners of the ceiling from two or three feet below. Depending on the shape and acoustical qualities of the room, you may need to move the mics around a bit to find the positions where they best pick up the sound of the echo or reverb.

For optimum results, send a dry signal to the speaker by using an aux send on your console. (You may also need some type of adapter to accommodate the connectors on the board and the speaker.) If you can't get enough gain from your board to drive the speaker, you can try using a combo guitar amp as the "monitor." Just remember that anything but the lowest, cleanest setting on the amp may compromise the quality of the source signal. Return the signal (or signals, if you're miking for stereo) on a console input channel so you can mix in and EQ the chamber ambience to your liking. Creating your own reverb or delay in this manner can be very gratifying. And if you have a good-sounding chamber to start with, chances are you'll end up with a sound that, although not nearly as versatile as a digital "room" reverb, sounds decidedly more natural.

A Closet Case

Creating effects like reverb and echo isn't the only recording application your house is good for. After all, what's sometimes needed is an absence of reverb and delay. Specifically, any signal that you intend to process heavily in the mix is usually best recorded dry so that ambient artifacts aren't processed along with the source signal. The only problem is that not every home recordist has a padded isolation booth at his disposal. But every home does have a closet or two, and in a pinch a closet can serve double duty as an iso booth. Just be sure to pick a closet that's well stuffed with clothes or other sound-absorbing material (blankets, towels, etc.). For maximum absorption, it should have a carpeted floor as well.

A classic application for the closet is recording a bass amp (see **Fig. 20.9**). For the best results, elevate the amplifier at least six inches off the ground (a foot or two is even better) to help dampen the signal. Then put down a layer of blankets or towels on the floor directly in front of the speaker to provide more sound absorption. The goal is to reduce reflections to increase the presence of the bass signal. Position the amp against the back wall of the closet and avoid putting it in the corner, because the low frequencies will tend to linger too long there.

FIG. 20.9:
A well-appointed closet provides considerable sound absorption for capturing a dry, present bass-guitar signal. This Harmony 525 bass amp is miked with an AKG D 112 dynamic mic.

Professional engineers often use two or three signals to record electric bass guitar: a DI box plus one or two microphones. The first mic can be either a dynamic (a kick-drum mic often works well) or a condenser set to a cardioid polar pattern. The exact mic position will vary, depending on the sound you want. Some engineers prefer to position the mic directly in front of the speaker. Others will place the mic three or four inches from the cabinet, facing the speaker at an angle of about 30 degrees off center. Feel free to experiment with the angle of the mic in relation to the speaker. Each position will yield a slightly different sound.

The second mic—either a condenser or a dynamic—is positioned about three feet back from the speaker. (If you use a dynamic mic here, the bass sound will be a bit punchier; with a condenser, it will be more bottom heavy.) The far mic is important because the low frequencies of a bass guitar need physical space in which to "stretch out." So why not just use one microphone positioned back from the cabinet? Because the close mic is needed to capture the punch from the strings. Without it, all you'll hear is rumble.

Electric bass can also be recorded in a carpeted bedroom—a good choice if the player is using a really large bass rig at a loud volume. However, it is not necessary to play the bass amp at a loud volume while you're recording. In fact, a medium volume is generally best because it's less likely to cause sympathetic vibrations in the speaker cabinet or elsewhere in the room.

You might consider putting your singer in the closet and recording a dry vocal track if you're not comfortable working with the reverberant nature of a bathroom or if your song simply doesn't warrant a lot of ambience. Have the singer stand near the back of the closet and put the mic in front of him at the same height and angle as outlined earlier for recording vocals in the bathroom. You can track electric guitars in a closet, too. For this application, you should probably also drape both the amp and the mic with a blanket, to further eliminate reflections.

A Slight Delay

As great as the sound of a double-tracked guitar is, sometimes using a delay is more appropriate. Although you could employ a digital delay to achieve this effect, consider using the real deal, which, if done properly, will sound more convincing than any DSP box. To do this, you'll need a carpeted room with furniture removed. Place the amp in a corner facing outward and close-mic it with a dynamic microphone.

You can position the delay mic in one of two ways. The first method is easy: Simply place a condenser mic facing the amp from across the room. Move the condenser closer to the amp to decrease delay time, or farther back to increase delay. Be sure to check for phase cancellation.

The second method is a little trickier. It involves placing two condenser mics in front of the amp, but facing them away from the amp toward the far walls of the room (see **Fig. 20.10**). This setup allows the signal to travel across the room and back, bounced from the opposite walls, before being picked up by the mics. The result is a really spacious, natural stereo delay.

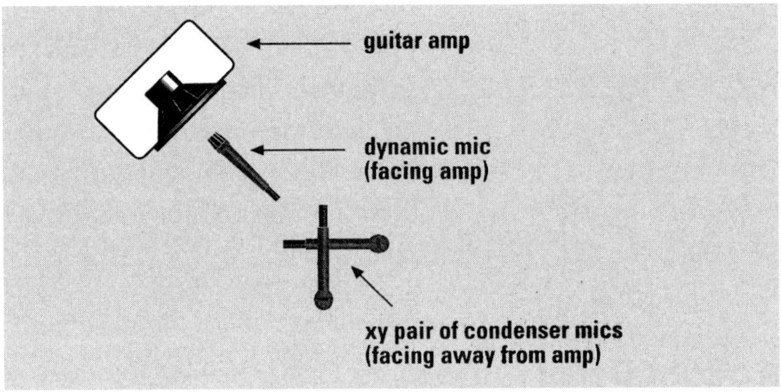

FIG. 20.10:
One interesting technique for capturing natural delay when recording electric guitar is to face the two condenser mics away from the amp, allowing them to capture the reverberant and delayed sound in stereo.

Come Together

Things get a little more complicated when it comes to recording two or more instruments—say, a whole band—simultaneously. Ideally, each mic should capture only the sound of the instrument it is positioned to record. To make this happen, you'll need to physically isolate each instrument from all the others, especially when using sensitive condenser mics. Usually, the most difficult instrument to isolate is the drum kit, due to its volume.

Thanks to having multiple rooms, most homes make isolation relatively easy to achieve. The obvious approach is to put each instrument in a different room of the house—for example, place the drums in a spare bedroom, the rhythm guitar amp in the bathroom, and the bass amp in the closet of another bedroom. Then have all the players perform in the drum room while wearing headphones. This setup requires plenty of cable, but it will keep instrument bleed to a minimum.

If it's not possible to isolate each instrument, consider piecing the song together through overdubs—starting, say, with the drums, bass, and electric guitar or keyboard. The bass and the guitar or keyboard can be recorded directly through the board or through DI boxes. These tracks can then be rerecorded, either by sending the recorded instruments to amps and speaker cabinets that are appropriately miked (referred to in the recording industry as *reamping*), or by completely redoing them through miked amps and speaker cabinets.

If the group insists on recording the rhythm section together, complete with amps blaring, and you have only one room to work in, you'll have to do some baffling. In that case, place baffling around the drum kit, put the amps as far away as possible (and baffle them, too), and record the bass directly. If you have a vocal going down at the same time, put the singer in another room (if one is available) with a pair of headphones. It's a compromise, but at least you'll maintain the band's energy, and in many cases, that's more important than getting a pristine recording.

Baffles can be fashioned from a variety of household items. Mattresses make very effective baffles, as do futons (if you can figure out how to prop them up). Freestanding, folding screens also work decently, especially when draped with blankets. Sleeping bags and quilts are quite handy, too, and can help to isolate guitar amps, bass drums, and other instruments. You can also easily build your own baffles: Simply cover a sheet of plywood or particle board (the standard 4-by-8-foot size works well) with foam or some other acoustically absorbent material and attach "L" brackets along the short end to help it stand.

Surround Sound

An acoustically neutral studio may be preferable for many applications, but it's not the only way to go. In fact, there's an impressive tradition of great records that have been made utilizing the various rooms in normal houses, including treasures from Motown, Fleetwood Mac, Led Zeppelin, and the Red Hot Chili Peppers. Hopefully this little guided tour of house sounds inspires you to investigate the sonic potentials available under your own roof.

Part III

Effects Basics

CHAPTER 21

Dynamics Processing

Dynamics processors—limiters, compressors, expanders, and noise gates—are the most misunderstood of all signal processors. And they can be touchy—mishandle a compressor, and it'll squash the life from a good recording. But don't be scared. Once you understand them, dynamics processors can make the difference between a good recording and a great one. And they're not at all difficult to use.

Dynamics processors alter the dynamic range of audio signals by changing the relationship of the loud parts to the soft parts, dramatically affecting how a sound is recorded and reproduced. Dynamic range is a ratio between the amplitudes of the softest and loudest sounds that a musical instrument can produce.

Dynamically speaking, not all sounds are created equal. A symphony orchestra is capable of fantastic dynamic range: typically more than 70 decibels between its quietest and loudest levels. The harpsichord, however, registers a smaller dynamic range, because there isn't much of a difference in amplitude between a soft touch and a forceful pluck.

Compressors and limiters, the best-known dynamics processors, are used to reduce a signal's dynamic range. On the other side are expanders and gates, which increase dynamic range. When should these tools be used? How do they differ? Let's find out.

Compressors

Vocalists are capable of tremendous dynamic range. That's great, but it's difficult to find optimum recording levels when a singer alternately throws screams and whispers at you. Riding the faders up and down to track signal levels is madness; you'll never react fast enough to catch sudden peaks.

A compressor frees you from "fader riding" by acting as a gain control. The user specifies an input threshold below which signals pass through unaffected. However, when signals rise above the threshold, the compressor kicks in and reduces their level by a user-selected ratio. (See the sidebar "The Dynamic Control Panel.") A compressor helps an engineer set an average recording level between high- and low-amplitude signals (see **Figs. 21.1** and **21.2**). A common misconception is that compressors make loud passages quieter and quiet passages louder. Here's what really happens: Because loud signals are reduced, the dynamic range between loud and quiet passages is also reduced. The quiet passages seem louder, even though they're not processed.

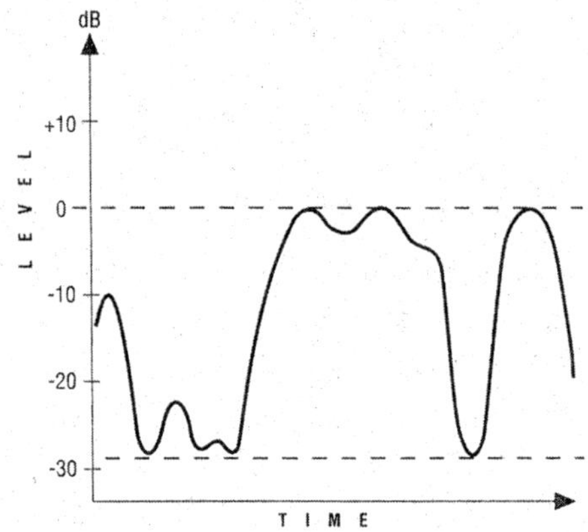

FIG. 21.1:
The amplitude envelope of an unprocessed audio signal.

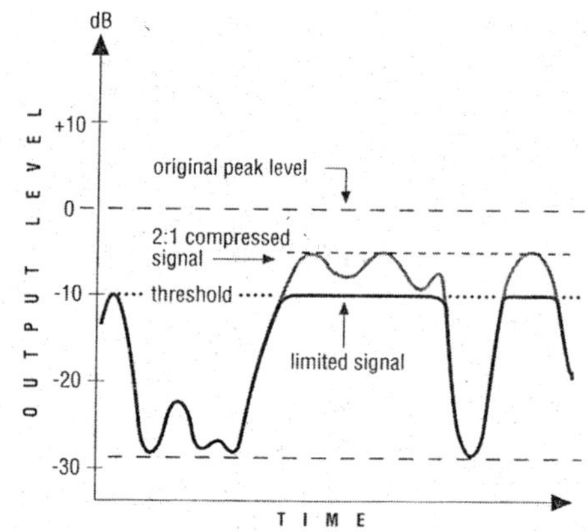

FIG. 21.2:
The same signal envelope, illustrating compression at a 2:1 ratio and limiting. The threshold in each case is set at 10 dB below the uncompressed peak.

Limiters

Limiting is an extreme form of compression, such as when the ratio is 10:1 or beyond. A good limiter lets you set an absolute maximum signal level; if the level exceeds the set threshold, it is effectively stopped from getting any louder.

Limiters typically are used as safety devices. For example, anyone who has played live knows it's easy to produce sounds that are capable of destroying a speaker. To prevent these mishaps, most professional sound systems are equipped with limiters to catch surprise signal peaks.

In the studio, however, limiters are used to prevent overloading the recorder so that distorted signals are not printed to tape or hard disk. Although vocals and drums are the main offenders, any source with a quick, unpredictably loud attack is a candidate for a "safety limit."

Duckers and De-essers

Duckers and de-essers are variants of the basic compressor and perform very specific—and extremely useful—tasks. Duckers often are used in broadcast advertising (jingles, voiceovers, etc.) to automatically reduce the volume of the music bed when an announcer is speaking. Basically, a ducker is a compressor controlled by a sidechain input. (See the sidebar "VCAs and Sidechains.") The music bed is put through the normal compressor input(s), and the announcer's voice is routed to the sidechain input. When the level of the announcer's voice exceeds the threshold set by the user, the level of the music is reduced in proportion to the level of the voice.

De-essing is a frequency-dependent dynamics process that also is based on the sidechain trigger. De-essers are indispensable for taming the annoying sibilants produced by some singers during recording. (Sibilants are those searing "sss," "sshhh," and "tsch" sounds that can compromise a good vocal performance.)

For de-essing, an EQ (parametric or graphic) is connected to the compressor's sidechain input. Now that the equalized signal is controlling the compressor—just as the level of an announcer's voice triggers ducking—the engineer simply boosts the sibilant frequencies (typically between 3 and 8 kHz) so that the compressor reacts to them more aggressively than the rest of the tonal spectrum. The result is a smooth attenuation of sibilants. There also are dedicated de-essers available that include some type of onboard EQ and a sidechain.

VCAs and Sidechains

Central to many dynamics processors is a small circuit known as a voltage-controlled amplifier (VCA). Once incoming signals cross the threshold level, the VCA kicks in and begins to *attenuate*, or reduce, levels. The amount and rate of reduction depends upon the type of processing (compression, expansion, limiting, gating) and the various control settings.

Normally, the VCA is controlled by whatever signal is at the processor's input. However, many processors allow you to access the VCA's electronic control input via an external sidechain. (Some boxes call it a *detector, key, control*, or *trigger input*.) You can connect something other than the signal to be processed to the sidechain input, and that external source will control how much dynamic processing occurs and when it starts (see **Fig. 21.3**). For example, let's look at the conventional noise-gate application of silencing an electric bass between performances. In this situation, the gate's VCA is controlled by level changes in the bass signal. (When the bassist stops playing, the input signal falls below the set threshold, and the gate shuts down the audio.) But if you were to connect the "kick drum" output of a drum machine to the sidechain input, the level of the kick drum would control the VCA. In effect, the kick drum would turn the bass "off and on" with each kick, producing an ultra-tight bass/drum groove.

Keep in mind that sidechain signals control only when and how much the incoming audio is processed; the sidechain signal is not fed to the processor's outputs. Therefore, unless you simultaneously fed the kick-drum signal to the mixer, you wouldn't hear it at all.

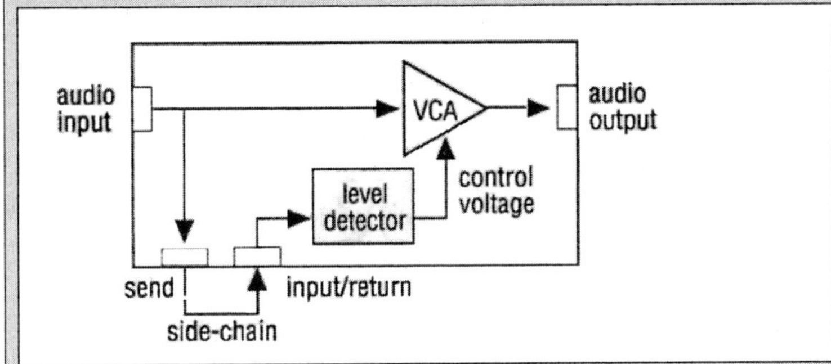

FIG. 21.3: *A block diagram of a generic dynamics processor with a sidechain.*

Expanders

When you need to increase dynamic range, call in an expander. In oversimplified terms, an *expander* is like a backward compressor: Expansion kicks in when a signal drops below a user-set threshold, resulting in a gradual reduction of gain.

There are three main uses for an expander: restoring dynamic range to "squashed" or overcompressed signals; reducing low-level background noises, such as hiss and microphone bleed (you can always count on rhythm-track leakage from the headphones into vocal mics); and cutting unwanted decay from a signal.

Noise Gates

Just as limiting is a form of maximum compression, noise gating is expansion taken to its most extreme. When a signal drops below the set threshold, its level is not just reduced but shut off completely. Only signals that rise above the threshold can "open" the gate and become audible.

Gates are perfect for eliminating hum and buzz when an instrument is not playing. Electric guitars, for instance, are notorious noisemakers; a gate can shut down the unwanted cacophony during silent passages. Gates also can be used to shut out background noises, such as lip smacks and page turning, from miked sources. The key to success, as with any dynamics processor, is careful adjustment. An improper setting can "clip" the attack from lyrical phrases or cause audible "stuttering" if a signal wavers around the threshold level.

The Dynamic Control Panel

Threshold. Determines the level at which processing kicks in. With compressors and limiters, signals that cross above the threshold level get processed; with expanders and gates, only signals below the threshold are processed.

Ratio. Refers to the ratio between a change in input level and the corresponding change in output. For example, if you set a compressor to a 3:1 ratio, a 3 dB increase in the input will be reduced to a 1 dB increase in the output. Ratio range depends upon the job at hand. Compression calls for ratios of 2:1 to 10:1. Limiting implies very high compression ratios of 10:1, 20:1, or even ∞:1.

For expanders, the ratios work the opposite way: A 3:1 ratio setting on the box really should be thought of as a 1:3 setting, since a 1 dB drop in input level will be expanded to a 3 dB drop in output level once the signal drops below threshold.

Attack and release. The attack control determines how quickly—from milliseconds to a full second or longer—processing kicks in once a signal has crossed the set threshold. A release control lets you set how much time passes before the processing stops, once the signal crosses back under or over the threshold. Quick releases are best for peak control, and moderate or longer release times are better for more natural-sounding processing.

Gain reduction meter. Usually calibrated in decibels (dB), this meter shows how much processing takes place once signals cross the threshold.

Sidechain input. Sometimes referred to as "Key In," this input engages the external sidechain return so that external signals control the VCA. (See the sidebar "VCAs and Sidechains.")

Slave. Dual-channel processors usually sport a slave switch, which puts the "slave" channel (usually the right channel, or channel 2) under the complete control of the "master channel" (usually the left channel, or channel 1).

Practical Processing

Now that you know the basics about how dynamics processors work, what can you do with these devices? Plenty! Here are some favorite "tricks of the trade" that engineers have used on countless productions. This list of applications is not comprehensive—signal processing of any type is limited only by the user's imagination and ingenuity—but it should get you excited about the ultimate power of dynamics processing.

Smooth vocals. This classic vocal compression is very subtle and even. Set your compression ratio anywhere between 2:1 and 5:1 (adjust to taste, of course), with a threshold level of 2 to 6 dB below the peak. The attack time should be moderately fast, and the release time slow. If excessive peaks ruin the effect, run the source into a limiter first (using fast attack and release times), and adjust the threshold to limit troublesome peaks.

Breathy vocals. To create whispery, highly present vocals, set your compression ratio between 5:1 and 10:1, with a threshold level of 6 to 20 dB below the peak. Attack time should be very fast, with a moderate release time. The effect is better articulated when a bit of reverb is used as well. Beware, because achieving this effect requires compression so intense that breaths, lip smacks, and other background noise will seem incredibly loud. A pop filter is recommended while recording.

Sustained bass. A smooth, legato bass sound can be achieved by setting your compression ratio between 3:1 and 6:1, with a threshold level 2 to 9 dB below the peak. The attack time should be very fast, and release time moderate to slow. After the instrument's initial attack, sustained notes will increase in gain, resulting in a sensual sustain. The length of the sustain can be modified by adjusting the threshold and attack-time parameters.

Gated Reverb. The classic '80s drum sound, popularized by Phil Collins, employs an outboard reverb unit to provide maximum ambience, a compressor to squash the drum sounds, and a noise gate to abruptly silence the track(s). The sound of the signal "recovering" after being severely compressed and reverberated intensifies the effect of the noise gate. The onset of gating should be timed to suit the music.

The reverb unit is first in the chain (after the source sound) and should be set to a concert hall or plate program with a long decay. Make sure that the reverb's predelay is null (0 milliseconds).

The compression ratio should be an over-the-top ∞:1, with a very fast attack time and a threshold level 15 to 40 dB below the peak. You can vary the release time to taste. The noise gate should have an expansion ratio of 1:∞, with a moderately fast release time. Attack and hold times and the threshold level can be set to suit the demands of the music.

Thick 'n' chunky guitar. Power chords! By applying different amounts of compression to two different mic perspectives, you could put even AC/DC to shame. Place microphone A close to the guitar-amp speaker and set a compression ratio of 8:1 on compressor A. The high compression mixed with a fast attack time will cause the guitar sound to "pump." The release time also should be moderately fast, and the threshold level should be 6 to 20 dB below the peak. Use microphone B as a room mic, placing it at least six to ten feet away from the speaker cabinet. You're going for a warm, sustained sound on this mic, so set compressor B's compression ratio to 5:1 with a moderate attack time and a slow release time. The threshold level should be 6 to 20 dB below the peak.

Radio mix. Want to produce a tight, slamming dance-club or radio mix? Set your compression ratio between 2:1 and 3:1, with a threshold level 2 to 4 dB below the peak. Use a moderate attack time and a slow release time.

Fast Release

Dynamics processing is easy once you understand it, and it not only solves nagging sonic problems but can also produce some pretty hip effects. In your informed hands, a dynamics processor is a powerful and versatile tool.

CHAPTER 22

PDQ EQ

Most musical sounds include four distinct attributes: pitch, volume, duration, and timbre. An *equalizer* is a type of device that affects timbre.

Equalizers got their name during the early days of telephone communication. The pioneers of telephony discovered that various frequencies within the sound carried on telephone cables were attenuated in different amounts over long distances. Special amplifiers were designed to selectively boost the strength of those frequency bands back to their original (input) levels, which made the spectrum at the output equal to the spectrum at the input.

The Drawmer 1961 is a dual-channel vacuum-tube parametric equalizer. Notice that each of the six bands can be switched in or out at the touch of a button.

These days, equalizers can not only boost certain frequencies but also cut selected frequencies in the input signal by combining a set of filters and amplifiers into a single device. This lets you alter the harmonic content, or *timbre*, of the signal as well as reduce feedback and acoustic anomalies. In this section, you'll learn how equalizers work. Refer to Chapter 25, "Creating the Ultimate Mix," for tips on using EQ in mixing.

The Right Connections

As discussed in Chapter 7, "Maximizing Your Mixer," most mixers include some form of EQ in each input channel, which is used to affect the timbre of the signal in each channel independently. However, you can also use an external equalizer for more precise control. In this case, the equalizer is connected to the mixer somewhat differently than most other effects.

Many other effects units split the input signal into two copies and mix the processed and unprocessed versions. An equalizer, on the other hand, outputs only a single, processed signal; after all, the whole point of equalization is that you don't want to hear the original timbre at all.

As a result, an external equalizer is connected to the mixer's insert points, rather than the effects or aux send/return loops (see **Fig. 22.1**). This routes the entire signal out of the mixer, through the equalizer, and back into the mixer.

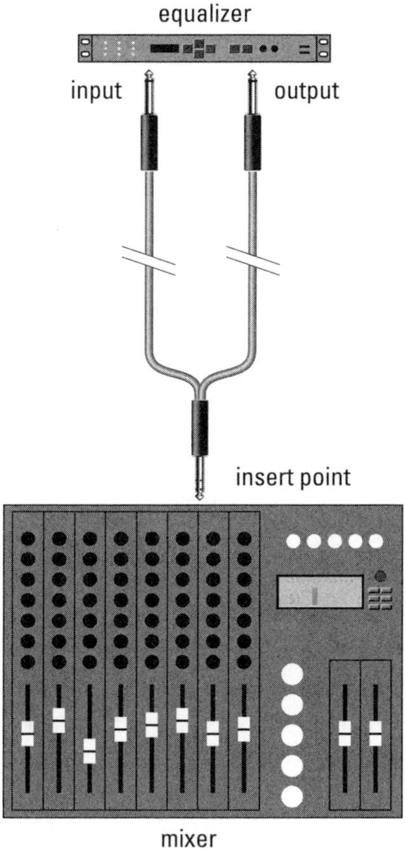

FIG. 22.1: Outboard equalizers are connected to a mixer's insert point, which routes the entire signal out of the mixer, through the EQ, and back into the mixer.

This connection usually requires an insert or Y cable with one 1/4-inch TRS (tip-ring-sleeve) stereo plug at one end and a pair of two conductor cables that terminate in standard TS (tip-sleeve) 1/4-inch plugs at the other end (see **Fig. 22.2**). The ring of the stereo plug is connected to the hot wire in one mono cable, which carries the signal from the mixer to the equalizer. The other mono cable returns the signal from the equalizer to the mixer via the stereo plug's tip. (This is reversed in some mixers; check your mixer's specs to be sure.)

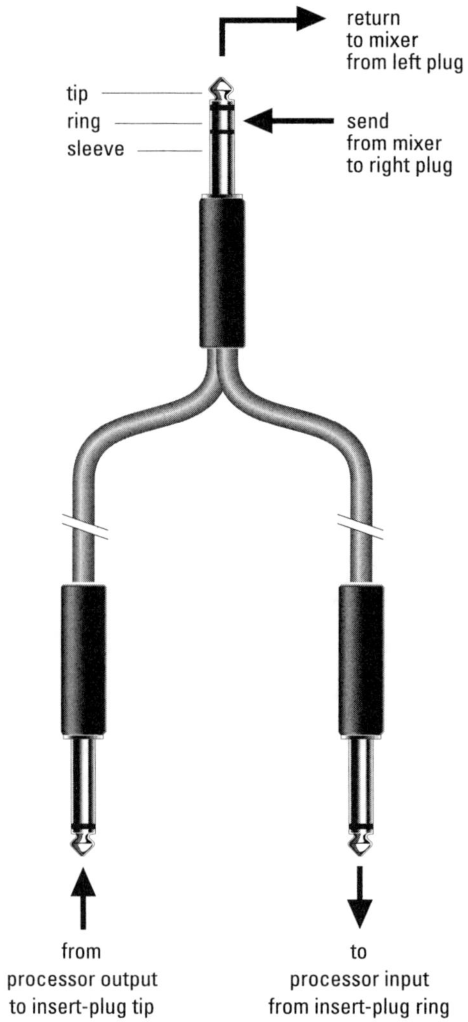

FIG. 22.2:
An insert cable consists of a TRS plug at one end and a pair of two-conductor 1/4-inch or XLR plugs at the other end. In most mixers, the TRS ring sends the signal to the processor, and the tip returns the signal to the mixer.

On the Shelf

Almost everyone has used an equalizer at one time or another. Virtually all stereo systems in cars and homes include bass and treble controls, which are a rudimentary form of EQ. (Most mixers also include these controls in each channel input; see Chapter 7.) This type of EQ is often called *shelving EQ* because the graph of frequency versus amount of boost/cut looks like a shelf (see **Fig. 22.3**). The bass control lets you boost or cut all frequencies below a preset threshold (called the *knee* or *shelving frequency*), which is usually 100 Hz. The treble control boosts or cuts all frequencies above its knee frequency, usually 10 kHz.

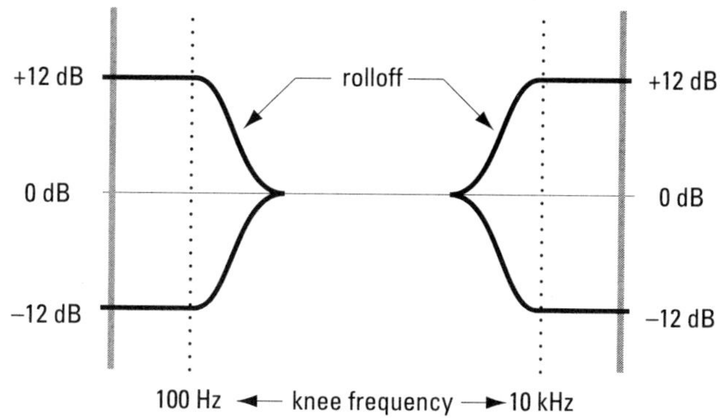

FIG. 22.3: High- and low-shelving EQ boosts or cuts all frequencies above or below the knee frequency, respectively. The EQ has progressively less effect as frequencies get farther outside these boundaries.

The amount by which the high or low frequencies are boosted or cut is measured in decibels (dB). The decibels used in EQ settings indicate changes in the relative levels of the incoming signal and the processed (equalized) signal; they do not refer to absolute values. In addition, EQ decibels are related to power rather than voltage, so a change of 3 dB halves or doubles the level of the electrical signal. For example, a setting of 0 dB allows the appropriate frequencies to pass unaffected. A setting of –3 dB cuts the amplitude of the affected frequencies in half, while a setting of +3 dB doubles their level. Most EQs have a boost/cut range of ±12 dB, which means the level of the corresponding frequencies can be boosted or cut by a factor of 16.

All frequencies below the bass knee or above the treble knee of a shelving EQ are affected equally by their respective settings. But what about the frequencies outside these boundaries?

In Fig. 22.3, notice that the curves depicting the effect of the bass and treble controls taper down to 0 dB as you move farther from the knee. This indicates that frequencies are affected less by the EQ the farther they are from the knee boundary.

The slope of the curve outside the knee boundary is called the *rolloff*. In reference to equalizers, you'll often hear specs such as "a rolloff of 6 dB per octave." This simply means that a frequency one octave away from the knee will be affected one-fourth as much as a frequency that is within the knee boundary. If the rolloff is 12 dB/octave, a frequency one octave away from the knee will be affected one-sixteenth as much as a frequency that is within the boundary.

Getting Graphic

Bass and treble controls are fine for broad tonal adjustments, but what if you need more detailed control? One answer is a graphic EQ. This device divides the entire frequency spectrum into several fixed bands. The controls include a set of sliders that let you boost or cut the frequencies in each band independently. The positions of the sliders form a graph of the EQ's frequency response, hence the name "graphic."

Each band is identified by its center frequency, and each can be boosted or cut by as much as 12 dB or more. The range of effect for each band forms a hump in the graph of frequency versus boost/cut (see **Fig. 22.4**). The setting of each band is applied fully to the center frequency only; the effect on other frequencies lessens the farther they are away from the center frequency.

As you can see in Fig. 22.4, however, the bands overlap. If you boost two neighboring bands, the frequencies between them are boosted as well. In extreme cases, the frequencies between the bands can be affected more than the center frequencies. In addition, you can create an uneven frequency response called the *ripple effect*, if you boost all bands to their maximum setting.

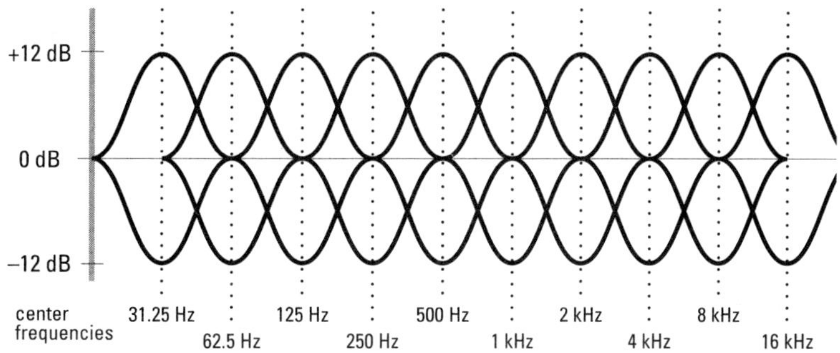

FIG. 22.4: This graphic EQ divides the frequency spectrum into 10 bands. Notice how the bands overlap.

One important characteristic of graphic EQ bands is the bandwidth, which is defined as the range of frequencies that are affected within 3 dB of the band's setting. For example, if a band is set to boost by 12 dB, the bandwidth is the range of frequencies on either side of the center frequency that are boosted by at least 9 dB. The points on the frequency-versus-boost/cut curve that correspond to the boundaries of the bandwidth are called the *3 dB down points*.

The range of frequencies that define bandwidth can be expressed in two ways: as the difference between the boundary frequencies, or as the ratio of these frequencies. Most people use the ratio, which is equivalent to expressing the bandwidth as a musical interval. For example, consider two bands, one centered at 150 Hz and the other at 1,500 Hz. The 3 dB down points of the 150 Hz band are at 100 and 200 Hz, while the

3 dB down points of the 1,500 Hz band are at 1,000 and 2,000 Hz. Both bands have a bandwidth of one octave. As you can see, the difference between the boundary frequencies depends on the center frequency of the band, whereas equal bandwidths can always be expressed as the same interval, regardless of their center frequency.

As a result, electrical engineers came up with another way to express bandwidth in relative terms: quality factor, or Q. This expression is calculated by dividing the center frequency by the difference in boundary frequencies. Returning to the previous example, if the center frequency is 150 Hz and the bandwidth is 100 Hz, again, Q = 1.5; if the center is 1,500 Hz and the bandwidth is 1,000 Hz, Q = 1.5. In a graphic EQ, both the center frequency and bandwidth of each band are fixed, so each band's Q is also fixed.

You might think that the bandwidth remains constant regardless of the band's boost/cut setting, but this isn't quite true. At low settings, the bandwidth tends to be wider than it is at the maximum setting. As a result, companies such as Rane make "constant-Q" graphic EQs, which maintain a constant bandwidth at all boost/cut settings.

Graphic EQs are often found on mixers designed for live-sound applications. These mixers generally include two separate graphic EQs—one for each stereo output—and each EQ typically includes 5 to 10 bands. These EQs are used to reduce feedback at certain frequencies and tailor the sound to the room. Outboard graphic EQs comprise 10 to 31 bands; the latter variety is often called a *1/3-octave graphic EQ*, which describes the width of each band.

Many people start by setting the sliders on a graphic EQ in the shape of a smile. This compensates for the fact that the human ear is less sensitive to high and low frequencies and more sensitive to the midrange, particularly in the 3 to 4 kHz region. As a result, it helps to boost the low and high frequencies and cut the midrange, particularly at low to moderate volumes. (At high volumes, the ear's frequency response flattens out, in which case this EQ configuration can actually damage the sound quality.) The loudness control on many stereo systems activates a fixed version of this concept. Following this initial setting, it's important to adjust the EQ for any room resonances or speaker anomalies (discussed shortly).

Parametric Power

The most flexible type of equalization is the parametric EQ (see **Fig. 22.5**). Unlike graphic models, the center frequency and bandwidth of each band in a parametric EQ are fully user-adjustable. Parametric EQs generally have fewer bands than graphic EQs, because their primary purpose is to tailor a few precisely defined problem frequencies.

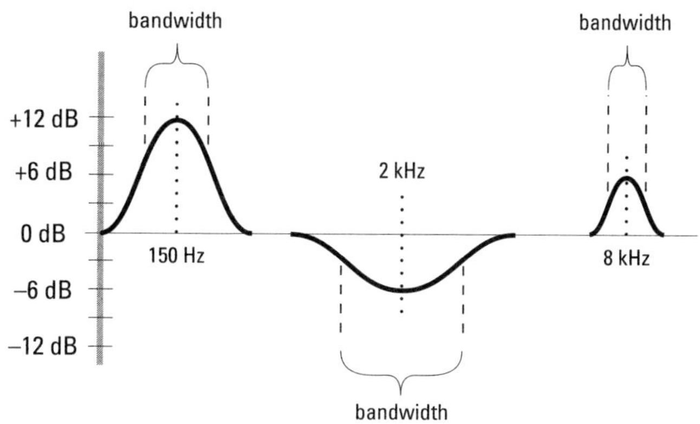

FIG. 22.5: This parametric EQ is set to boost 150 Hz by 12 dB, with a moderate bandwidth; to cut 2 kHz by -6 dB, with a wide bandwidth; and to boost 8 kHz by 6 dB, with a narrow bandwidth.

A variation of this is quasiparametric EQ, which offers full control over center frequency and boost/cut level but only provides a few preset bandwidths from which to choose. More common is the semiparametric, or sweepable, EQ. In this case, the center frequency and boost/cut level are user-definable, but the bandwidth is fixed. Many mixers include one or more sweepable bands in each channel input.

Applications

Tonal correction is among the most common application for EQ. If a sound or recorded track seems too bright, too boomy, or too dull, an EQ can help. The trick is to determine the offending frequency and the amount to cut or boost it. This takes some experimentation. If the track is too bright, the high frequencies should be cut; if the track is too boomy, the lower mid frequencies (in the 150 to 300 Hz range) should be cut.

To remedy such cases, begin by setting a sweepable band to boost by a relatively large amount (12 dB or more) and play the track, while sweeping the frequency knob back and forth until you hear the offending frequency as loudly as possible. Then play the track again while cutting the offending frequency to taste.

Another important application is tonal matching. For example, sometimes two singers' voices don't blend as well as you would wish. In addition, the same singer's voice can vary on different days, which can be a problem if you want to combine recordings from separate sessions. These timbral mismatches can sometimes be addressed by applying EQ. Once again, the trick is to identify the frequencies that are different and boost or cut them to match. This requires a trained ear that can identify the specific frequencies within a complex timbre that are too loud or too soft.

If you've ever used amplified sound, you have probably encountered feedback. All acoustical environments (rooms, auditoriums, etc.) and audio circuits exhibit resonances at specific frequencies. If these resonant frequencies are stimulated, you get feedback. EQ can be instrumental in reducing feedback by attenuating the resonant frequencies in the sound.

However, this also affects the timbre of the sound, so exercise care when using EQ to reduce feedback. Parametric EQs are commonly used for this task, because you can dial in a specific frequency and use a narrow bandwidth to minimize the effect on other parts of the sound. The Sabine FBX-series Feedback Exterminators expand on this idea, identifying which frequencies are feeding back and automatically applying narrow-band (0.1-octave), dynamic EQ to reduce the offending frequencies.

Room resonances can color the sound of a PA or monitor system drastically. In addition, many speaker systems distort the timbre of the sounds they reproduce. Graphic EQs are often used to correct these anomalies. Many engineers place a microphone in the room, play pink noise (which generates the whole range of frequencies at equal amplitudes) over the sound system, measure the frequency response at the mic position, and adjust a 1/3-octave graphic EQ to flatten the response. However, this might not fix the anomalies at other positions in the room.

Generally, you should make as few EQ adjustments as possible. In particular, boosting can be a big help in many situations, but it also increases the noise level. If a band of frequencies is too low, try cutting the frequencies around it first.

Any application of EQ (or any type of filter, for that matter) shifts the phase of the signal. This may not matter in some applications, but it is critical in others. For example, if nearby frequencies are phase-shifted with respect to each other, they might cancel or reinforce each other, leading to unexpected tonal results. To deal with this problem, savvy engineers will use linear-phase equalizers to keep depth and imaging from smearing due to phase anomalies.

Final Cut

Equalizers are among the most common signal processors used in music. They have many uses and help the sound engineer tailor timbre, reduce feedback, and tame room and speaker anomalies.

If you haven't done so already, experiment with the various types of EQ. Trying them out on recordings you know well will give you a better sense of how they sound and behave. A good place to begin is with the high and low shelving EQ on your mixer. If you use a digital audio sequencer, it usually includes basic EQ plug-ins for you to work with.

Over time, you will gain the ability to distinguish and identify frequencies within a complex timbre. The more you work with EQ, the more your ability will improve, which will help your overall music production skills.

CHAPTER 23

Reflecting on Reverb

Back when Phil Spector invented the "wall of sound," outboard reverb units consisted of long springs, heavy plates, and specially designed acoustic chambers. Obviously, few of today's personal recording studios have the space to accommodate these signal-processing monsters from the past.

These days, a smorgasbord of acoustic environments is readily available in software and in hardware devices that fit into a 19-inch rackspace. Effectively using the bounty of easily accessible acoustical environments is another matter; heavy-handed application of reverb can turn a well-recorded track into a soupy mess.

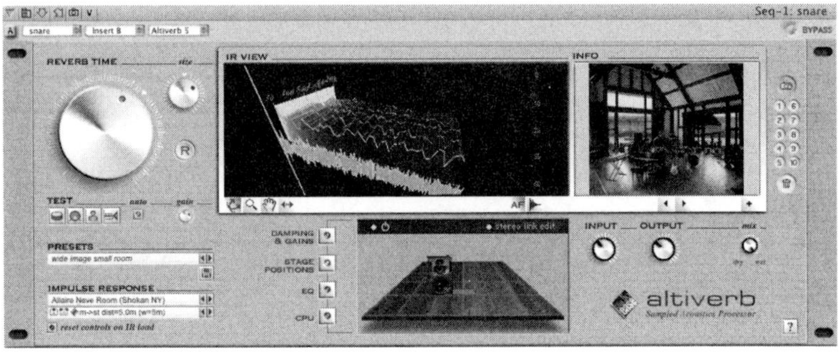

The Audio Ease Altiverb 5

The Audio Ease Altiverb 5 is a reverb plug-in that takes an impulse response from a real acoustic environment, and through a mathematical process called *convolution*, it produces rich, realistic reverb. The upper-right portion of the previous screen shot shows you a photo of the environment in which the impulse response was recorded.

We Are Family

One of the major mixing applications for reverb is putting diverse elements into a common acoustical environment. An engineer often designates a particular reverb as the "master" reverb. This overall reverb, which often is set to a medium or large room (or plate) with a decay time somewhere between 1.5 and 2.5 seconds, is used to process each instrument in the mix in varying amounts.

In effect, the master reverb gives the track an illusion of cohesiveness: A synthesizer without a natural (or internally processed) environment can sound like it was recorded in the same room as an electric guitar. Because instruments in multitrack sessions are often recorded at different times and in diverse acoustical environments, a master reverb can be used to make a mix sound more organic by bestowing identical acoustic qualities upon each instrument.

Hitting the Tracks

While using a master reverb is the most organic method of environmental control, it isn't the only way to spice up tracks—or even always the most appropriate. Some engineers first match individual reverb programs to specific instruments, and then mix the processed tracks in a common "room" created with a master reverb. Other engineers couldn't care less about a cohesive environment and purposely create diverse programs that highlight particular sounds and instruments. If you want to break up the band (sonically speaking), here are some specific reverb applications and ideas.

Drums

Although less fashionable today, gated reverb has been a popular percussion enhancement for years. In the past, a gated-reverb sound was produced by sending the reverb returns (or outputs) into a noise gate and setting the threshold and release parameters to abruptly snap off the reverb decay. Now, almost every multieffects processor offers this sound as a factory preset. A short decay tail can add punch to snare tracks, although the resulting effect is considered by some to be rather cliché. Playing with the gated reverb's room size and decay time can produce anything from pistol-shot slapbacks (cool on snares) to bizarre "percussive" reverb tails (great for toms).

If you want punchy tracks but can't stomach gated-reverb effects, try a short decay on a moderately large room or plate program. This big/short combo maximizes the impact of the drum without allowing a long decay to obscure other instruments.

When constructing reverb environments, keep in mind that plate programs often accentuate the highs, while rooms tend to exhibit warmer timbres. Also, take care with the amount and time of early reflections, diffusion, and predelay. These parameters provide aural clues that help indicate not only room size, but also where the listener is sitting relative to the sound source and reflective surfaces. If preliminary reflections or reverberation anticipate the direct percussion sound, you may end up with some weird, disorienting timing anomalies.

Guitars

When it comes to putting reverb on guitars, almost anything goes. Just make sure the decay time isn't so long that it washes out the track—a common mixing problem. If you really want ripping guitar tracks, critically assess whether reverb treatment is necessary. A typical miked amplifier usually produces suitable ambience (depending on the room in which the guitar was recorded); if further treated with a guitarist's favorite effects processor, the guitar signal may become overprocessed. Depending on the mix and performance style, adding more reverb can actually diminish the power of the guitar.

A good rule of thumb is to start with a completely dry track. If the guitars burn, leave them alone. If not, sneak in some reverb until you're happy; then quit while you're ahead. It's always better to use less reverb than you think you need.

Keyboards

Except for lush string programs, few synth and sample tracks survive being washed in reverb. The overwhelming ambience reduces most sounds to audio mush. But electronic instruments often benefit from a little extra substance.

A common trick for fattening up synth tracks involves running the signal into a reverb unit that has a large room setting with a short decay time. Route the output of this reverb into another reverb unit set with a medium plate and a long decay. The first reverb setting emulates the acoustics that would have existed if the sound source were miked, and the second reverb blends the synth into the overall mix. Be sure to adjust the wet/dry mix of the second reverb (or the effects return levels, if you're routing the outputs of both units into your mixer) to prevent the long decay from compromising overall clarity.

The Ursa Major Space Station SST-206, by Seven Woods Audio, is a digital effects processor small enough to sit on the desktop. The device, which uses only digital I/O, offers reverb and multitap delay-based echo.

Vocals

Lead vocal tracks often scream for reverb. Actually, the lead vocalist often screams for reverb. And he always demands tons more than is appropriate. Unfortunately, a voice submerged under a sea of reverb only serves to sink your mix. Because the vocal often is the primary element of a track, you must stop reverb overkill by any means necessary. A subtly processed voice punches out from the track; a reverb-doused mess usually gets lost in the wash.

If you insist on using a reverb with a long decay, try holding back on the effects-return level. A barely audible reverb wash provides a nice background ambience without overwhelming the track. And don't forget that adjusting a short reverb's pre-delay can make a relatively dry vocal treatment sound "wet": You simply move the onset of the reverb closer to the direct signal (voice). In addition, keep in mind that every voice has a different quality and timbre, so audition plate and room reverbs until you find the program that works best.

Cleaning House

One of the major causes of compromised sound in effects devices is failure to maximize the signal input. If you want to get more reverb out of your box, don't instantly crank up the output. Such a maneuver increases your chances of adding hiss to a clean mix. First, make sure that the signal-input level of the unit is as hot as it can get without distorting; then boost your output to the desired level. This simple technique maximizes your signal-to-noise ceiling.

It also pays to solo your reverb returns to check noise levels. Many low- and midpriced hardware processors exhibit some level of audible hiss, so you may need to put a noise gate on the effects return. The gate ensures that residual noise is silenced when no signal is running through the reverb unit. Take care to set the gate's threshold and release parameters so that the reverb can decay completely. Some processors have internal EQ, and you can always run your effects returns into a mixer channel for equalization purposes, so there is almost no excuse for muddy reverb. In addition, engineers usually cut out a small amount of the bass frequencies to enhance clarity.

A little-known problem is signal phasing caused by using two or more models of the same reverb unit in line. Try reversing the left and right outputs of each unit if you notice that your mids and highs are compromised.

Quick Delay

Reverb can make your mix sound larger than life, or it can flush audio clarity down the drain. If you employ reverb in a mix, don't forget that the effect plays as much a part in the overall sound as the instrument you are processing.

Ultimately, all the elements of a track influence the final sonic mix. So don't let that paranoid vocalist talk you into decorating his voice with the "Grand Canyon" reverb program. (This warning goes double if you are the vocalist.) And remember, keeping your tracks clean doesn't mean you can't have fun. Once you've maximized your signal levels, toss the manuals into a drawer and start experimenting with every reverb parameter you can get your hands on.

CHAPTER 24

Deploying Delay

From the whisper of a butterfly's wings beating in the air to the loudest crescendo of a symphony orchestra, all sound can be defined by four parameters: amplitude, pitch, timbre, and time. In essence, the terms we use to describe music—rhythm, melody, and so on—are simply elaborations on these parameters.

We perceive changes in amplitude because our ears are sensitive to how air moves. The tiny twitches of air molecules against our eardrums tell us the location and nature of people and objects in our environment. Acoustically, we sense time in day-to-day life in the form of acoustic echoes. These delays are so much a part of aural perception that we seldom notice them, yet they form much of the basis of our ability to locate and identify sounds.

The upshot of all this is that when we apply delay in recording and performance, we are controlling amplitude and time at an extremely basic level. Whether creating audio illusions impossible in any real acoustic space or trying to simulate a specific acoustic environment accurately, delay is a powerful tool for playing with a listener's perception.

How time delay affects sound depends on the delay time itself, along with the amplitude and frequency content of the delayed signal as compared to the original. The presence of any other delays and any differences between the sounds that arrive at the left and right ears also are critical factors (see **Fig. 24.1**).

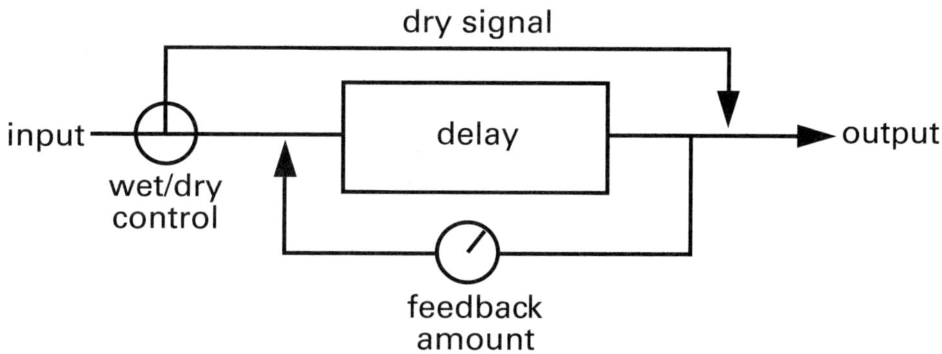

FIG. 24.1: In a simple, single delay, the input signal is split in two: One signal proceeds directly to the output, and the other is delayed by a certain amount of time before it is mixed with the original signal. The delayed signal can also be split in two, and one of these signals fed back into the delay's input to be delayed yet again.

The sonic characteristics of different delays usually are related to specific time ranges. In reality, these ranges cannot be defined so precisely. In particular, at short delay times, the effect is vastly different for stereo and mono signals. With that caveat in mind, here are some typical effects correlated to approximate delay times (see **Fig. 24.2**).

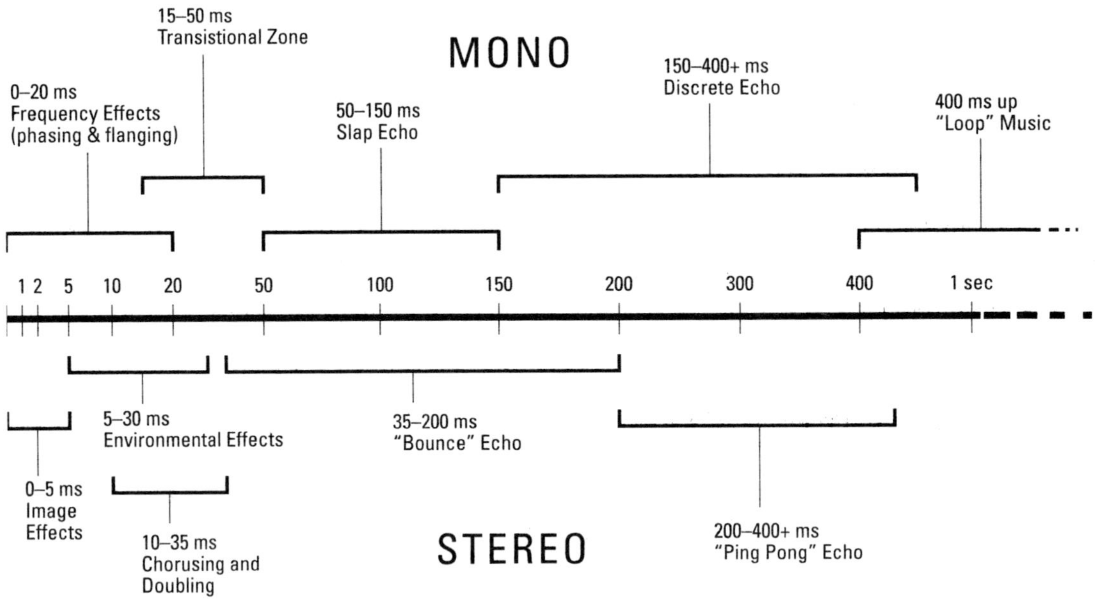

FIG. 24.2: The continuum of delay effects in mono and stereo.

Stereo-Image Effects

0 to 5 milliseconds. Delay times of just a couple milliseconds primarily affect stereo imaging, but only when the original signal predominates in one ear and the delayed signal predominates in the other. When heard through headphones, the sonic image tilts strongly to the ear receiving the nondelayed signal. This happens because our auditory system uses the difference in path length from one ear to the other as a key cue in determining the lateral direction of sound in nature.

Over loudspeakers, the effect is less distinct, due to the blending of sound from the speakers with reflected sound from the listening environment. Generally, you'll hear a spread of the stereo image that changes as you turn your head or change position. Small time delays between channels can help build separations between tracks in a sonically cluttered production. To embed imaging information in the tracks, use small delays of differing values for different tracks, and alternate which speaker channel receives the nondelayed signal (see **Fig. 24.3**). Be careful when applying this technique, because effects that sound subtle over loudspeakers can be excessive when monitored on headphones.

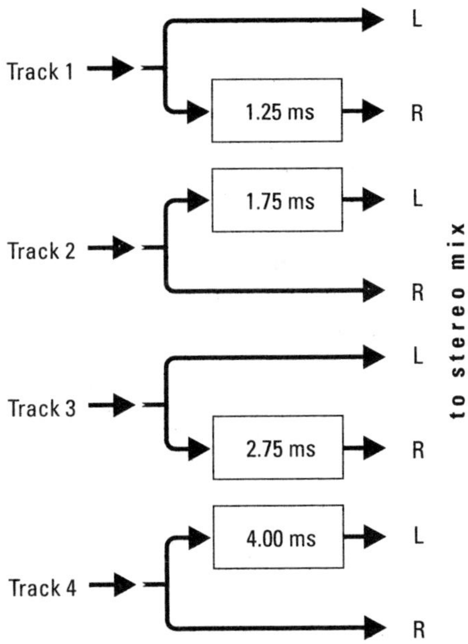

FIG. 24.3: Using delays to add imaging to a stereo mix. Note the use of different delay times and the alternation of which channel precedes the other.

Separation Effects

10 to 35 milliseconds. You can set delay levels and pans that create the effect of a separate but equal sound source, rather than merely suggesting environmental reflections. The principle behind doubling is that the ear will treat the delayed signal as another sound source, because the two occur at different times. However, in practice, a simple delay is not enough to create a credible doubling effect. You will need to introduce small pitch shifts by altering the delay time to produce a more realistic effect. Periodic LFO-induced shifts are less convincing than random shifts, but not if the random changes occur too quickly. Also, one of the traditional ways of generating random shifts—the sample-and-hold waveform—often changes too abruptly to be usable. It's better to use a smoothed sample-and-hold, which acts more like a triangle-wave LFO with speed that varies randomly within a certain range.

Using a pitch shifter tuned at, or very near, unity creates a very convincing illusion of two independent sources, if you pan the unshifted and shifted signals to opposite stereo channels. When the tuning is placed very close to unity, the result is a kind of random phase modulation.

In theory, chorusing creates the sound of a large number of sources playing identical lines ensemble. In reality, chorusing can be a wonderful means of enriching a sound that simulates, rather than duplicates, the ensemble effect. The line between doubling and chorusing is a blurry one, and sometimes it seems that any doubling setting that is too pronounced to be realistic is called "chorusing."

Slap Echo

50 to 150 milliseconds. In this range, a sound's delayed repeat is very distinct from the original. However, sounds with very slow attacks and decays may tend to blend. (Such sounds often obscure many of the effects we are talking about, because the ear usually uses the sounds' initial transients to correlate the direct and delayed sounds.)

In mono, the effect is that of a fast stutter or a repeat of the sound. Depending on the characteristics of the sound and the relationship between the levels, slap echo also may "fatten" the sound, or broaden the attack. In stereo, a "ricochet" effect occurs, which may cause the listener's attention to jerk from the undelayed to the delayed speaker. To accentuate this effect, route the delayed signal through a bandpass filter to cut the high and low end, feed the signal to a reverb unit, and delay one channel of the reverb output (the one opposite the "dry" version of the delayed sound) by 50 to 100 milliseconds.

Discrete Echo Effects

150 to 400 milliseconds. In this range—the classic "Echoplex" zone—delayed sounds are clearly and fully distinct from the original and are heard as separate repetitions. (Is there a guitarist or vocalist who is not thrilled to hear the repeat of their licks fading into the ether?)

Often, it is important to select delay times that work rhythmically with the music. For some musical styles, it's best if delay times synchronize with the beat. You can figure out a complementary delay time by using the following equation: delay time in milliseconds = 60,000 ÷ tempo in beats per minute (bpm).

In other instances, you may want delays that do not correspond to the beat. These tend to "cut across" the dominant beat and gain their power from their very lack of an easily discernible relationship to the main beat.

It is easy to overuse echo, so exercise caution; crowding too many repeating delays into a mix turns it into an indistinct wash. Controlling the signal going to the delay, either with effects sends at a mixing console or with foot pedals, can regulate the amount of echo. This also lets you do tricks such as adding echoes selectively (just to the tail ends of phrases, for example) by feeding only the target signal into the delay line. When you pull back on the input level, the echoes will continue, but no subsequent sound will be processed.

Delay Loops

400 milliseconds and up. When delays become long enough to equal musical bars, phrases, and sections, we get into an area that some call *loop music*. Guitarist Robert Fripp popularized this effect, constructing sonic symphonies of undulating guitar lines (and sounds) in real time, which he dubbed "Frippertronics." Other early practitioners of loop music include Brian Eno, David Torn, Steve Tibbetts, and Andy Summers. This technique extends into more contemporary styles too numerous to list, with loops being created in hardware and software.

Tricks of the Trade

Besides the obvious uses for delay, here are a few tricks you can use to give your tracks a professionally produced sound.

Vocal slapback. Delay can be used subtly to add depth to a voice. A 75-millisecond setting with no repeats (or feedback) delivers a classic slapback effect. Panning the delayed or slapback signal a little to the right or left of the original (centered) vocal helps clarify the effect. Sometimes, it may be appropriate to pan the original vocal full left and the delayed signal full right. Obviously, the delayed signal has to sound as clear as the actual vocal for this trick to work; however, the ragged resolution of inexpensive, guitar-oriented processors will not give you this clarity.

The never-ending vocal echo. Long delays with moderate repeats provide the foundation for adding dimension to a predominantly dry vocal. Set the delay unit to approximately 375 milliseconds with 10 to 15 repeats; don't forget to match the tempo of the repeats to the song. Fade this percolating chorus of echoes far below the level of the original vocal track. At first listen, the voice may appear almost completely dry. Certain phrases, however, should reveal the delay effect and help pull the listener into the song.

Some producers mix the multiple repeats as loud as (or louder than) the lead vocal to add importance to selected lyrical phrases. This application is an old dub (Jamaican club music) standard and has been adopted by the current generation of rap, techno, and other dance-oriented artists.

Aural ghosts. Another classic trick is using delay to retard the onset of a reverb. Basically, you send the selected tape track into the delay unit and route the delayed signal into a reverb. You won't hear the actual delayed signal, only the delayed reverb. Set the delay unit to zero feedback, because you just want the signal to arrive at the reverb unit a few milliseconds "late." How late the delayed signal triggers the reverb effect is up to you. Start with a rather languid timing of 250 to 500 ms, depending on the tempo and feel of the track. The reverb unit—again, depending on the atmosphere you're trying to achieve—should have a large or medium room setting, with a long decay time.

At its best, this application produces a spooky effect that sounds great on lead vocals or slow, melodic solos. (The delay ping-pongs caused by high-speed soloing usually are too intense for this use.) On vocals, the lyrics seem to "shadow" the lead vocal: The lush reverb softly repeats the words a fraction of a second after the actual vocal track is heard. This effect is more sensual than the chopped repeats produced by pure echo. Some multieffects processors allow you to place a delay before the reverb in a single algorithm, so this ghosting effect often can be accomplished with one box.

Faux stereo. One of the simplest delay tricks involves transforming a monaural signal into a pseudostereo image. A mono signal can be "cloned" through a delay processor, returned on an effects return, and panned opposite the original track. Begin with the delay time at 10 ms to produce a "snapshot" copy of the original track. You can widen the spectrum a little by adjusting the delay time to between 30 and 50 ms.

Return Signal

Signal processing does not occur in a vacuum; there's always a rich interaction of one sound with another. As you experiment with delay, use your ears and your mind together, and consider the nature of the sounds themselves and the music in which you use them. If you use these delay techniques wisely, you'll achieve sounds that can leap out and grab the listener's attention.

Part IV

Mixing and Mastering Your Demo

CHAPTER 25

Creating the Ultimate Mix

Whether the listener is aware of it or not, his response to a recording depends greatly on the mix. No matter how well the instruments were recorded, if they're not well placed in relation to one another, the results will be boring and lifeless.

In the world of major-label projects, it's common for a project to be recorded by one engineer, mixed by another engineer, and mastered by yet another. Because each stage requires highly specialized skills, it makes sense to let the experts do the work.

If you're producing anything mainstream, from alternative to Top 40, the mix needs to be aggressive and have an attitude. It needs to be in your face. So what is it that the pros do that makes even an average song sound great? This chapter will give you some insight.

Subtly using a high-end stereo dynamics processor, such as the tube-based Manley Stereo Variable Mu limiter/compressor, on the mix bus can help you solidify a mix.

The Three-Dimensional Space

Because the first recordings were recorded with a single microphone and without the benefits of overdubbing and mixing, the first recording engineers relied on the placement of the musicians in a room, relative to the microphone, to get the right mix. For example, the instruments that needed to be "up front" in the mix were placed closer to the mic. To get a natural blend from an orchestra, the softer instruments (such as the string section) were placed nearer to the mic than the louder instruments (such as the brass and percussion). If the music included vocals, the singer needed to be as close to the microphone as possible for maximum vocal intelligibility.

In the modern multitrack recording environment, it is no longer necessary to record this way. However, when it comes time to mix a multitrack project, it is helpful to imagine the instruments placed in a three-dimensional space right behind your monitors (see **Fig. 25.1**). Whether the final mix duplicates the realism of a stage setup or creates a surrealistic one, you need to visualize the exact position of each instrument in front of you. If you spent time tuning your room, acquiring sonically accurate gear, and placing it in the sweet spot of the room, everything should be in place and ready for you to visualize as you mix.

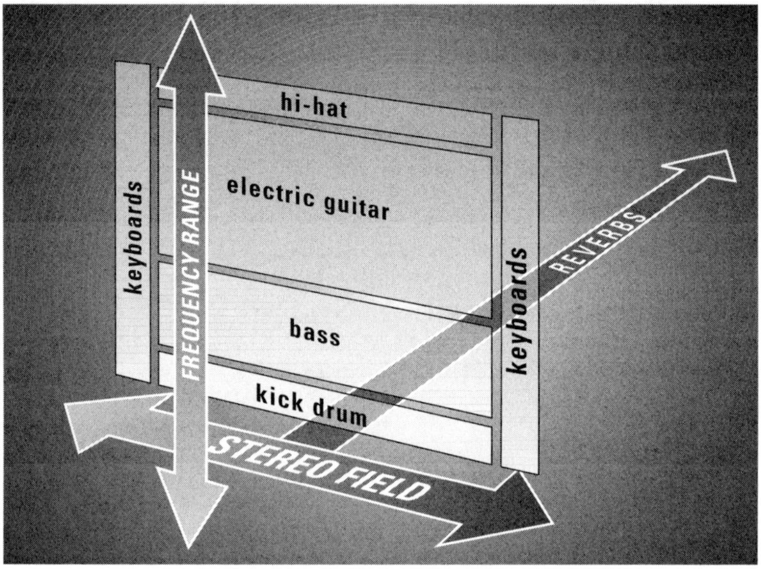

FIG 25.1: By conceptualizing the mix as a three-dimensional stage where the vertical axis represents the frequency range, you can graph the soundstage from the front or above and see the frequency/pan position or volume/pan position, respectively. Make sure that no two components are in the same place in either axis.

Anatomy of a Mix

Producing pristine masters requires "transparent mixing." This means that all the elements of a recording must be sonically well defined and subservient to the demands of the music.

What defines a good mix? Unfortunately, there are no absolute guidelines. Music is a subjective medium, and arguments regarding a production's sonic quality can rage for hours. However, a professional mix is easy to identify: You can hear everything. The rhythm section is tight, the vocals are crisp, and the background material (such as keyboard pads and counterpoint lines) is clear and well articulated.

In a pro mix, the ear is drawn to certain elements deemed by the artist or producer to be the work's focal points. On a pop record, these elements often are the lead vocal, rhythm section, and instrumental hooks. Jazz producers typically highlight the soloists. In every case, a professional mixer ensures that the appropriate musical hooks are loud, clear, and unfettered by competing sonic elements.

It takes years of practice, ear training, and intensive study before you can begin churning out "hot" mixes. The first step to producing transparent, professional mixes is to keep an open mind about learning new things and unlearning old habits. Be prepared to change the way you do things to get your mixes to the next level. Begin by listening to classic and contemporary recordings. Try to identify the elements that comprise a sharp, clean mix: What sounds are generally mixed up front? How many different instrumental and vocal parts are featured, and what tonal ranges do they fill? What is the basic sonic personality of the mix (a full tonal spectrum, predominant midrange frequencies, etc.)?

Once you've developed an ear for the components of professional mixes, reference your own mixes to commercial CDs within your stylistic genre. By critically assessing how your mixes stack up against professional products, you will begin to get ideas of how you want your mixes to sound and how to get them there.

Analyzing Your Favorite Recordings

Each musician has his favorite recordings. As you begin thinking about mixing your own tracks, reference these classic recordings. If your music fits into a specific genre, listen to other recordings in that style and think about what makes each track sound unique. To get the process rolling, here are a few questions to ask yourself:

1. How do the vocals sit in the mix? Are they up front, or do they sit back within the accompaniment?

2. What is the overall blend like? Can you hear the "room" around each instrument, or is everything in the same "room"?

3. Where are the various instruments placed in the stereo field? Which instruments appear in the center, which instruments appear on the sides, and which have a stereo spread? Does this sound natural or artificial? Which do you prefer?

4. What is the overall feel of the track? Does it sound large and "live" as if it were recorded in an arena, or is it more intimate?

Different effects, such as panning, reverb, and echo, often are the defining characteristics of a musical genre. Before you begin mixing, it is useful to be able to identify both the obvious and the subtle effects that pertain to the style of music you make.

A useful exercise is to pick a musical genre and compare a record that was mixed 20 years ago with one that was mixed last year. Begin by focusing on one instrument. For now, let's look at the drums. Many drummers in the mid- to late-1970s used some degree of dampening on their drums. This gave the instrument a tight, dry sound but with good projection.

As you go through records in your collection, notice whether the drums sound dry and muffled, or have a tone and are ringy.

Compare your findings with well-produced records from the '90s. Do the drums sound larger and more resonant? Do you hear different reverb characteristics in comparison to the earlier tracks?

It's also a good idea to step out of the genre you're most familiar with and listen to how different styles are recorded and mixed. You may not like the sound of rap, the feel of country and western, or the intensity of heavy metal, but major releases in these genres are often recorded and mixed by the same people. You may find one particular element in this unfamiliar music that you can use in your own music, whether it's the sound of a bass drum or an effect used on a voice. The more you listen to unfamiliar styles, the more likely that you will be able to bring new ideas to your own.

Referencing

If you're planning on mixing a project that will be heard by anyone other than yourself, in any environment other than your own studio, you need to reference through a variety of monitor speakers. Most professional studios have two or three sets of monitors set up, and mixing engineers routinely check the mix through each set of monitors as they progress.

Begin by working on your favorite speakers. Then check the relative levels of the instruments using a set of smaller, inexpensive speakers. Make sure they are positioned next to your favorite monitors so that you are sitting in the sweet spot for both sets of speakers. If the tracks sound good on the low-quality speakers, and you can hear everything clearly, the mix will probably translate well on any system.

Mono compatibility is another big part of a successful mix. Keep in mind that people often listen to music without the benefit of true stereo: FM radio is not true stereo, car speakers don't give you a great stereo image, and boom boxes essentially produce a mono signal as soon as you step away from them. It's a good idea to flip the mono switch on your console frequently, or pan the tracks to the center, to ensure that your mix is mono compatible. If your mix sounds just as good in mono as it does in stereo, you're going in the right direction. If portions of the audio spectrum become quieter or disappear, you may have some phase problems within the tracks.

From the Top

When you first bring up all the tracks on a song, listen closely to how the various parts are blending. Don't immediately assume that everything needs tweaking. If you did a good job of recording the basic tracks, you may find that you have the beginnings of a decent mix right away.

Remember that a good mix is mainly subtractive: You should try to clean it up rather than add things to mask problems. If you're not satisfied with your progress at any point during the mix, don't be afraid to go back and change things. Inevitably, the first tracks you tweak won't sit right with the other instruments, no matter how good they sounded by themselves.

Although soloing tracks is great for fixing problems, creating your individual tracks in solo mode is generally a bad practice. Only solo a track if you hear a problem. For the most part, you want to listen to a track in context with the other instruments in the mix. For example, you could work on a soloed bass sound for hours, only to find it doesn't sit right with the kick drum in the mix. Then you're back to square one.

Another important element in doing a good mix is the ability to relate to all of the instruments. If you play a particular instrument, it's important that you don't favor that instrument in the mix. Many engineers fall into this trap. You need to appreciate what each track has to offer. That's why it is always a good idea to have an extra set of ears, such as a band member, present for input.

The Big Picture

Savvy producers conceptualize the final mix as the project is being recorded. This means they have an idea of how the end product should sound as they go through the entire recording process, from tracking basics to doing overdubs.

If you prepare supportive musical and sonic arrangements before committing a single sound to tape, the technical aspects of the mixing process—issues such as equalization tweaks and the relative volume of instruments—should be almost automatic. Such preparation is rewarded by allowing you more time to concentrate on the creative aspects of mixing, such as imaging (the placement of instruments within the stereo spectrum) and signal processing. All of this preproduction is important because the "fix it in the mix" scenario is a myth. Therefore, a little preproduction planning can save you hours of mixing frustration.

The Mix Elements

Every mix decision should be committed to creating a supportive environment for the lead vocal, solo instrument, or other musical hook. When you begin playing with track levels and EQ, make sure that nothing interferes with these critical elements.

A transparent mix can only be achieved with slavish attention to detail. Only after you've identified a production's musical focal points, however, should you risk obsessing over the individual components of your multitrack master.

For a good pop-music mix, you must find the optimal balance between the rhythm instruments and the vocal. Let's break down the mix into four sections that represent the most important elements of a top-notch mix and discuss some techniques to make your tracks sound as good as they can.

Drums. The most critical relationship in the rhythm section is between the kick drum and the bass guitar. These two things drive the song. Although what you want your kick drum to sound like largely depends on the style of music you're mixing, you must make sure that its punchiness does not interfere with any of the frequencies generated by the bass. Therefore, you should always tweak it while listening to the bass track.

Sometimes, you'll hear something wrong in the mix, but you can't put your finger on it. Often, the snare is the culprit. The snare acts as the song's metronome. As with a tambourine, it's very noticeable when the snare is either too soft or too loud. Don't just assume that a quick level adjustment is the solution. Many times EQ can bring out the snare, by either adding some mid frequencies or subtracting some low end. Try that before boosting the level.

Many people also like to use a bit of compression on the snare drum, especially if the dynamics of the performance are uneven. Overcompression can be used to create a particular effect. By playing with the attack and release times on your compressor (adjusting them relative to the song's tempo), you can get a snare hit that sustains the resolution of the note, creating a more full-bodied sound.

You can also use a noise gate to produce a well-defined snare sound. Set the gate so that it cuts out everything except the actual snare hit. Then send the signal to a compressor to even out the dynamics and produce more impact. Be sure that the noise gate eradicates any stray cymbal crashes, as compression can noticeably raise their relative levels.

Finally, keep in mind that people love percussion. Almost any song can be improved and any mix fattened up by adding percussion. Tambourines and shakers are always good additives. If you have done everything you can to a mix and it still sounds empty, try throwing in these two instruments as a quick fix. By panning them left and right (nine o'clock and three o'clock), you can often improve a mix dramatically.

Bass. Compression and EQ are used to fatten up a bass track. Compression is usually needed because each string on the bass guitar produces different dynamics, and the dynamic range of the track can be pretty large. Smooth compression will tame flabby dynamic levels and allow you to bring up the level so that the track provides the desired sonic backbone.

A compression ratio of 2:1 or 4:1 at a threshold level of –10 dB usually tightens up the low end quite nicely. If you're going for "big bottom," boost 100 Hz by 5 to 10 dB, and cut the low mids to keep the lowest information from muddying up the track. If a funkier bass is needed, cut 100 Hz by about 7 dB, and boost the mids to taste.

Typically, the bass signal is routed to an EQ and then through a dynamics processor. You may want to patch in a second EQ after the compressor/limiter. This will allow you to make minor adjustments to the sound after it has been dynamically processed. Sometimes, compression will sustain certain frequencies that may clash with other instruments. The second EQ lets you find those frequencies and cut them from the mix.

The bass provides the fundamental pitches for a song, so always listen to how the bass fits into the mix. To hear the instrument's low pitches clearly, you need to find a balance between the low- and high-end frequencies. Having the right balance gives the bass the definition needed so that pitches, rather than "woofs" or rumble, are clearly heard.

Guitars. Guitars should sound natural and unobtrusive. Except for the lead or solo, the guitar tracks should be mixed in well with the other instruments. A slight amount of compression is generally added to help accomplish this. Depending on how many rhythm guitar tracks you have, you may want to group them to a stereo pair and add the compression at the bus insert.

A common practice is to double the rhythm guitars. This sounds most natural when the guitarist simply plays the part twice on two separate tracks. However, many tracking engineers mic the cabinet from two distances, using a close mic and an ambient mic. This creates a natural delay that fattens up the sound.

It's also very important to consider the tonal characteristics of the guitars when you blend them with the other instruments. Make sure that your guitar tracks are not laden with unnecessary low frequencies that will clash with the bass. Sure, the tracks may sound fat when soloed, but when you mix them in, you'll have a muddy bottom end. Also, try not to make the guitars too bright; nothing is more annoying than screeching guitars.

A noise gate is essential for shutting down ugly, amp-related noises when the guitarist is not playing. Compressing the guitar brings out hums and hisses; gating or downward expansion can be used to minimize the unwanted sounds.

Vocal Intelligibility. Undoubtedly, the lead vocal is the most important track in almost any song. It needs to stand out because, like it or not, the singer usually sells the song or band. However, the vocal is also one of the most difficult things to get to work because of the frequency content of the voice.

A vocal track needs to have body, presence, and air, but not so much that it interferes with the rest of the mix. Compression is often necessary to keep the level constant and to help separate the vocal from the rest of the music. Subtle boosting of the midrange also helps the vocals move to the front of a mix. This is the most sensitive track you will have to EQ, and because there are so many variables, making categorical statements about it is difficult. You'll have to listen carefully and make EQ decisions based on the sound of the particular voice you're working on.

Among the trickiest songs to sit vocals in are ballads. Ballads usually begin with just the vocal and a simple accompaniment, with the full band coming in midsong. This is when the signer's dynamic range is typically the largest. You should isolate the two sections and address them as separate entities. If you have more than one compressor available, try setting up individual ones for different parts of the song.

A common trick that many mix engineers use to fatten a vocal track is to route the track to a delay unit through an aux send, process it with a slight amount of delay (10 to 15 ms), and bring it back into a separate channel fader. The delay is not long enough to hear as a discrete sound, but it increases the fatness of the vocal track.

Background vocals are another matter, and there are two major types: the simple harmony and the chorus. The first is your standard harmony that moves along with the lead vocal. Since this is almost like another lead vocal, you can EQ it in a similar fashion if you want the vocals to blend. If you want the harmony to stand out more, give it a slightly different EQ and perhaps give it its own place in the stereo field.

The other type of background vocal is the choral effect, where you may have three or more vocalists in various octaves. These vocals typically sound better when they have a bit of "air" to them.

Begin by rolling off low frequencies, around 400 Hz, on the high harmonies and attenuate the extremely low frequencies, around 100 Hz, on low harmonies. Then remove as much mid-range as you can, usually between 1 and 4 kHz, without losing the clarity of the voice. Finally, add some upper mids and high frequencies with a shelving EQ set around 8 or 9 kHz until you get that angelic effect. It also helps to pan the voices across the soundstage.

Mixing Mandates

Don't disregard rough mixes. More often than not, any rough mixes you've made throughout the recording process will have desirable qualities that should be considered at the final mix session. Roughs are fresh and intuitive, and they often expose the raw truth of a performance. That's a rare and beautiful thing. Be careful not to "mix out" the passion by putting a magnifying glass over each and every track.

Mix with fresh ears. Morning mix sessions are ideal because your ears have not been abused by a typical day's activities. Ear fatigue is a real thing and can easily happen after a few hours of close-field monitoring.

Monitor at reasonable levels. Occasionally, it's good to blast the speakers to check bass frequencies, but for the most part, soft playback levels tell the truth. Monitoring at lower levels also helps protect your hearing.

Know when to quit. When the fatigue factor reaches the point of diminishing returns, bail out. There's no sense in forcing yourself to finish something that you'll probably end up remixing later when you've come back to your senses. Also, take short breaks throughout the mix session to rest your battered ears.

Put the mix in context. Be sure to mix on familiar speakers to ensure critical listening. However, once the mix is finished, see if the sound translates well to the outside world. Check the mix on different home stereo systems, portable players, car stereos, and boom boxes. After all, these are the means by which the public will hear your work.

Keep detailed notes. Don't rely on your memory to recall how much you compressed the snare track or gated the lead guitar. Keep detailed notes on every aspect of the mix, just in case you have to revisit the track for a remix. You can also refer to your notes later on as you tackle new projects and want to find out how you got a specific sound or effect.

Be open to remixing. From band members to band managers, everyone has a vision of how a record should sound. Be prepared to remix a track if some of those involved aren't happy with the sound. Fortunately, your copious notes will allow you to re-create the mix in a minimum amount of time.

The Stereo Spread

Creating a believable stereo image is one of the hardest things to do. The soundstage needs to be wide, but the mix must sound good in mono. In addition, the spread shouldn't be so wide that the image is unrealistic. The rule of thumb has traditionally been to position the instruments as you might hear them onstage from the audience. Many engineers will pan things hard left or right, especially guitars and drum toms. But then again, you can take a different approach.

For example, you might pan everything from the drummer's perspective, as if the listener were sitting on the drummer's stool. To do this, you would put the kick in the middle, the snare left of center, the hi-hat slightly left of the snare, and the cymbals and toms exactly where they appear on the kit. Next, pan the guitars at ten and two o'clock, and put the bass and vocals in the middle, with any background vocals just left and right of center. With this setup, you have all of your important information in the center (and in mono), while the supporting cast is on the outside.

But this is only one way to do it, and like everything else in mixing, there are no set rules. Remember the listening exercises I talked about earlier? This is where you can put to good use the information you gleaned from analyzing the stereo image of your favorite records.

Regardless of where you place everything, it's crucial to maintain an accurate representation of the instruments. Remember that panning instruments to the outermost edges of the left or right (farther than three o'clock or nine o'clock) invites phase problems when the mix is played in a mono or pseudostereo format (such as FM radio).

Mixing with EQ

There are two basic reasons to use your console EQ during a mix: to shape an instrument's tone so that it "sits" better in the overall track, or to alter the tone because you want the instrument to sound different. The first reason can be thought of as corrective EQ and the second as creative EQ. Often, a combination of the two yields the best results.

However, creative EQ is particularly useful when you have a tone in mind that's more appropriate to a groove or style of music than what's actually recorded on tape. As long as your board offers at least one (though preferably two) sweepable midrange band, as well as low and high shelving, you can usually tailor the sound of an existing track to better match the mood and style of a song. You can also get creative and dial in unusual or bizarre sounds.

Bass-ic EQ

Obviously, even the most creative equalization can't alter a bass player's style, technique, or musicality. For example, if you record a heavy-metal bassist playing a Gibson Ripper with a pick, no amount of tweaking in the world is going to make the track sound like Jaco Pastorius playing a fretless Fender. But if your bass track is just shy of hitting the yummy mark, twisting a few knobs can slam home a great tone. Of course, it helps if you have a general idea of which frequencies to boost or cut for some classic bass sounds.

Beatle bass. Paul McCartney's bass sound evolved over the years, but whether it was the early Hofner thump or the Rickenbacker rumble of Wings, his tone was always round and fat. Low-mids often predominated, and the attack was very articulate because McCartney usually played with a plectrum. To push a track toward the Beatle zone, start by boosting 80 or 100 Hz (depending on your board's EQ configuration) by 2 or 3 dB. If the bassist used a pick, there's probably sufficient mid-range "pluck" already; if not, try boosting 3 to 6 dB at 3 kHz. This should increase string intelligibility and punch.

If your mixer has high-shelving EQ in the 12 to 18 kHz range, you can make the sound a bit smoother and warmer by cutting 6 dB up there. But if all you have is a 10 kHz shelf, take care when cutting, or you may dull the sound too much.

For a similar sound with a little more warmth, again boost the 80 Hz range a few decibels; then boost 500 Hz by 6 dB or so. Next, cut 300 Hz by about 3 dB and 12 kHz by 6 dB. (Obviously, this application requires 4-band EQ with two sweepable mids.) Cutting at 300 Hz gets rid of any hollow, tin-can tones, and—in combination with the boosts—yields a warmth that can complement a ballad while retaining enough authority to drive a rockin' blues or clubhouse shuffle.

In your face. If the tune calls for an aggressive Chris Squire or John Entwistle sound, you'll need to roll off some low end and crank up the mids. First, add 6 to 9 dB of high-mids and sweep between 1 and 2 kHz until you find the appropriate flavor of honk. Next, cut 200 Hz by 6 dB. If you want an even more brittle sound, cut 80 Hz by another 2 or 3 dB. The result is a trebly, piano-string sound with enough attack to help a busy bass line slice through the mix.

Twang. If you want to accentuate the twang in a bass track, give this a try. First, cut 200 to 250 Hz by 6 dB or so. This is a good cut for reducing "mud." Now, boost an equivalent amount of 1 kHz for the twang. Finally, beef up the low end a tad by boosting a decibel or two at 80 Hz.

Motown. Legend has it that the classic "dead string" bass sound of Motown groove king James Jamerson depended on, well, dead strings. To achieve a similarly smooth, muted tone without dumpster-diving for discarded bass strings, simply cut 1 kHz by 5 or 6 dB, boost 200 Hz by 3 dB, and pump up the lows with a slight boost at 80 or 100 Hz. Then cut the high end (preferably 18 kHz, but 12 kHz will work) by 6 dB or so. Also, note that by boosting a few more decibels of low end, you can achieve a passable reggae bass sound as well.

Stax/Volt. This is basically a variation on the Motown sound, which is not surprising when you consider that Duck

Dunn (of Booker T. and the MGs) was also known for never changing his strings. But rather than cutting at 1 kHz, go for a more punchy, aggressive sound by scooping out six or more decibels at around 5 kHz. By staying "down in the basement," either the Motown or Stax/Volt sound works nicely in a mix cluttered with midrange elements such as guitar, piano, and horns.

Jaco jazz. The bass sound of jazz legend Jaco Pastorius has been described alternately as tight, animalistic, and hornlike. But however you describe it, the bottom line is that it takes a Jaco Pastorius (or a darn good clone) to get a true Jaco tone, since much of his sound was in his fingers.

But you can approach the Jaco sound—especially if working with a fretless bass—by boosting the midrange while reducing low mids. Start by cranking 1 kHz by 6 dB or so to get some honk. Then carve out a big dose of 200 Hz, cutting as much as 9 dB or more. Finally, boost the low end and cut the highs by 1 or 2 dB. Actually, this sound works well in a variety of progressive jazz applications. To get more of a Marcus Miller sound, cut the low mids around 800 Hz rather than 200 Hz.

Bass-in-the-Mix Tips

Keep in mind that small, close-field monitors don't provide subsonic bass response. If your monitors can't accurately reproduce frequencies below, say, 60 Hz, the plain fact is that you'll be stuck guessing what's going on below that point. This is another reason why it's very important to reference your mixes on several different playback systems.

In addition, as anyone who has done much mixing knows, there's a fine line between too much bass and too little. Finding that line is complicated by the fact that we typically perceive certain tones differently when we hear them at different volume levels. As it turns out, our ears have a flatter response at higher volumes than they do at lower. The lower the volume, the quieter that low frequencies (from 20 to 200 Hz) sound in relation to mids and high mids (from 1 to 6 kHz). In other words, what sounded like tons of bass while you were mixing at 100 dB will likely sound puny at 70 dB. That's why it's also vitally important to check your mixes at several different volume levels.

Creative Drum EQ

With EQ, you can improve the drum sound without ever going near the drums, and equalization can go a long way toward salvaging lousy-sounding tracks while still giving you a natural sound. Even if you're blessed with a drum kit that sounds splendid, a few tonal tweaks may still be in order to make what's recorded on tape better suit the style and mood of the song. There are also those times when you just feel like reshaping the sound for creative reasons.

Let's look at equalizer settings for the kick and snare, the two drums that are the driving force behind most styles of pop music. Armed only with console EQ that offers one or two sweepable midrange bands as well as high and low shelving, you can subtly enhance or drastically alter the sound of these two all-important instruments.

Kick Tricks

Before delving into problem-solving applications, let's map out some critical frequencies for the kick drum and specify how they affect the sound. This will also ensure that we're on the same page vocabularywise.

Boom, of course, is the low end, and you can boost or cut it with the low-shelving control (usually 80 or 100 Hz). *Click*, on the other hand, refers to the sound of the beater (specifically, a wood one) hitting the head, and it is the highest part of the sound. You can boost or cut click with the high-shelving EQ (typically 10 or 12 kHz).

Attack refers to the impact of a felt beater laying into the head. This could also be called *definition*. You can increase attack, or definition, by boosting at 5 kHz (or, obviously, decrease it by cutting at that frequency). *Punch* is the tight thud or thump in the sound and can be increased by boosting 1 kHz. *Wallop* is a visceral, chest-hitting whomp that can be increased by boosting around 220 Hz. On the other hand, cutting at 220 Hz will thin out the sound of the kick drum and make it more dry.

Rock sculpting. First, let's EQ a double-headed kick drum with no muffling whatsoever. If the drum is too boomy, begin by cutting 3 to 6 dB at 80 Hz (or wherever your console's low EQ shelves) to roll off the lowest of the lows. Then make an even steeper cut, say 9 to 12 dB, at 200 Hz. At this point you should definitely be hearing more of the head itself and far less resonance. Now, add 3 to 9 dB at 500 Hz to contribute a bit of "flap." If necessary, add a touch of 12 kHz (or whatever the high-shelving frequency is on your board) for beater definition.

These settings should give you a slightly wet, flappy kind of sound.

Funk it up. Let's say you have the same problem—a kick drum that's too boomy. But rather than a wet and flappy sound, you'd prefer a dry and funky-sounding kick, say a James Brown "Get On Up" kind of thing. Again, start by cutting 6 dB or so at 80 Hz to lose the boom. Then add 6 dB at 350 Hz for some midrange thud. Next, to impart definition, boost another 3 to 6 dB at 3 kHz. If necessary, add a bit of 12 kHz. As a finishing touch, add some compression with a 4:1 ratio, medium attack, and slow release.

Kick it down. You're just as likely to encounter a kick drum with no front head and a pillow and several packing blankets crammed as tightly as possible against the batter head. The sound? More like an oatmeal box than a drum.

The trick here is to inject some of those missing lows without overwhelming that nice, dry punch. This is easily accomplished by adding one or two dB at 80 Hz. If you need a rounder, darker sound, try cutting 3 to 6 dB at 1 kHz. However, if you're starting to lose definition at this point, you can always roll off a few decibels at 220 Hz.

Long tones. To approximate the sound of the Roland TR-808 "long" kick, first turn down your monitors and boost 80 Hz by 9 dB or more, depending on how much boom is already present in the signal. (The less that's there, the more boost you'll need.) Next, cut 9 dB at 300 Hz and another 9 dB at 1 kHz. Now add the signature beater click by cranking up 12 kHz. Finally, add a hall reverb with medium delay and long decay to provide some sustain.

Subtle tweaks. So far we've looked at major overhauls, but sometimes all you need is enhancement. If the kick already sounds pretty good as is, you might just want to tighten up and clarify the sound a bit with a few slight adjustments. First, using the high-mid band, boost 4.5 or 5 kHz anywhere from 2 to 6 dB. (If there's a Q control, put it at the widest setting.) Now, with the low-mid band, either boost 350 Hz by 2 to 3 dB or cut 220 Hz by 2 to 3 dB. Try both and see which works best.

Next, depending on the mix, either boost or cut 1 to 2 dB of 80 Hz shelving. Solo the kick with the bass guitar to determine which direction sounds best. Also, play with the relationship between the 5 kHz and 80 Hz frequencies. For example, if you add more 5 kHz, compensate with more 80 Hz. Finally, touch the sound off with a 1 to 2 dB boost of high shelving.

Snare Drum Specifics

Again, before getting into specific applications, let's map out critical tonalities and corresponding frequencies for snare drum. Think of snare in terms of four qualities: snap, crack, pop, and body.

Snap is the high, snappy sound of the snares, as well as the stick hit, and is centered around 5 kHz. *Crack* is just how it sounds, and it can be boosted or cut at 3 kHz. (Some people call this *bang.*) *Pop* is a throaty, honking kind of sound, centered at 1 kHz, which tends to emphasize the tonality of the drum shell (wood, stainless steel, brass, etc.). *Body* is located anywhere from 240 Hz down to 100 Hz. Because it makes the speaker move a lot of air, it can be very visceral and bone-shaking, especially in the lower realm.

To get a quick hit of the possibilities, try some basic combinations: for a military snare sound, combine body and snap; for a funky backbeat, combine body and crack; for rock, combine body and pop. Or, to get more precise, check out the following tailor-made applications.

Fatback. For a really fat but shredding backbeat, first boost 300 to 350 Hz by 6 or more decibels to lay in some "thonk." For the shred, boost 5 kHz by 3 to 6 dB and maybe add a touch of 12 kHz. Finally, depending on the sound that works best in the mix, either cut or boost the low-shelving frequency by 2 or 3 dB. Try both. I tend to like it with a cut at 80 Hz.

Paper trail. For a distinctive, postmodern tone, make the snare drum sound like paper tearing. Start with a radical 12 dB cut at 80 Hz. Then make another deep cut, say 9 dB or so, at 250 Hz. Now, using a 2-octave Q, boost 6 kHz by 3 or 4 dB. If desired, add a decibel or two of high shelving. Now run the whole thing through a flanger, and you're ready for the European trip-hop scene.

Deeper down. To make a standard, 5-inch snare sound like a deep-shell, parade drum—once again a popular sound for certain flavors of pop—first add some body to the sound by boosting 220 Hz by 6 dB or so. Then cut 1 kHz by 6 to 9 dB and 80 Hz by 3 dB. Finish off with a 3 dB boost at 12 kHz.

Pseudo piccolo. With a few easy tweaks, you can simulate piccolo snare. First, boost 1 kHz by 3 to 6 dB to attain the characteristic piccolo pop. Next, shave off 9 to 12 dB at 230 Hz, and another 9 dB at 80 Hz. To go the extra mile, use a pitch shifter and bring the sound up a fifth or so.

Watch Where You Notch

Whether or not you like the sound of these EQ templates for kick and snare, by giving them a whirl, you may come across some sounds that you do like. Also, as you experiment with the different EQ combinations, you'll find that there are more ways than one to achieve a particular result. That can be a useful thing to know if, for example, a certain EQ setting adds too much noise to the mix—because, generally, it's best to favor a combination that has more cuts than boosts.

Remember, the point of equalizing kick and snare is to define and clarify them so they can do a better job of driving the song. It's fun to dial up "out there" settings, and on some songs a radical drum tone can work wonders. But remember that context is king. While equalizing, bring in the rest of the instruments frequently—or else you may end up with a killer sound in solo mode that doesn't work at all in the mix.

Electric Guitar

As with the bass and drums, how you treat the electric guitar depends on the other elements of the mix. For example, if you have only one electric guitar in a mix with just drums and bass, you can make the track sound large. However, if you have three other electric guitars, a piano, keyboards, percussion—the works—then you have to fit it nicely into a spot on the soundstage. Let's look more closely at a couple of these scenarios.

Lone guitar. Let's say that you can do whatever you want to this guitar to make it sound as big as possible, as long as it doesn't conflict with the bass guitar. You can fatten up the low end with a boost of 3 dB around 160 Hz and another between 700 and 800 Hz. Depending on the sound of the amp, you may need to cut a few decibels around 3 kHz. The amount of high end you add depends on the sound you want: A boost of about 6 dB at 7 kHz will add crunch to the sound.

It's always good practice to roll off any frequencies above or below the ones you really need, but listen carefully before you cut, lest you accidentally eliminate desirable, but subtle, low-level subharmonics and high harmonics. At each step, check to make sure that the guitar sits well in the mix with the bass.

One of many. For our second scenario, let's assume you have to fit this guitar into a mix with a full band, including two other electric guitars. In this case, you may want to focus on the midrange. Roll off everything below 200 Hz and above 9 kHz. Then do some sweeps in the middle to see what needs to go in and what ought to come out. You'll find that, often, a boost around 4 kHz and a cut around 6 kHz generally work, although sometimes the opposite is true.

You have to listen to the track and decide according to the mix at hand. If you have more than one electric guitar, make sure that they sound a little different from each other. This could mean using different guitars, amps, mics, miking techniques, or processing. In addition, you can further differentiate the guitars by giving them their own space in the stereo field.

Gentle Reminder

Now that we have examined a number of bass, drum, and guitar EQ settings, keep in mind that not one of them is worth a hill of beans if the resulting sounds don't complement the song and work to enhance the other elements of the mix.

Although it's certainly no sin to tweak a track in solo mode, EQ settings should only be finalized in the context of the complete mix. The purpose of equalizing a mix, after all, is to minimize frequency conflicts among the various instruments so that they're not fighting for the same sonic space. In other words, you're trying to create an aural "niche" for each instrument—and this can only be done while listening to all the parts together. Often, after you've equalized a track in the context of the entire mix, an individual track will sound absolutely horrible when soloed. Well, so be it. All that really matters is that the sound works when it is joined by all the other elements of a (hopefully) well-balanced mix.

Use these EQ recommendations only as starting points. Some of these suggestions will work for your track, and some won't. But if nothing else, these "tonal templates" will help you get acquainted with the sonic capabilities of your console's EQ section. Then you can more readily find your own favorite EQ tweaks.

Polishing the Mix

Regardless of whether you have the project professionally mastered or do it yourself, your best bet is to leave the overall EQ of your mix as flat as possible, meaning that you haven't unnecessarily boosted or cut any frequencies. The golden rule here is that you can always add, but you can't always subtract. Be aware that the room you're working in can sometimes fool you, causing you to unnecessarily boost frequencies to compensate for the room's deficiencies.

However, you also want the mix to sound as good as it can when it leaves the studio. Don't assume that you can fix all of your mix's sonic problems during the mastering stage. If you hear something you don't like, fix it now.

Typically, engineers apply some premastering compression to the stereo mix (see **Fig. 25.2**). How you apply compression to the mix usually depends on the material. If you're working on a rock song that really needs to hit hard, try compressing the mix by 2 or 3 dB at a 2:1 ratio, with medium attack and release times. For fast, rhythmic music, such as dance or techno, you might shorten the attack time and lower the threshold. Generally, a little compression on the stereo mix is a good idea to smooth out the song. Just don't go crazy!

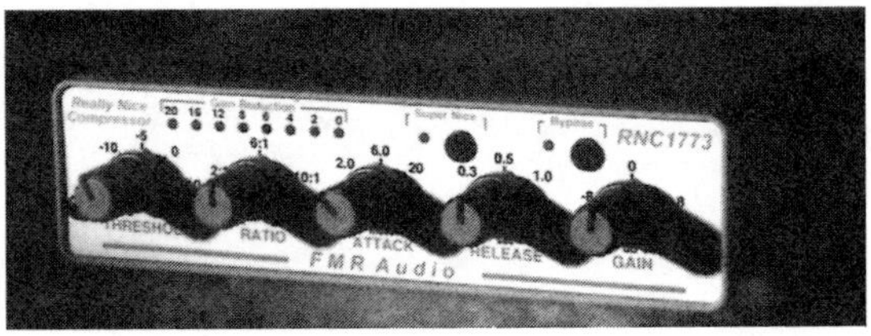

FIG. 25.2: FMR Audio's Real Nice Compressor (RNC) is an inexpensive yet transparent compressor that works well across the mix bus.

Most semipro analog stereo compressors add significant coloration to the signal chain. If you want the compression to be transparent, you will need to use a unit that doesn't color your mix. If your compressor has a hard-wired bypass, click it in and out to see how the circuitry affects a stereo mix before you use it on your mix. For units without a true bypass function, do trial mixes with and without the compressor in the chain and assess the differences.

Fade Out

Expensive equipment is not always the key to great-sounding mixes. The tricks that professionals use day in and day out are not dependent on SSL consoles or Sony multitracks (although these high-ticket items do make things easier). With a little patience and some practice, anyone can learn to produce rich, full, in-your-face mixes.

CHAPTER 26

Mastering Your Mix for Reproduction

After you have finished mixing your tracks, mastering is the next important step to take if you plan to release them as an album. The mastering process involves performing any final edits, putting the various tracks in their proper order, checking them for audio anomalies, and processing them (using EQ, compression, and normalization) so that the sound is uniform from one song to the next.

When the mastering engineer feels satisfied that the album has an overall consistency, he will create a production master that will be used by the manufacturing plant for replication. The sample rate and bit depth of the master must match that of a Red Book CD: 16-bit at 44.1 kHz.

Putting It All Together

"Mastering and editing a recording project is analogous to assembling an art exhibit. Every piece may be great on its own; however, the pieces will have a much greater impact as a collection once they are cleaned up, properly framed, and displayed in a way that shows each in the best possible light. This kind of attention to detail makes the whole artistic experience greater than the sum of its parts."—Myles Boisen, chief engineer, Headless Buddha Mastering Lab

Higher Ground

If you have the capability to mix to a resolution that's higher than the CD standard of 16-bit/44.1 kHz, do so. By keeping your mix at the highest resolution possible, you will ensure the sonic integrity of your music as it passes through the various editing and mastering phases.

The differences between 16-bit and 24-bit audio are not as subtle as you may think. The most obvious rewards of the higher resolution are improved dynamic range, quicker transients, greater low-level detail, and a smooth, even blend throughout the frequency spectrum. When you use noise-shaping algorithms to reduce the digital word length back to 16 bits during the final mastering phase (a process referred to as *dithering*), the results retain much of the clarity of the original version.

Food for Thought

If you want to take your mixing skills to the next level, it's a good idea to closely examine your work just as a mastering engineer would, even if you're not planning to master your mixes immediately.

Begin by listening to your mixes on a variety of monitoring systems and headphones. Compare the sound of your tracks to professionally mastered CDs and imagine what you would and would not do to them in a mastering situation. In addition, it's a good idea to check your mixes for mono compatibility, dropouts, and any noise and distortion that may have worked its way onto the masters.

If you are able to step back and look critically at your work, you will probably find room for improvement. Each time you notice problems and make corrections, you will get one step closer to becoming a better engineer.

Preparing for a Mastering Session

Begin by determining the final order of the songs. You can easily experiment with different song orders by using the playlist capabilities of an MP3 player or by programming them into your CD player. Things you will want to listen for include the timing between cuts; how the musical keys of the songs sound when they're played back-to-back (for instance, does it sound weird to have a song in F# follow a song in G?); and the overall flow of the album (such as the pattern of fast songs and slow songs, and how the CD ends).

If you are not comfortable editing your songs yourself, this process can be done during the mastering phase. However, you are the only person who knows how your album should sound. Whether you have one edit or a hundred, preparing for the editing session in advance will save you time and money. In fact, the amount of time you spend in preparation is proportional to the amount of money you will save. The more edits you need, the more planning you should do.

If there is editing to be done, determine which sections of music you want to use. For example, pick the take you want to use, or select the best parts of each take and decide how you want to piece them together. Mark down the exact time (in minutes and seconds) of each potential edit point. This is easy to do if you're using a CD-R as a reference, because you can read the timing off the player. Another way to do it is to view each song in the waveform editor of your digital audio sequencer and note the end time.

Your mission is to help the mastering engineer find edit points quickly. Knowing, for example, that the killer guitar solo begins 4 minutes and 12 seconds from the beginning of the song will help the engineer find it easily.

Now determine the order of the edits. The time it takes to complete each edit depends on how complex it is. To help move the session along quickly, you should have as much information in front of you as possible about each edit you want to make. If you are not sure whether one take is better than another, don't sweat it; just note both of their timings and make the final judgment when you assemble the parts into the final version.

As you go through these procedures, keep a list of any questions or thoughts that come up. When you hear the songs in a new sequence, keep your ears open for subtle variations in level, EQ, and mix. If you make a list of comments for each song, arrange them in an easy-to-read list by song title, so that you can check them off one at a time as you go through the session. This little exercise in anal retentiveness may save you from having to book another mastering session because you overlooked an important point during the first one.

Mastering Suite Etiquette

Mastering is one of the most crucial stages of the recording process. It can also be one of most tedious, because you may not be able to tell what the engineer is doing much of the time. Critical listening requires a lot of energy, as well as sustained patience for everyone involved. So how can you maximize the productivity of this all-important session?

For one thing, stay out of the engineer's way. It's okay to occasionally ask a question, especially if something is sounding different than you expected. But don't start up an unrelated conversation in the middle of the session. Not only does it waste time (and money!), but it breaks the engineer's concentration and makes it difficult for him to focus on the necessary sonic minutiae.

Be invisible. If your project requires a fair amount of work, the engineer will play small portions of each track over and over while listening carefully and adjusting various aspects of the sound. Therefore, it is important to be as quiet as possible when you are sharing the mastering lab with the engineer. If you need to conduct business or carry on a conversation with someone else, take it out of the room so the engineer can work. The engineer will come and get you when it's time for you to hear how the piece has progressed.

Assembly and Editing

A typical mastering session begins by loading the various songs for the project into a digital audio workstation (DAW). After previewing the mixes, some mastering engineers will record them into the computer in real time using a digital connection (if the master is in a digital format) or through analog-to-digital converters (if the master is on analog tape). During this stage, the engineer may decide to add a little preliminary processing, such as EQ, compression, limiting, or reverb (see **Fig. 26.1**). As the tracks are playing, the engineer will note the beginnings and endings of songs. If you did your homework before the session, you can use this time to let the engineer know where important edit points are, or any places where a large change in dynamics occurs so he can note them for future reference.

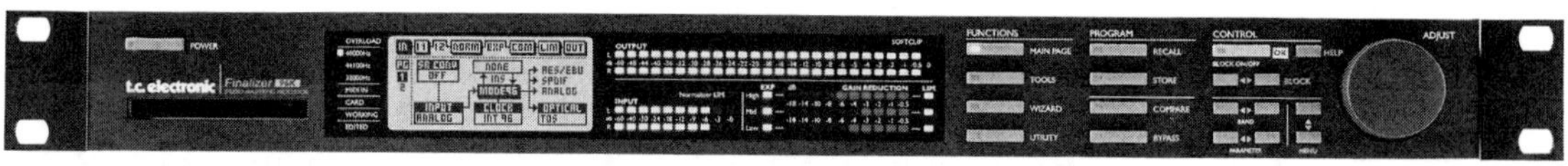

FIG. 26.1: The TC Electronic Finalizer 96K is a powerful and versatile tool that combines several mastering processes (A/D and D/A conversion, EQ, spectral enhancement, normalization, and dithering) in a single box.

Once everything is loaded on the DAW and the data is saved as a file, the engineer will begin creating In and Out points for the sections you want to edit, as well as the beginning and ending of each song. The In point is a marker that tells the computer where in the digital file to begin, and the Out point tells the computer where the file ends. This creates regions of data that can be played at any time and in any order. Once the engineer has finished creating the regions, it's time to put them into the correct order and assemble the record.

There are several other things you can do in a DAW environment, such as shaping crossfades between tracks, auditioning different versions of an edit without destroying the original (this is called *nondestructive editing*), or changing the length of a song by deleting a chorus or verse.

After the tracks have been edited and mastered, it's a good idea to make a safety copy of the final results. It doesn't matter whether you back up the data to hard disk, CD-R, or DVD-R, but keep the safety copy in a secure place, away from the master, in case disaster strikes.

Money Well Spent

If you want to create a pro-sounding release, the mastering phase is a crucial step. Although much of the work (such as editing or assembling the songs in the correct order for the album) can be done on your own, a mastering engineer has the know-how to raise the audio quality to professional standards.

If you've never mastered an album project before, consider taking it to a professional before trying it at home. When you hear the results, you will see how the added expense was money well spent.

Index